photographed by Kōichi Uchida

比叡山千日回峰行………光永圓道阿闍梨写真集

写真：打田浩一

プロローグ | Prologue

1990年2月28日、比叡山無動寺谷明王堂で一人の少年との不思議な出会いがあった。師匠である光永覚道阿闍梨から得度式の記念写真の撮影依頼があり、年若い僧侶の誕生に遭遇することになったのである。天台声明が唱えられるなか、黒の法衣と白い袈裟を着け、名も「圓道」と改めた15歳の僧侶が誕生した。
1999年3月29日、明王堂輪番であった師匠・覚道阿闍梨のもと、圓道師の百日回峰がはじまった。初日は行者以外には門外不出の「手文」に記されている回峰行のコース、礼拝する場所、真言などが伝授されるという。初百日の行者を新行者と呼ぶが、真摯に取り組む姿が印象的であった。
初百日から4年後、2003年3月1日、28歳になったばかりの圓道師は12年間比叡山に籠り、千日回峰行に入行。その日の比叡山はすっぽりと綿帽子をかぶったような雪景色で、これからの行の厳しさを物語っているかのように感じられた。

February 28, 1990 I had an unexpected encounter with a young man at Myōōdō temple, which is located in the Mudōji Valley of Mount Hiei. I had received a request to do a commemorative photo shoot from Ajari Kakudō Mitsunaga. The event was a *tokudo* ceremony; the initiation for a monk. The young man was wearing a black robe and a white *kesa* (type of robe). While *Tendai Shōmyō* was sung, the *Dharma* name "Endō", was given to the 15-year-old as he became a young monk.
On March 29, 1999 Endō's first one-hundred day *kaihōgyō* training began. He was taught by Kakudō Mitsunaga, his *shishō* (Master), and also the guardian monk of Myōōdō temple. On the first day, trainees read a special book called *tebumi*. Inside the book is a detailed recording of the *kaihōgyō* training route, including instruction on pilgrimage sites, mantras and sutras to be recited, etc. The *tebumi* is never to be removed from the premises except by *gyōja* (*kaihōgyō* trainees). During the first day of the *kaihōgyō*, the new trainees are called by trainees who have already completed their *kaihōgyō*. At that time Endō's sincerity and determination left a deep impression.
Four years later, Endō began his thousand day *kaihōgyō* training on March 1, 2003 (The then) Reverend Endō had just turned 28 years old. This was the beginning of his 12-year confinement on Mount Hiei. The mountain that day was blanketed in snow, as if it had been sprinkled with cotton. Looking at that snowy landscape, I felt how difficult the coming *kaihōgyō* would be.

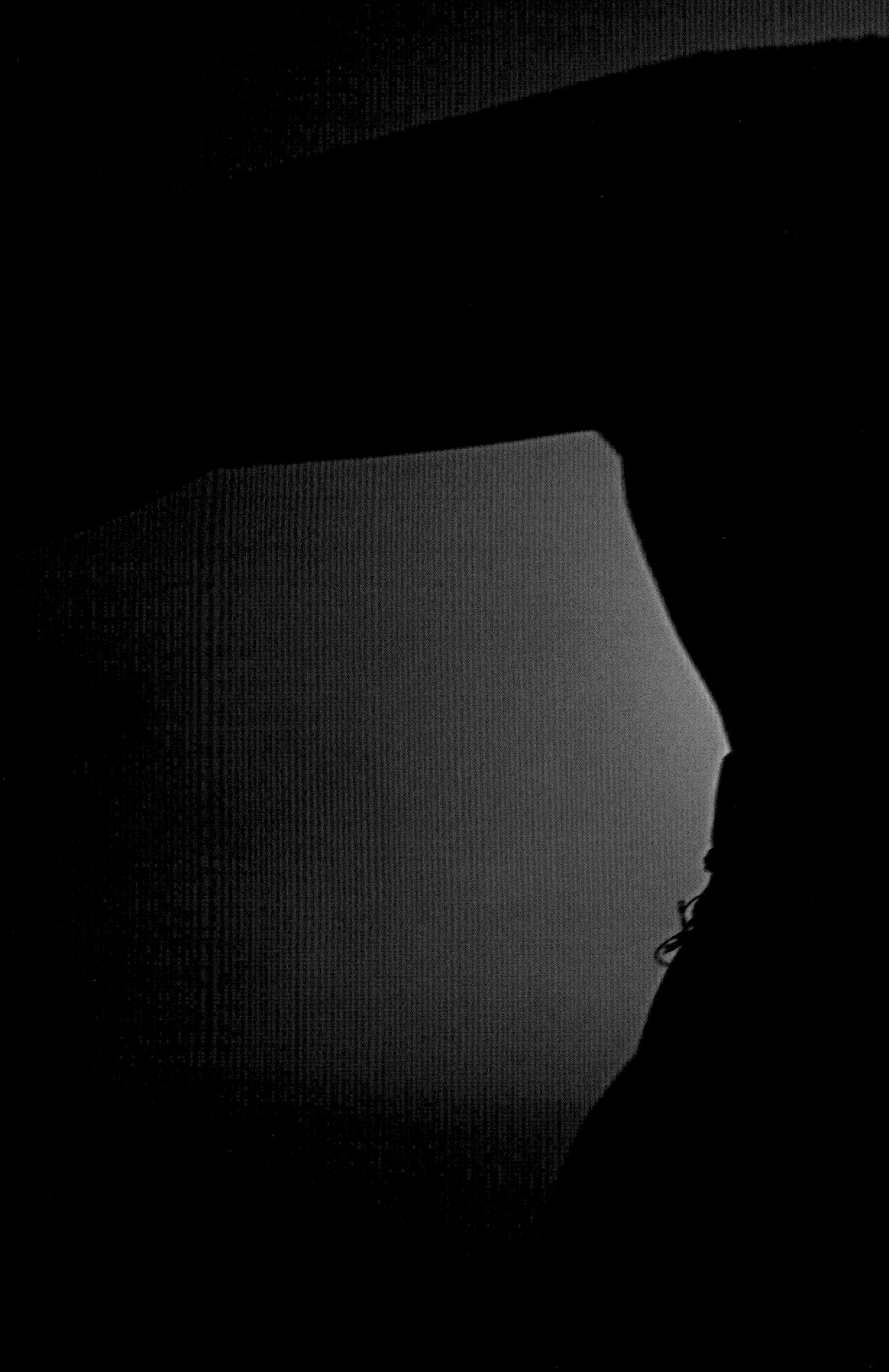

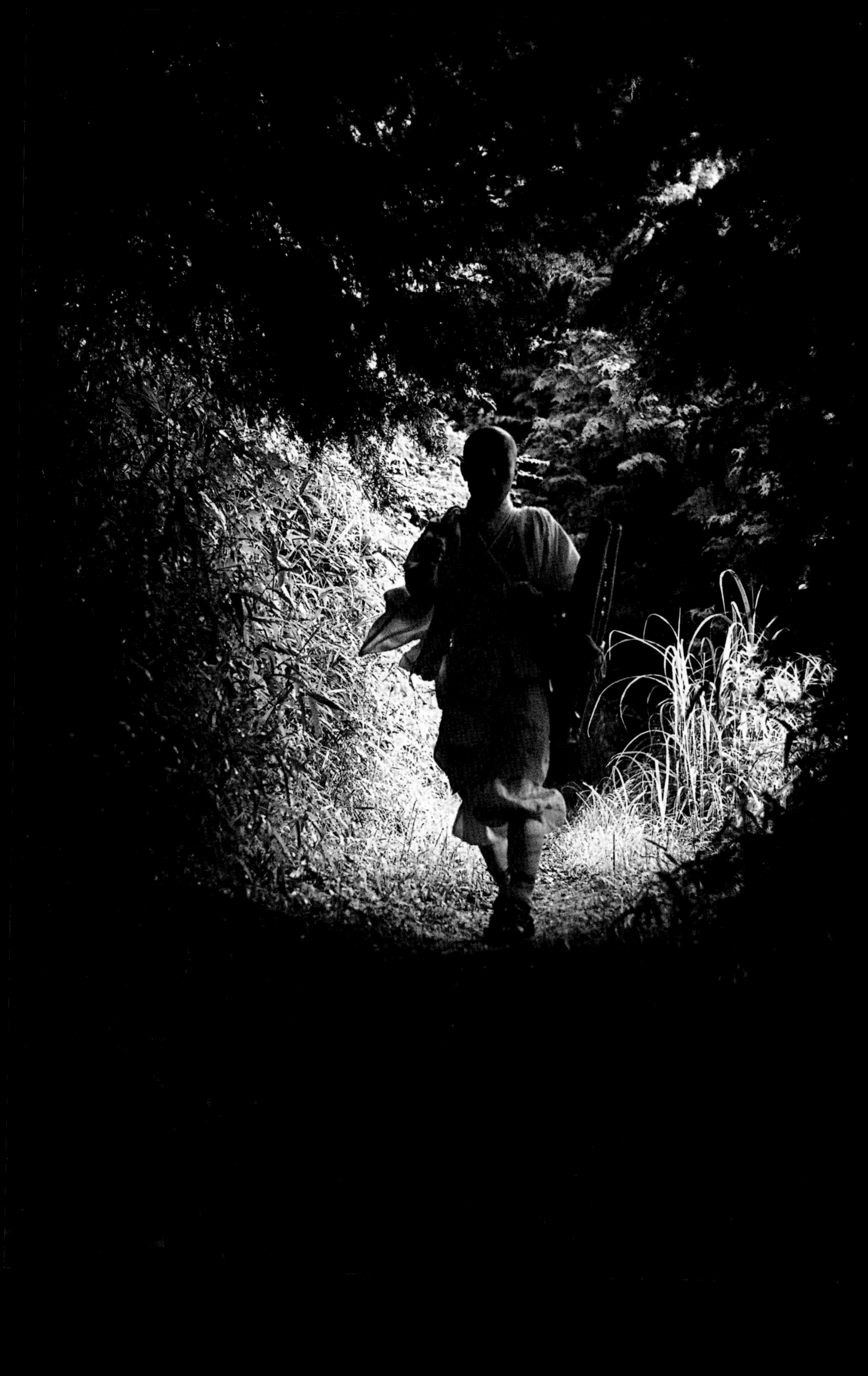

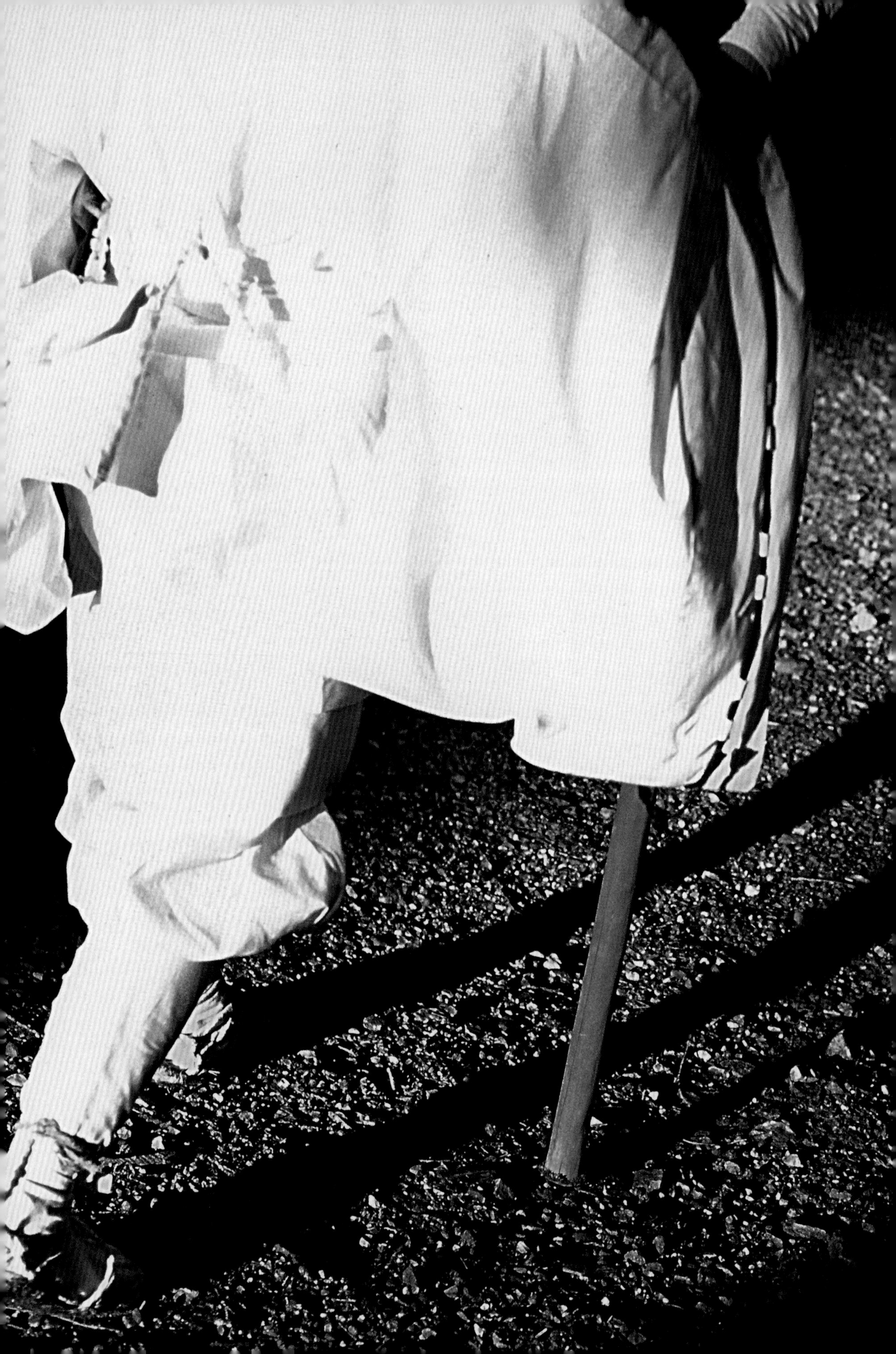

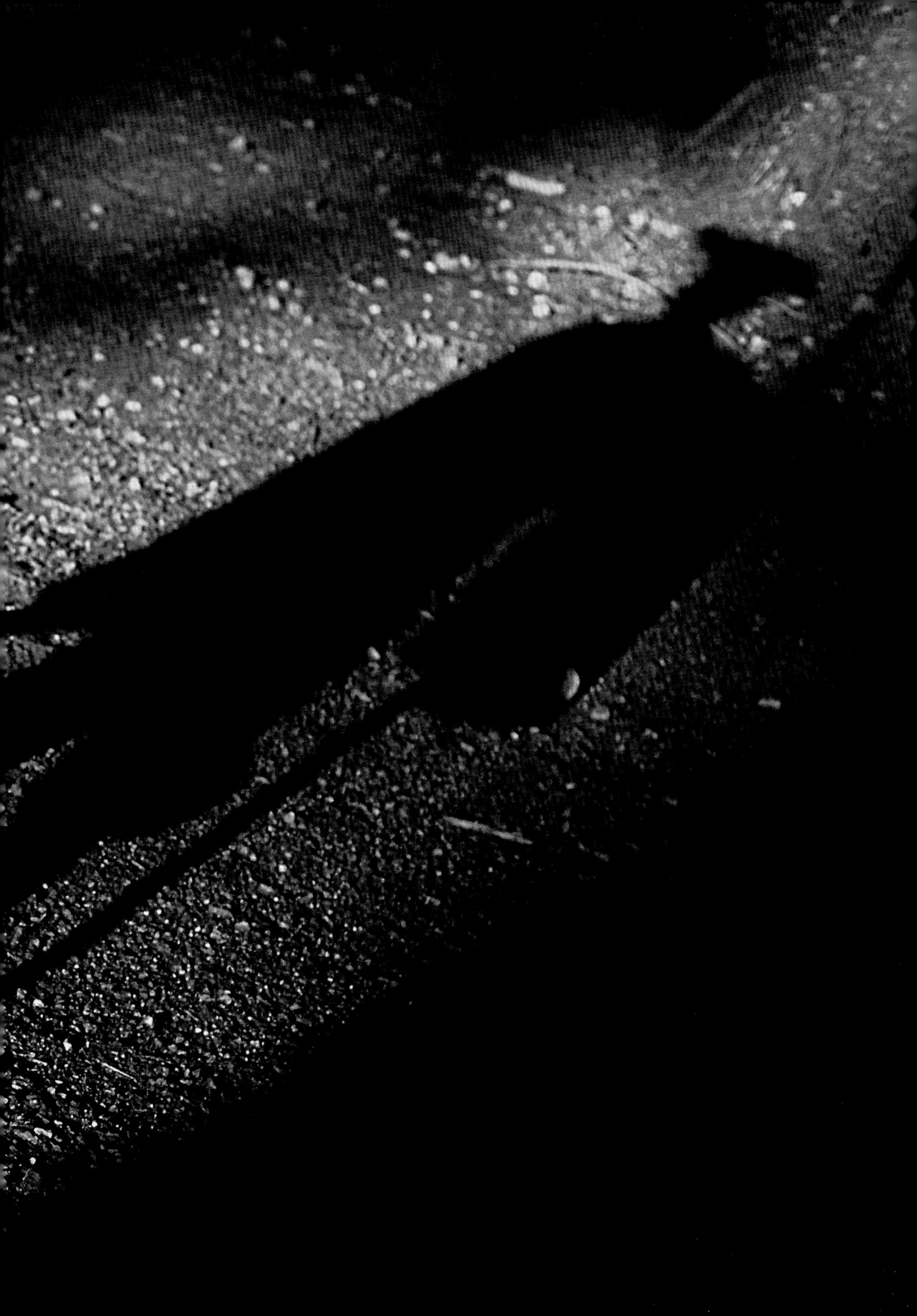

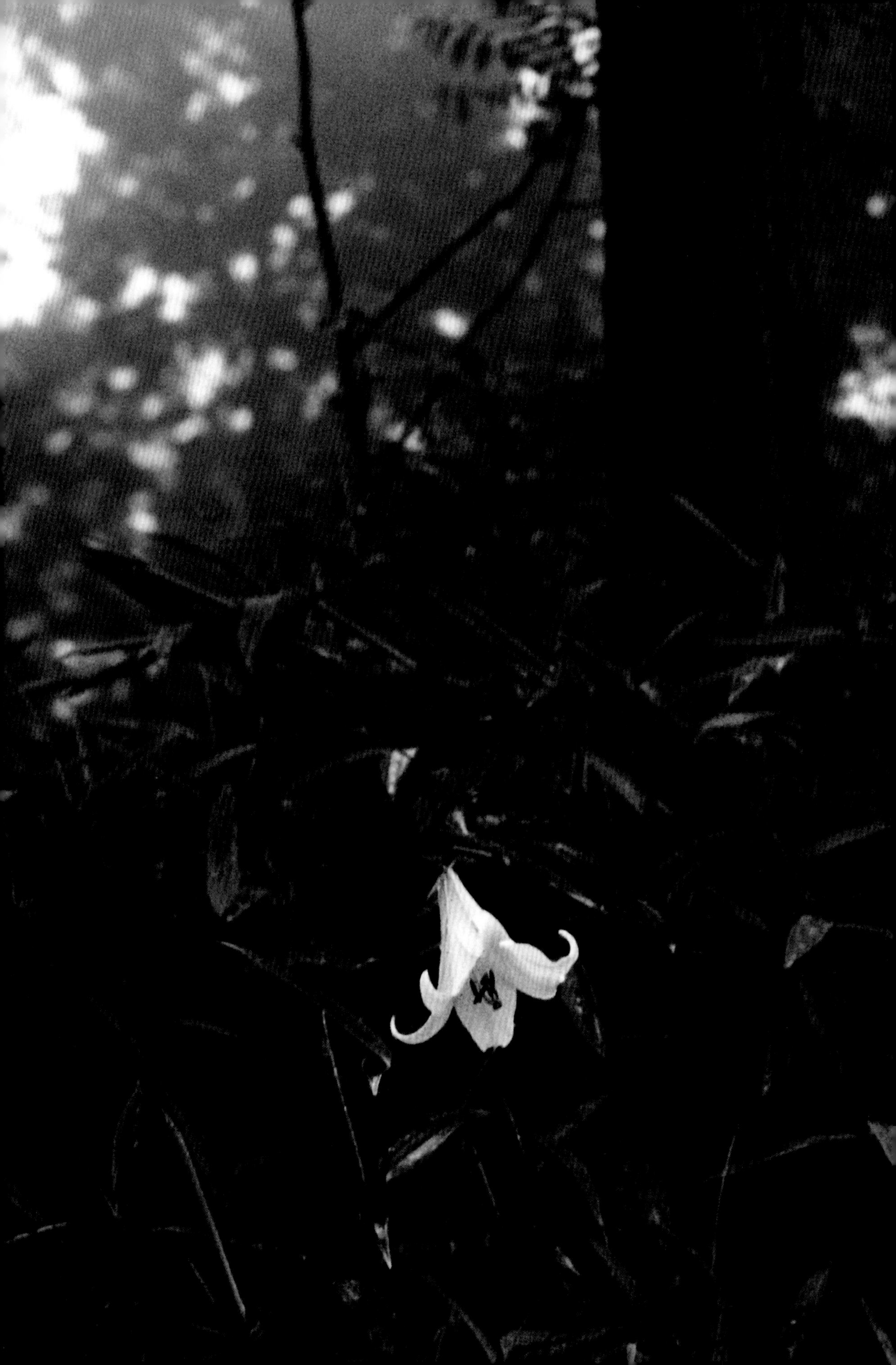

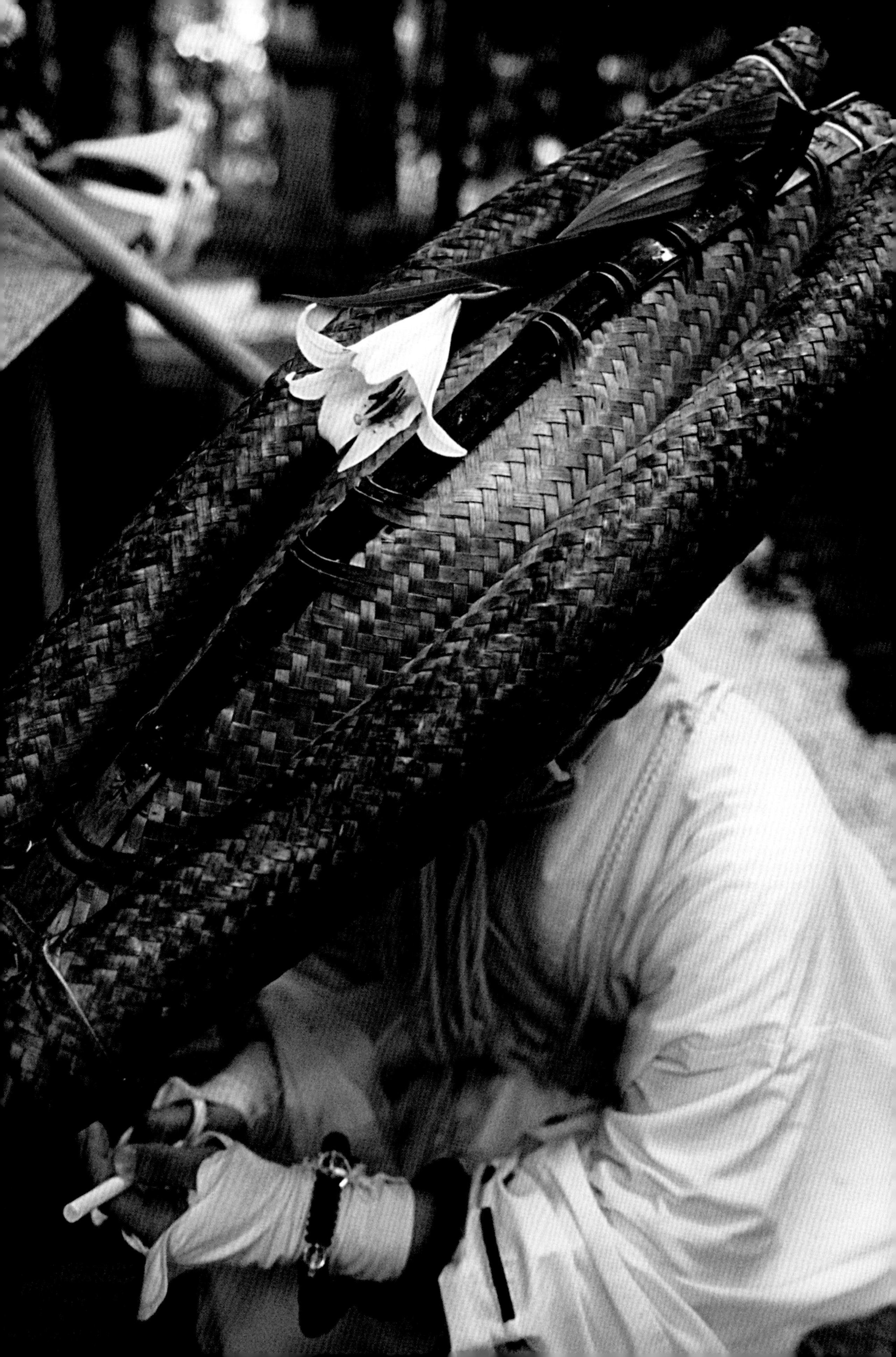

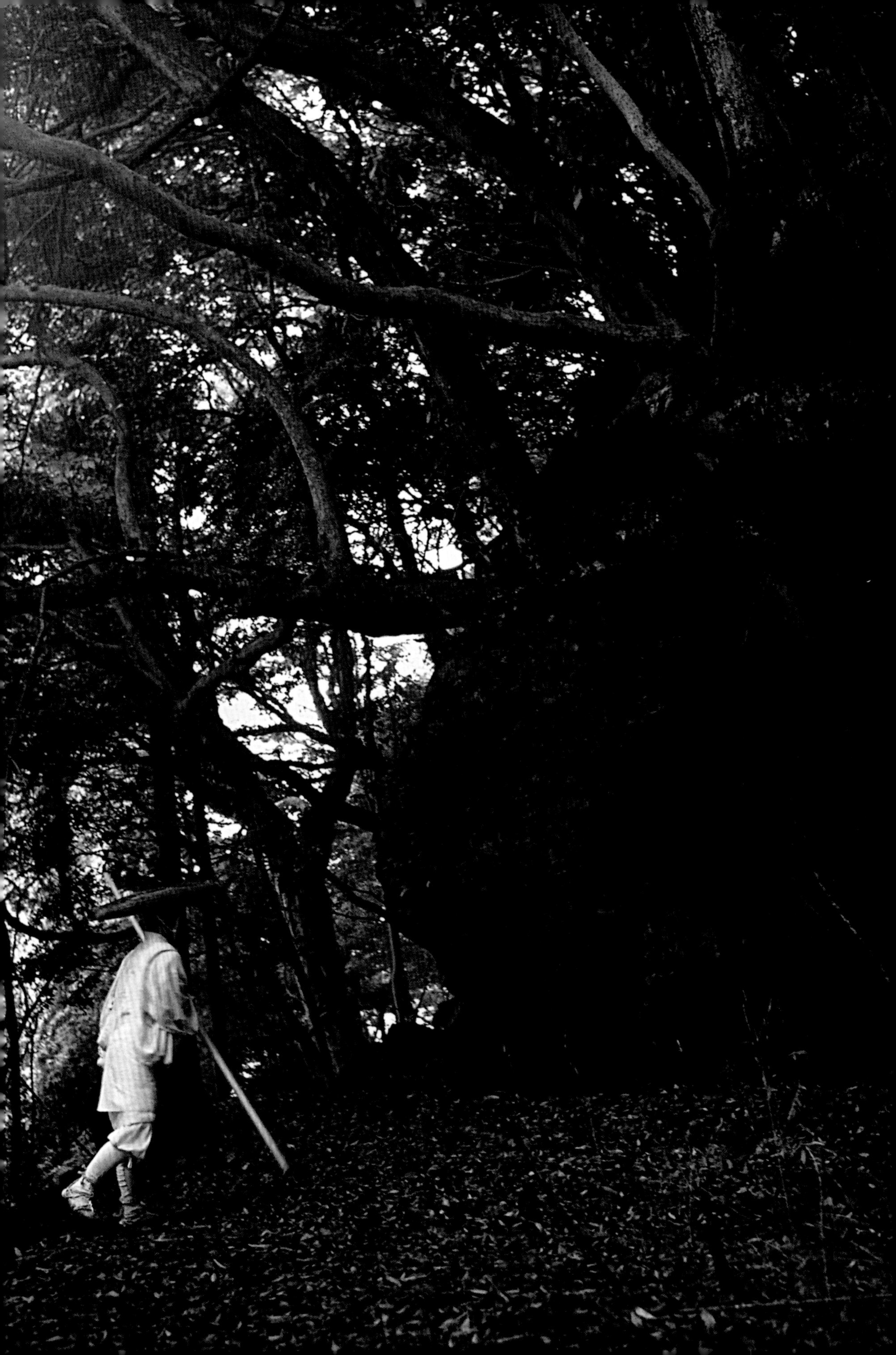

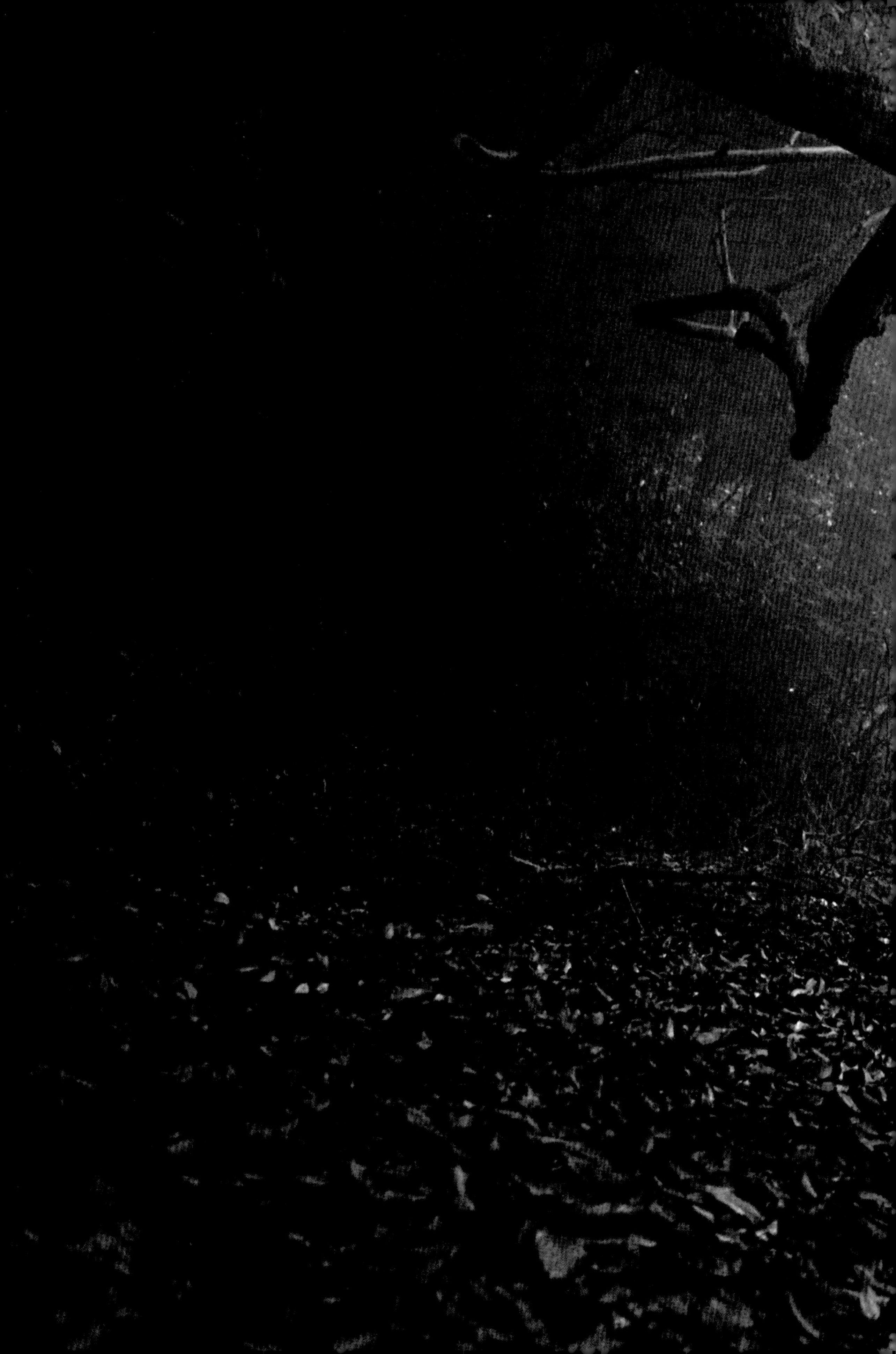

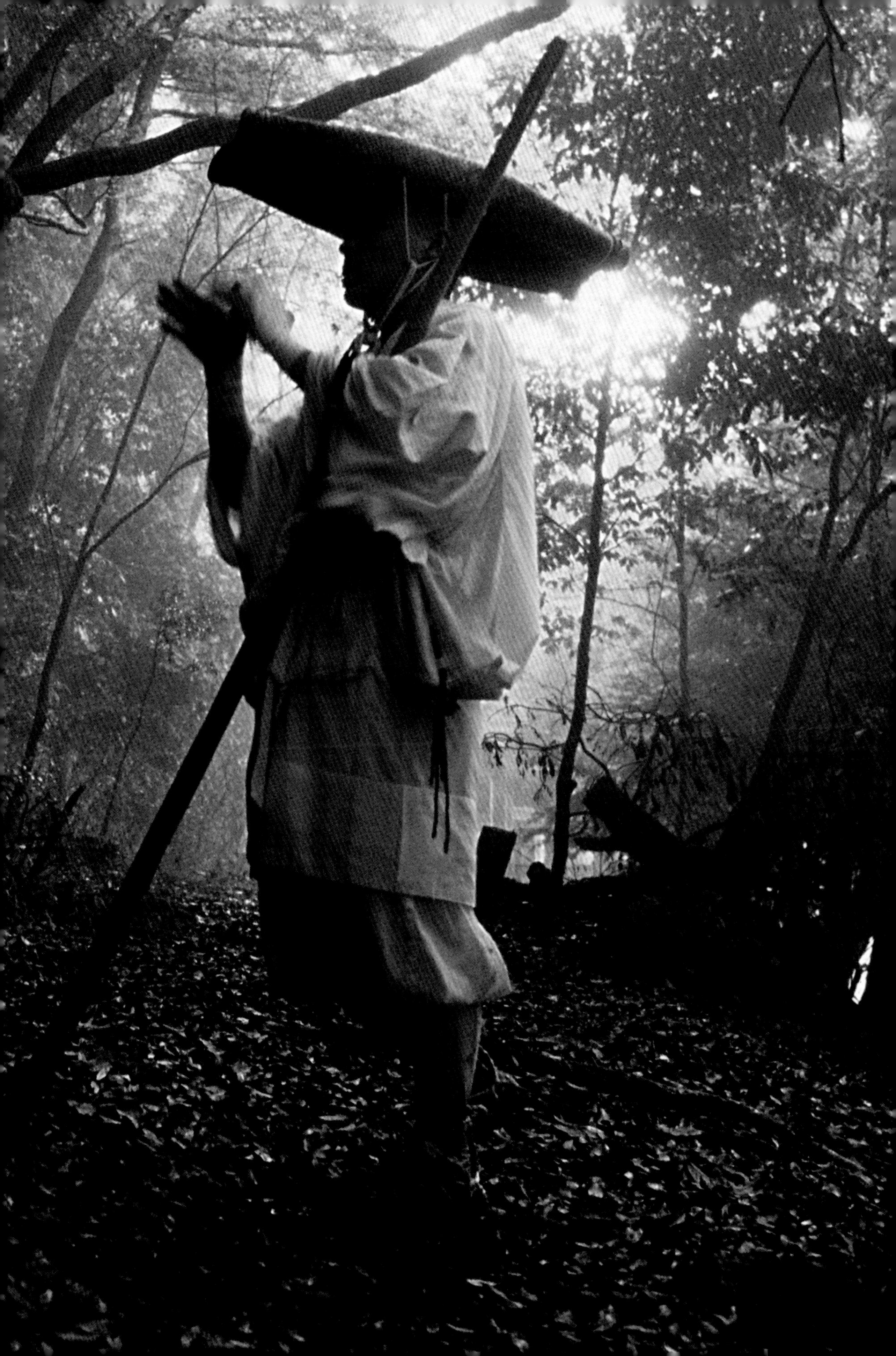

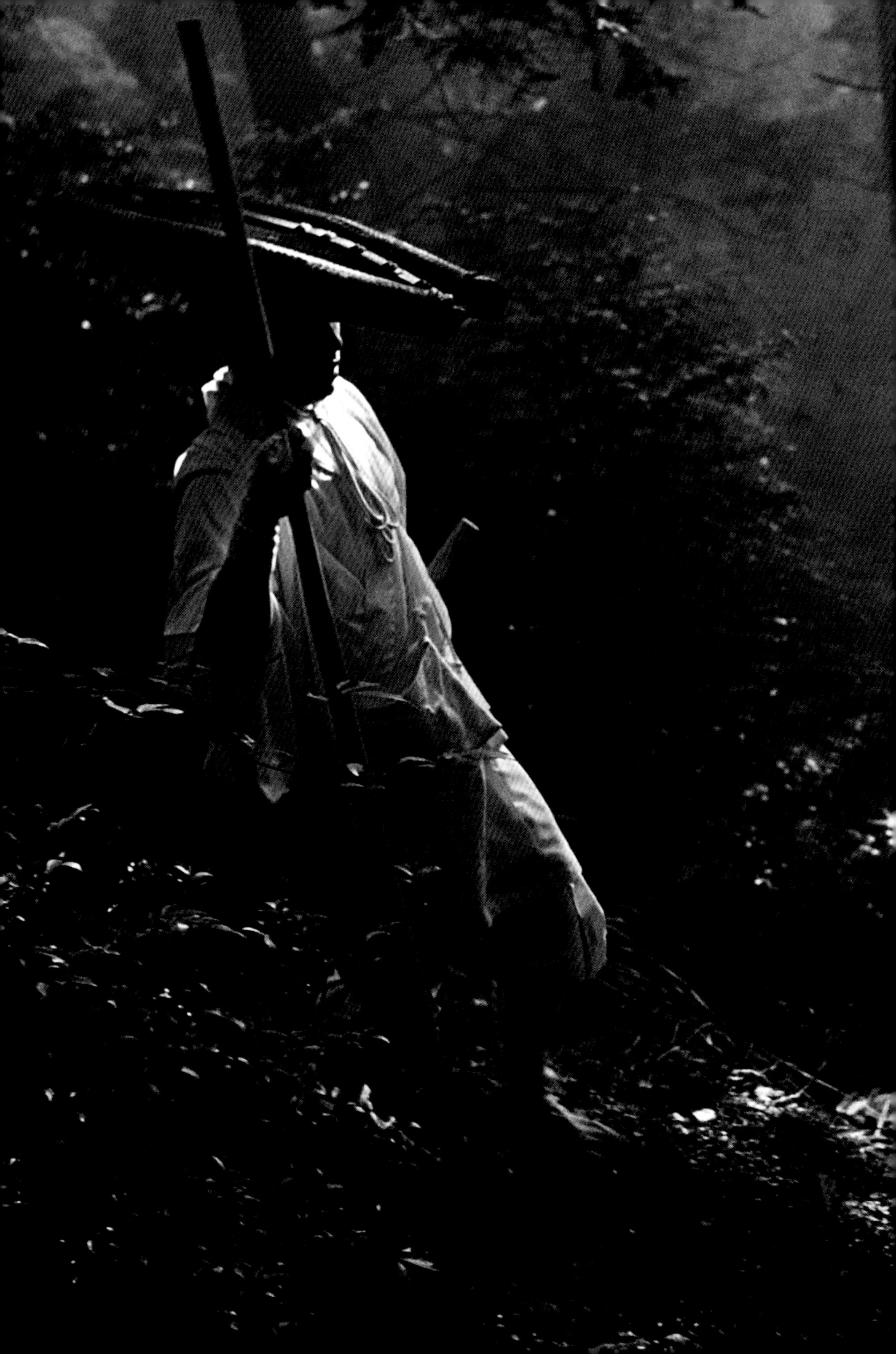

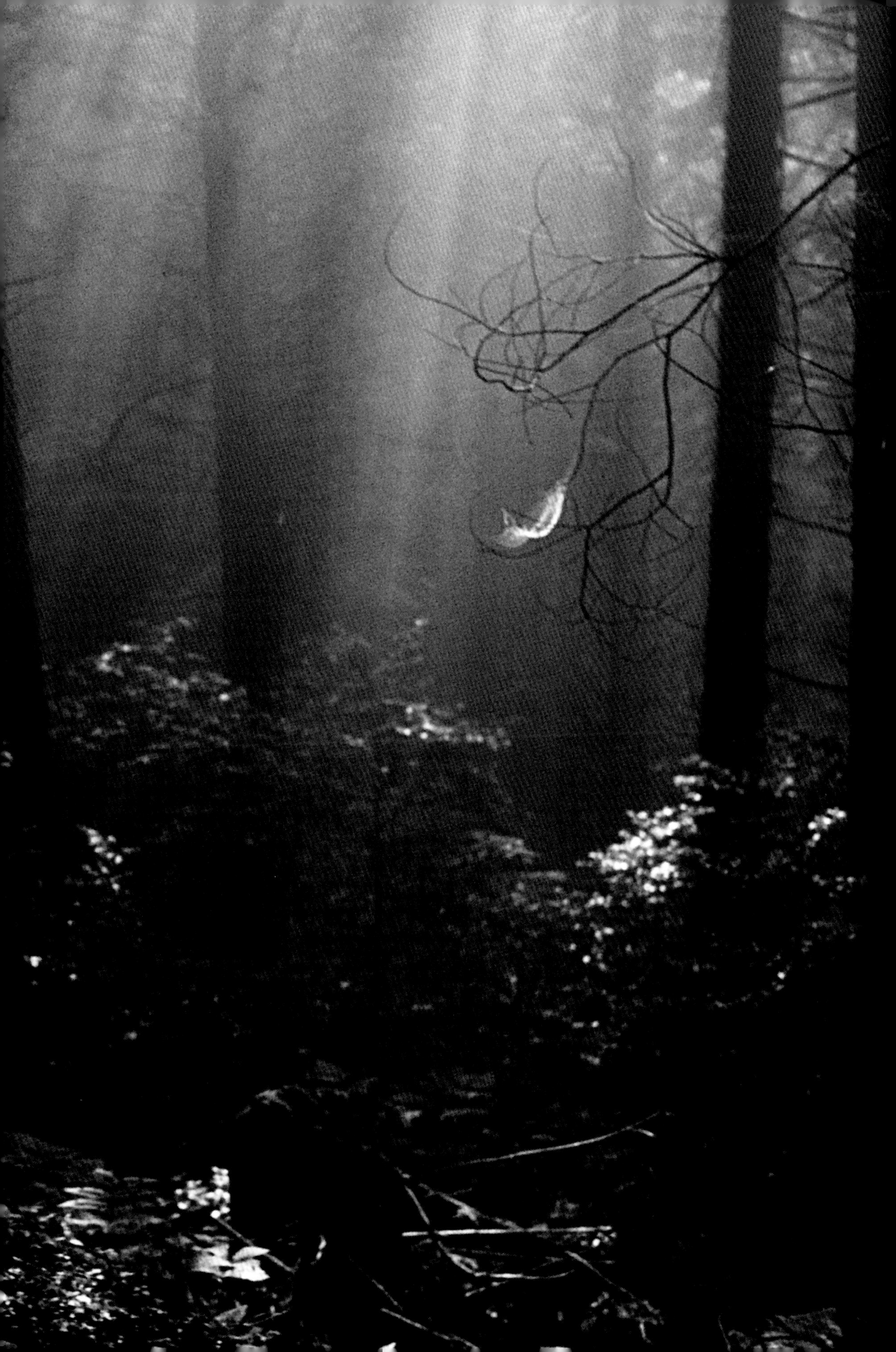

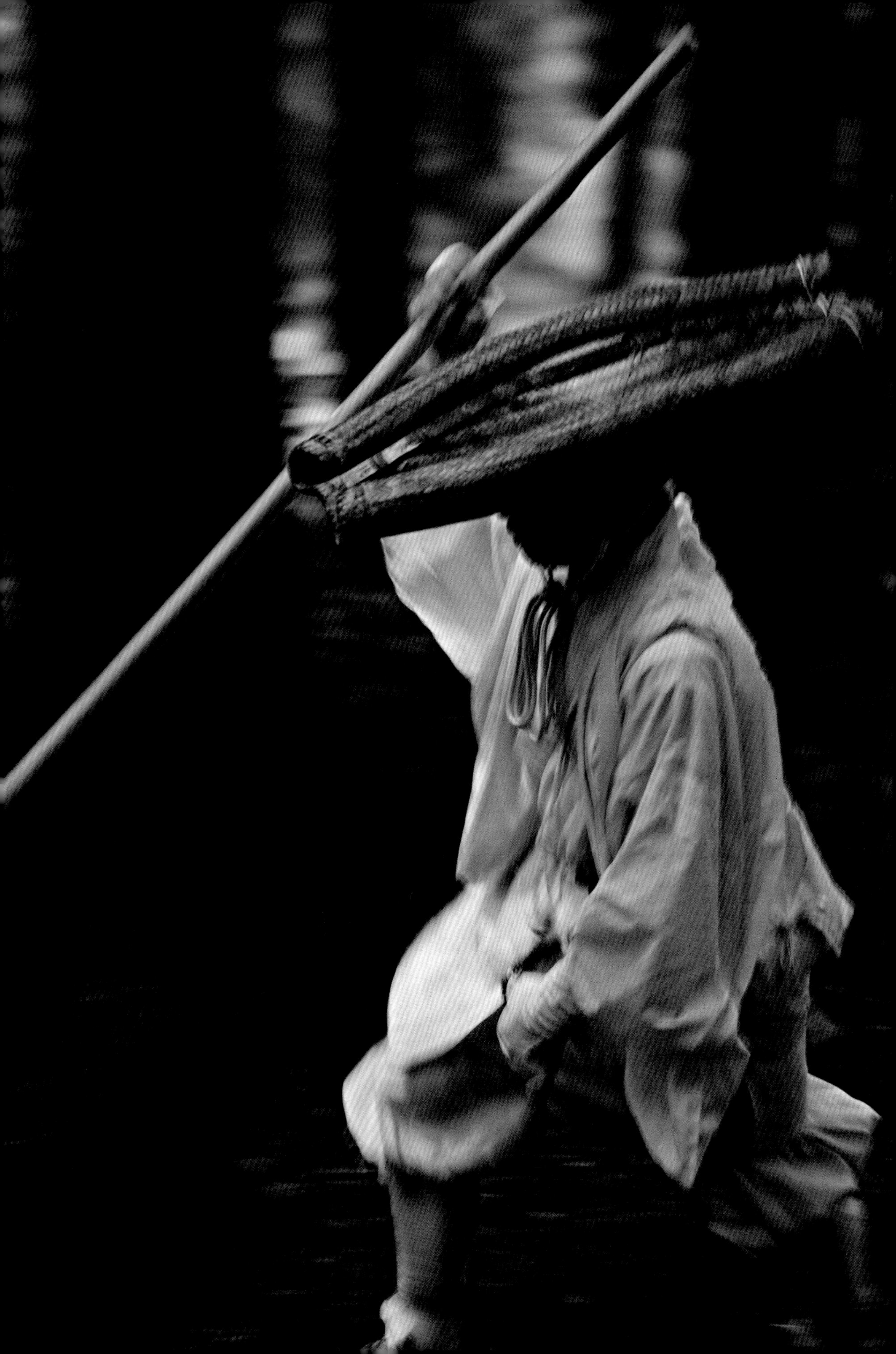

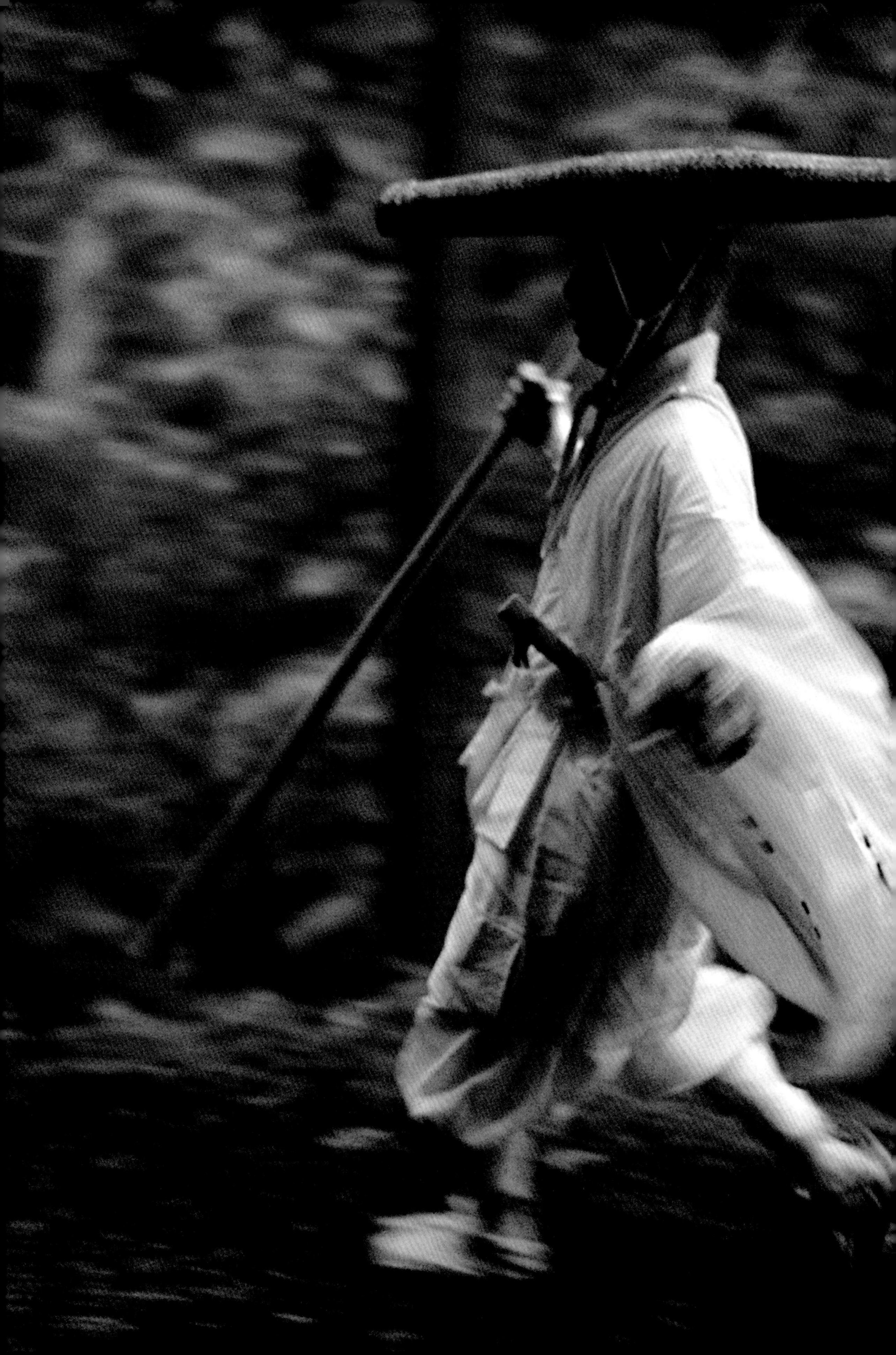

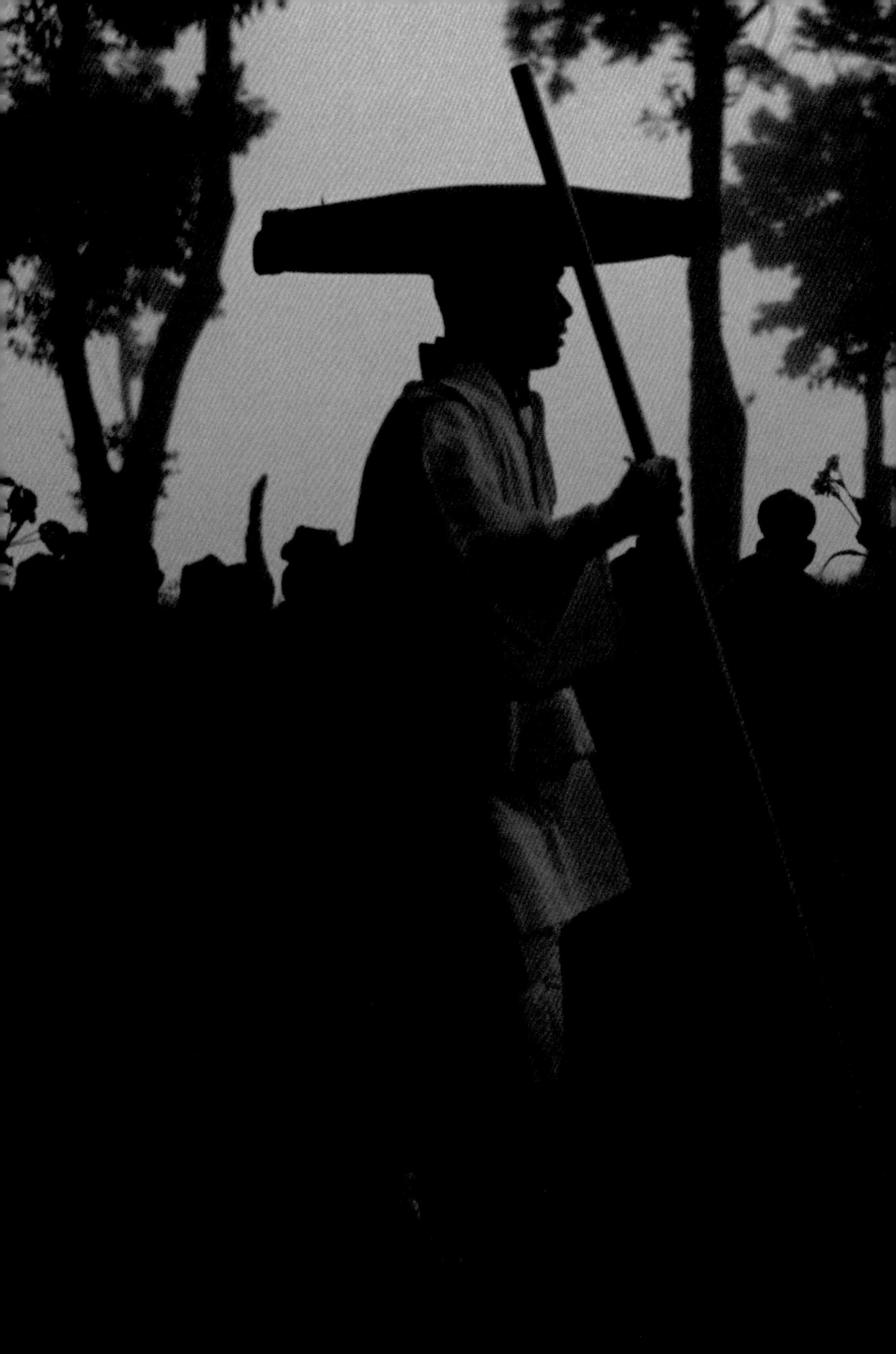

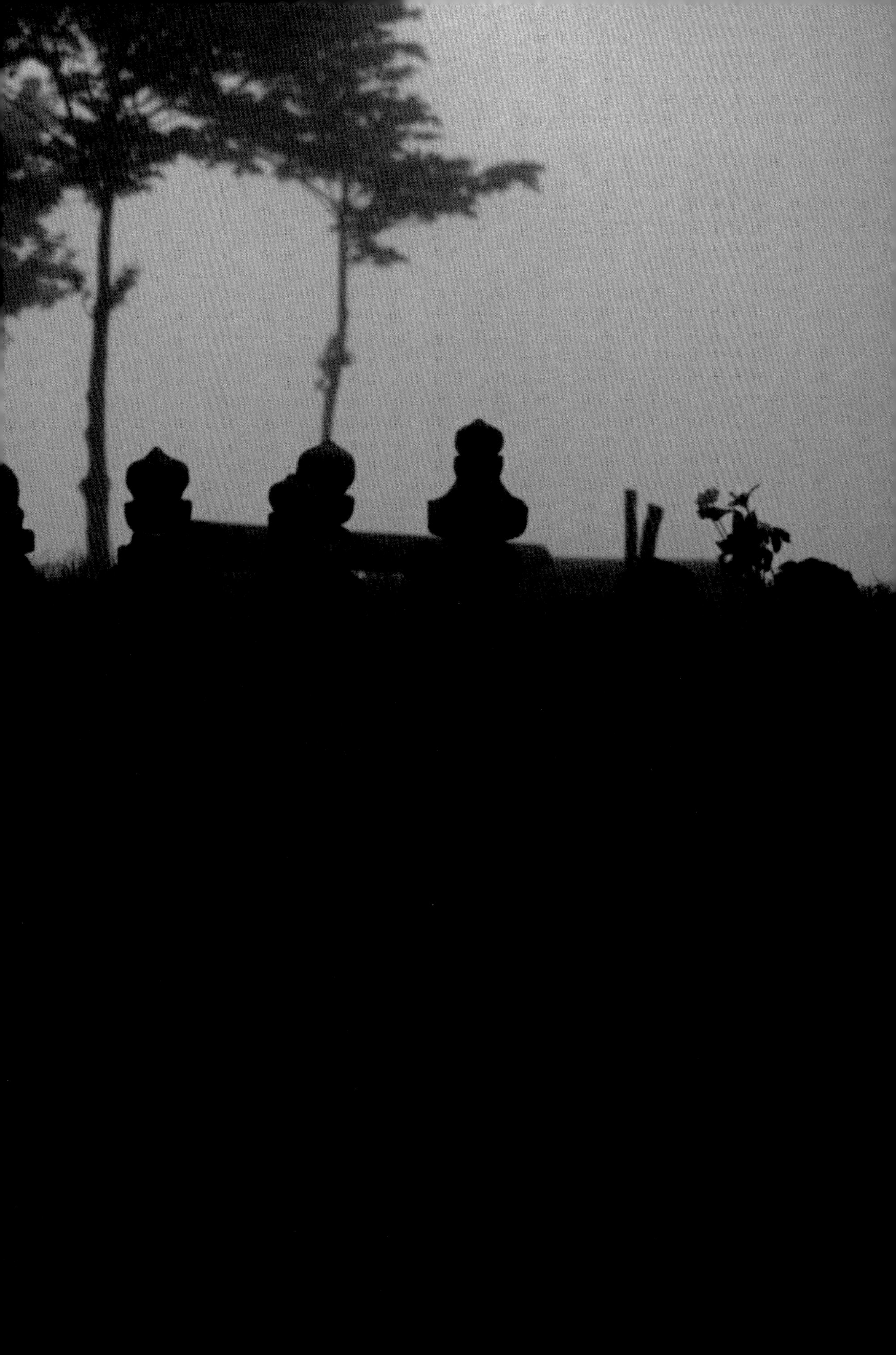

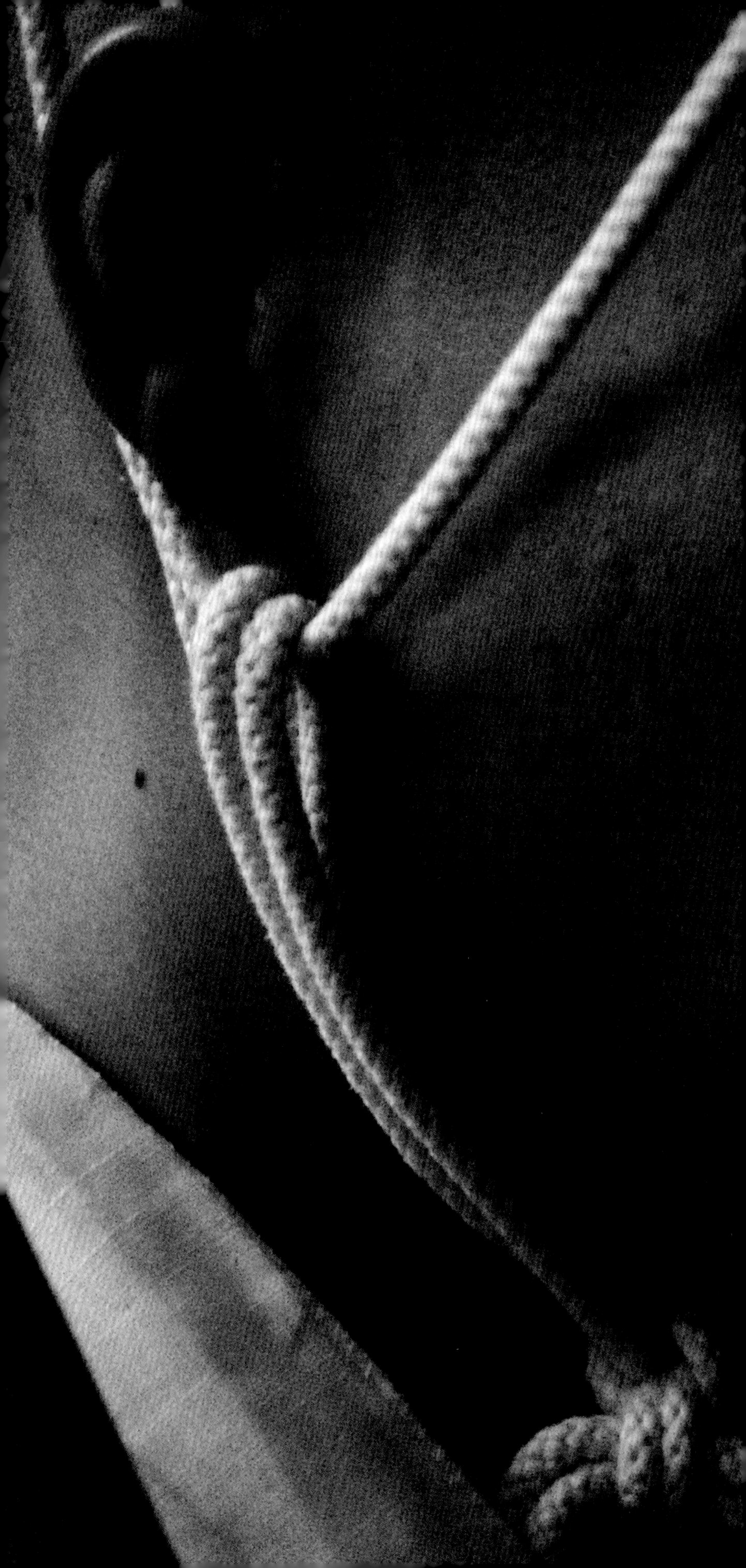

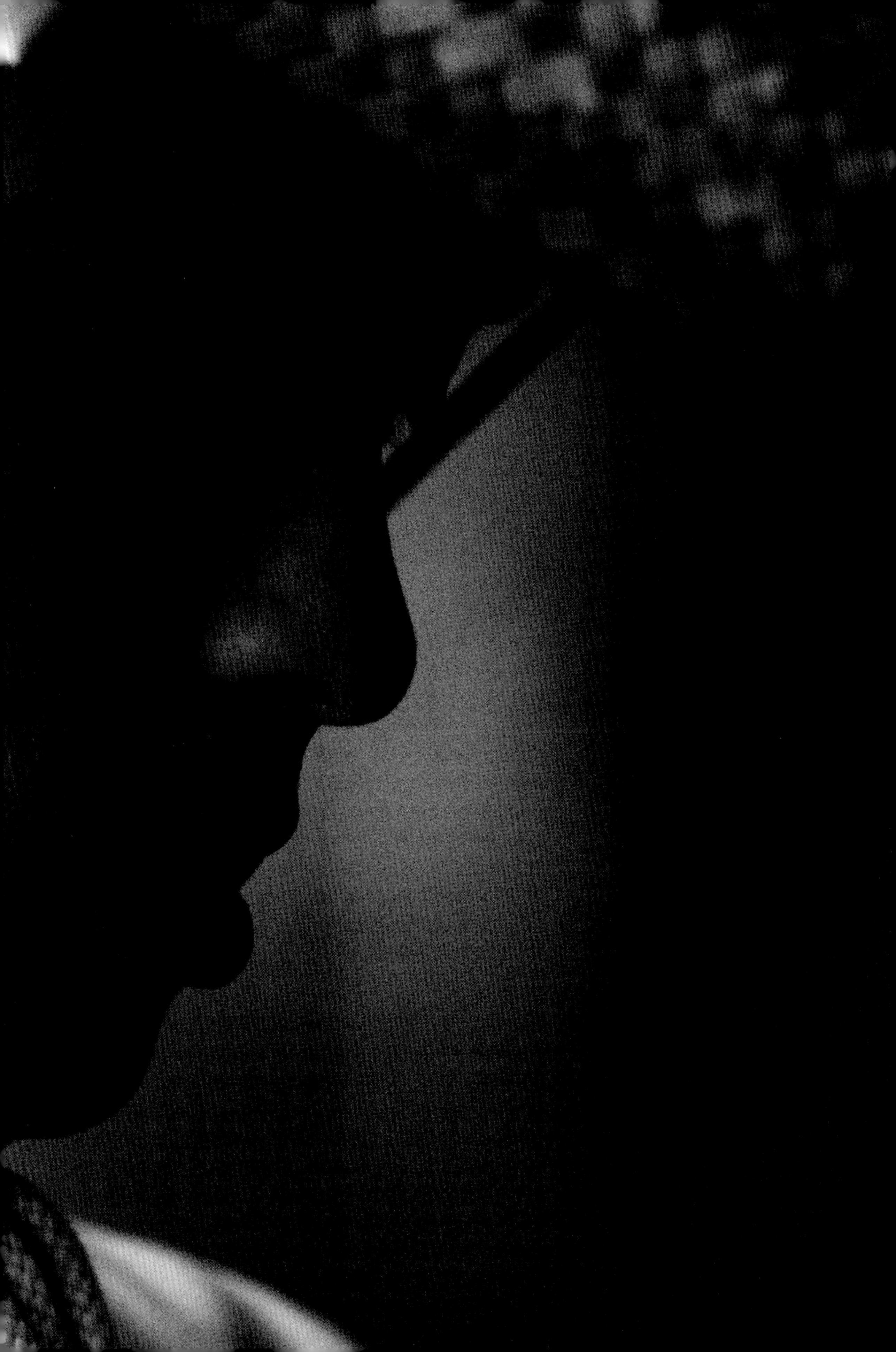

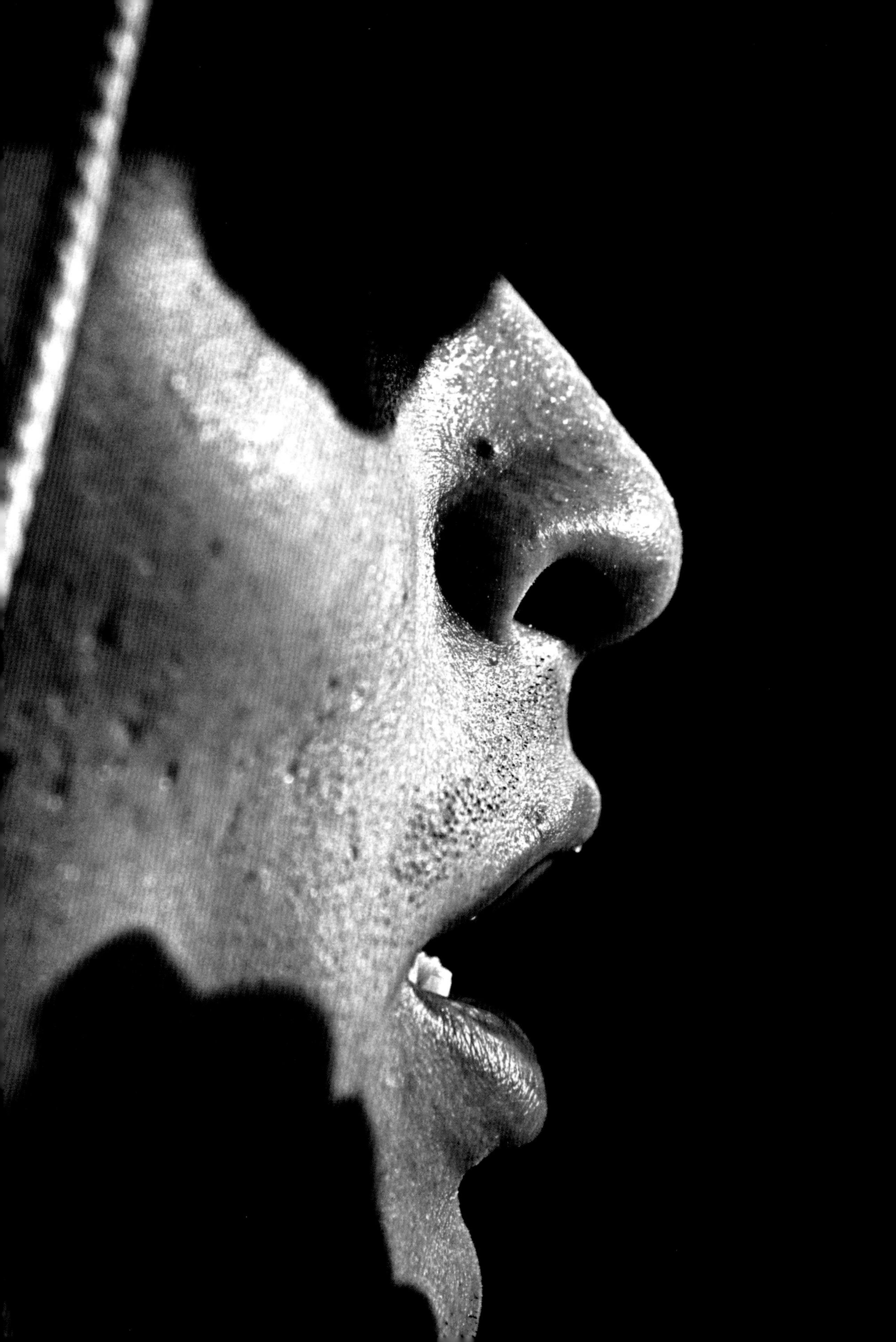

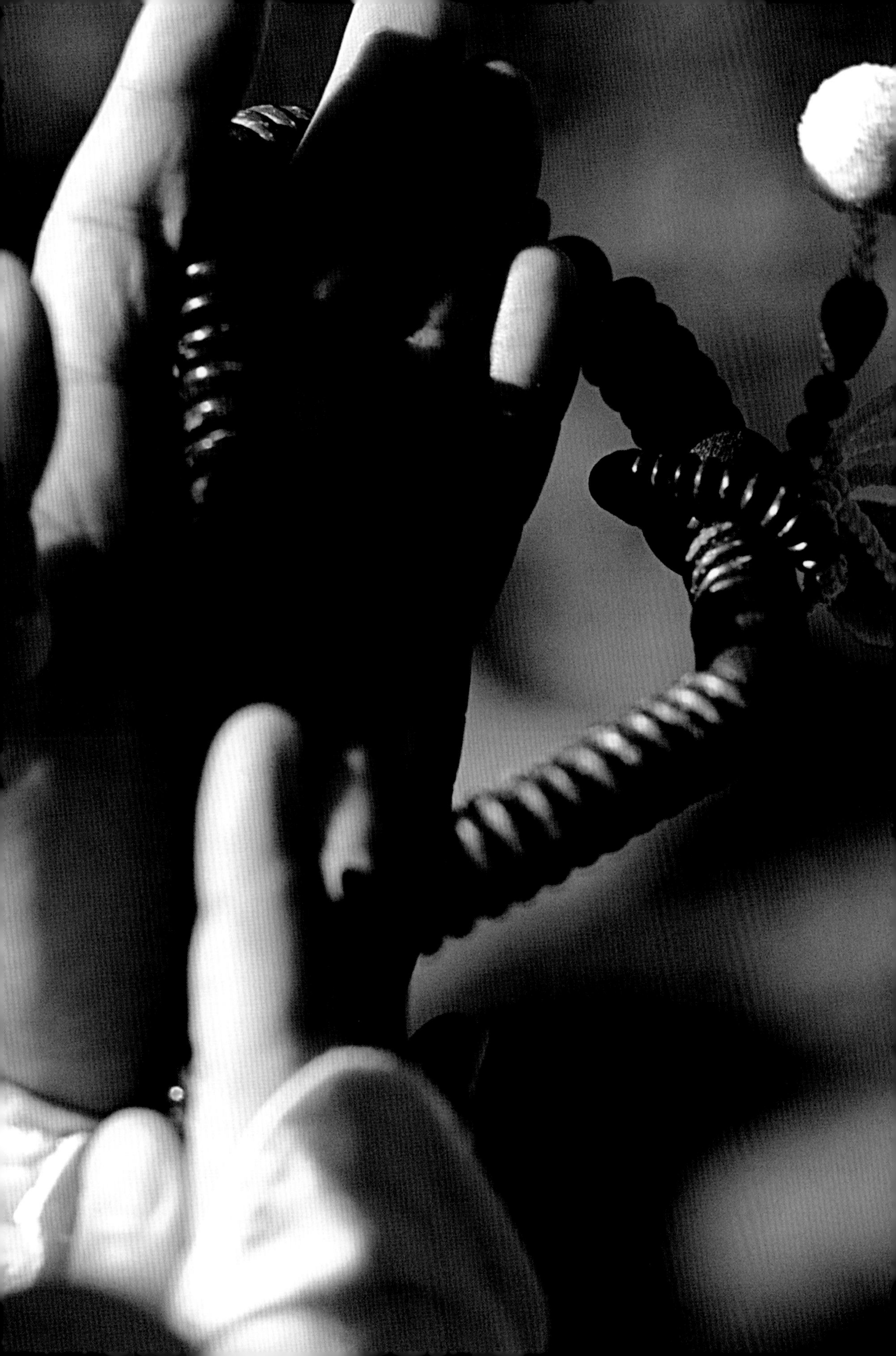

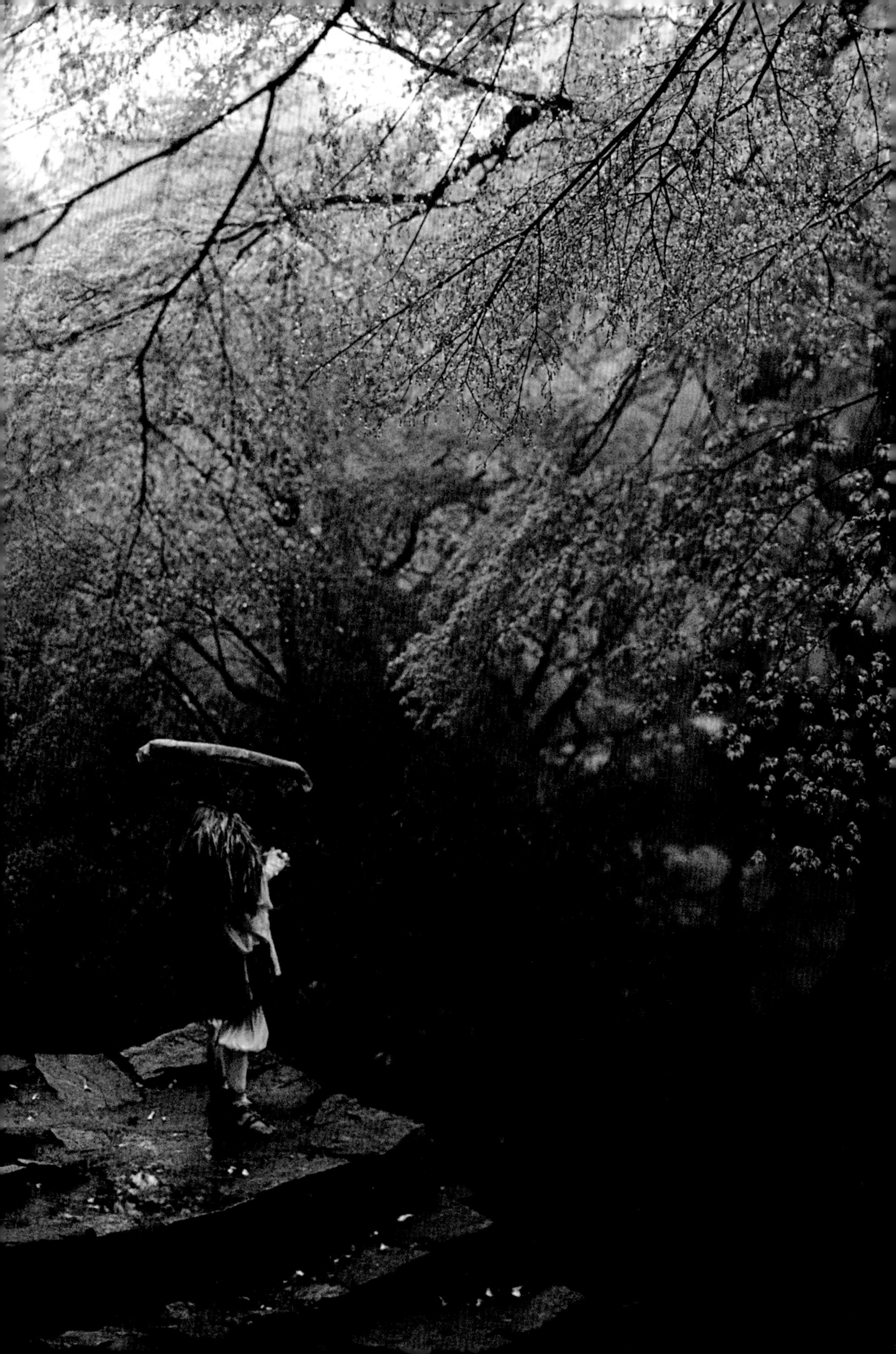

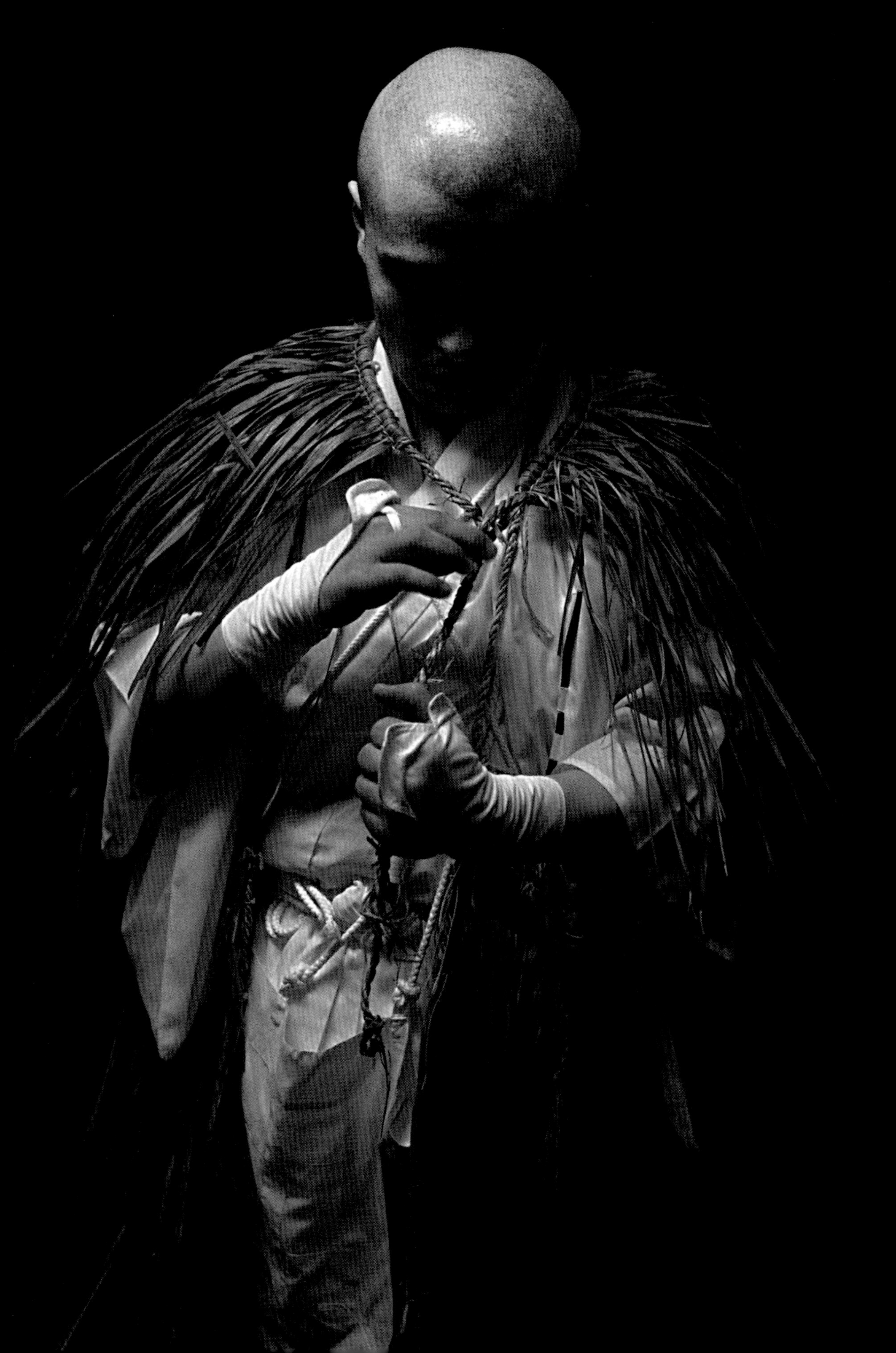

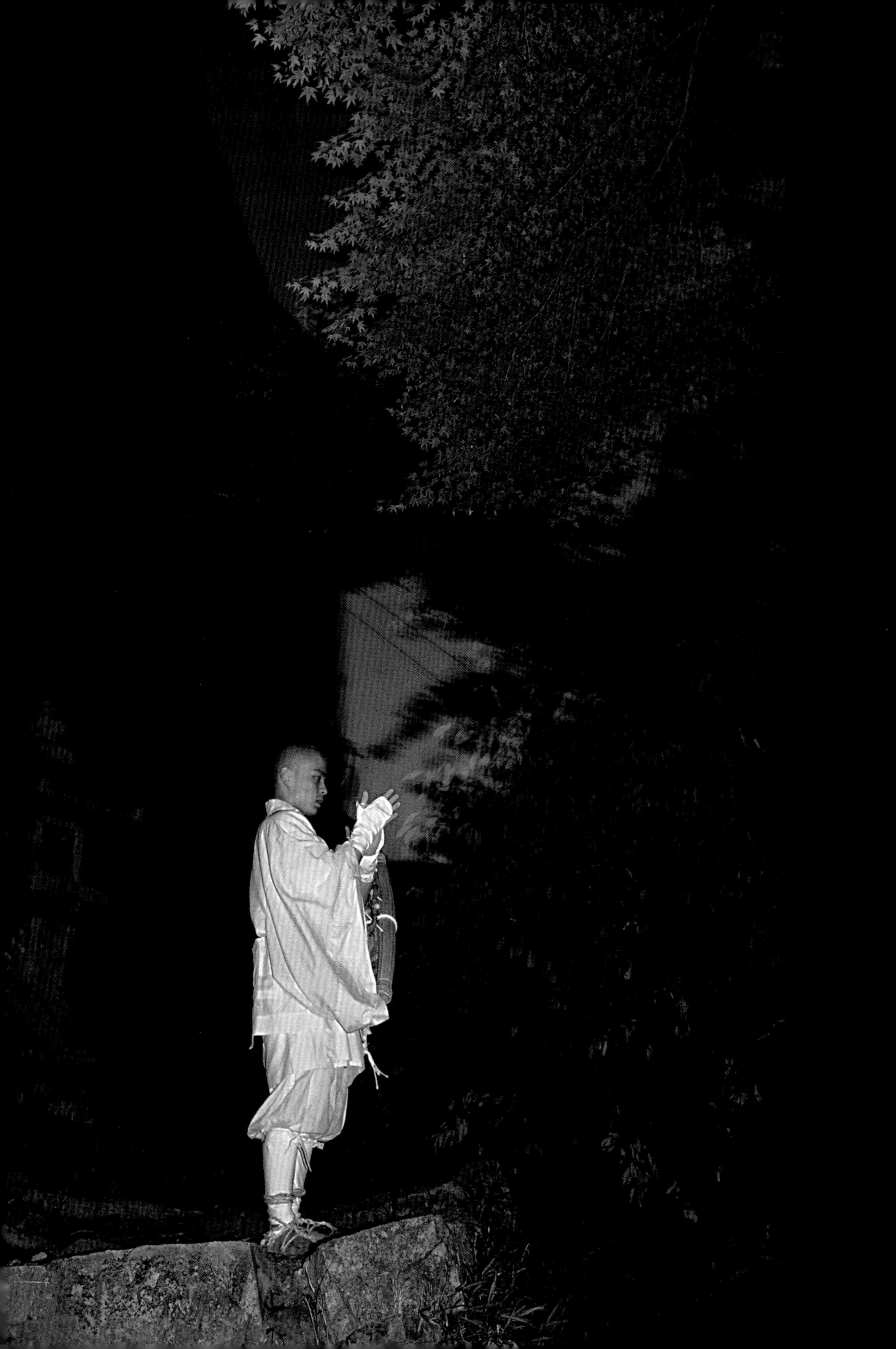

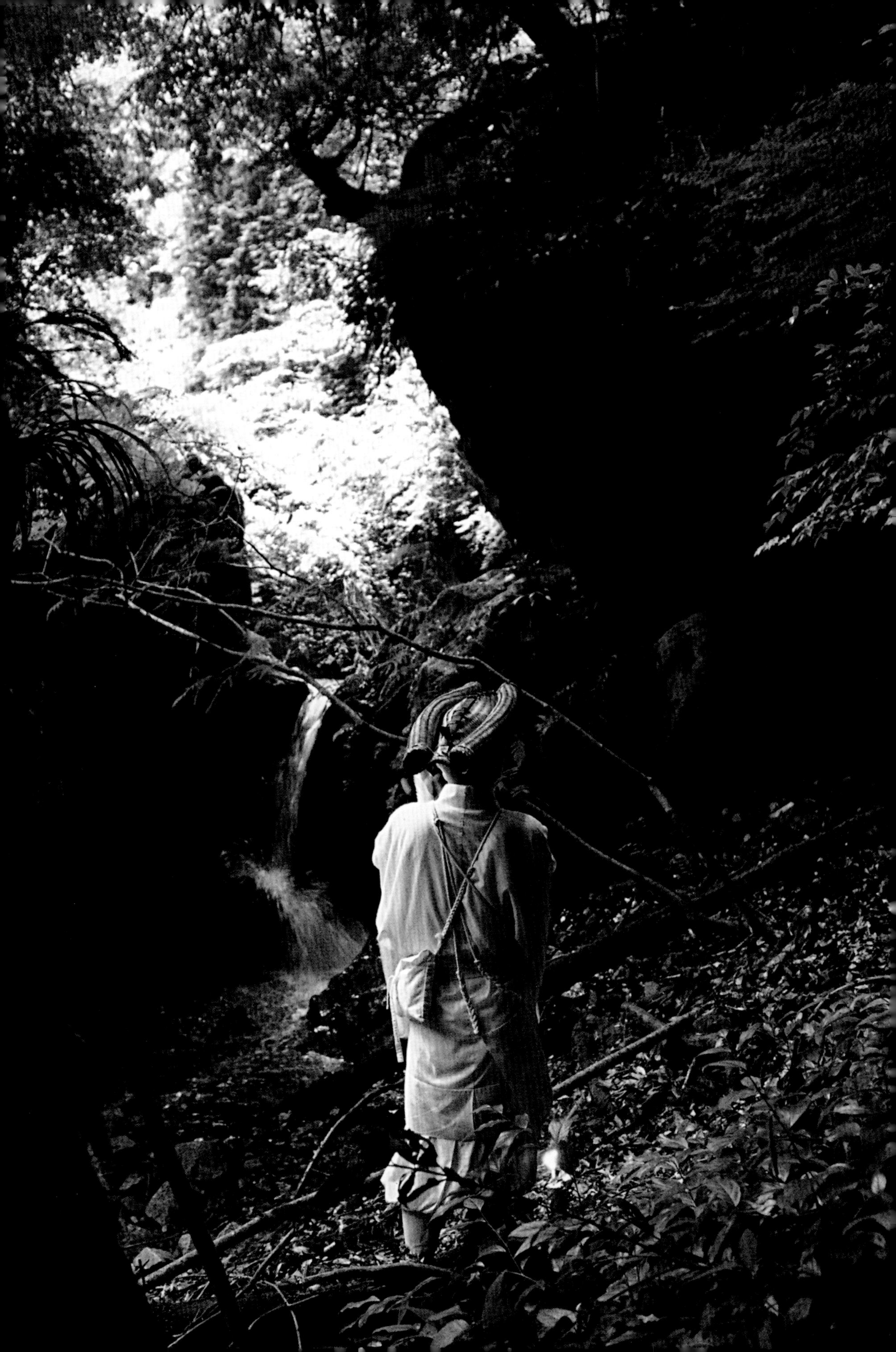

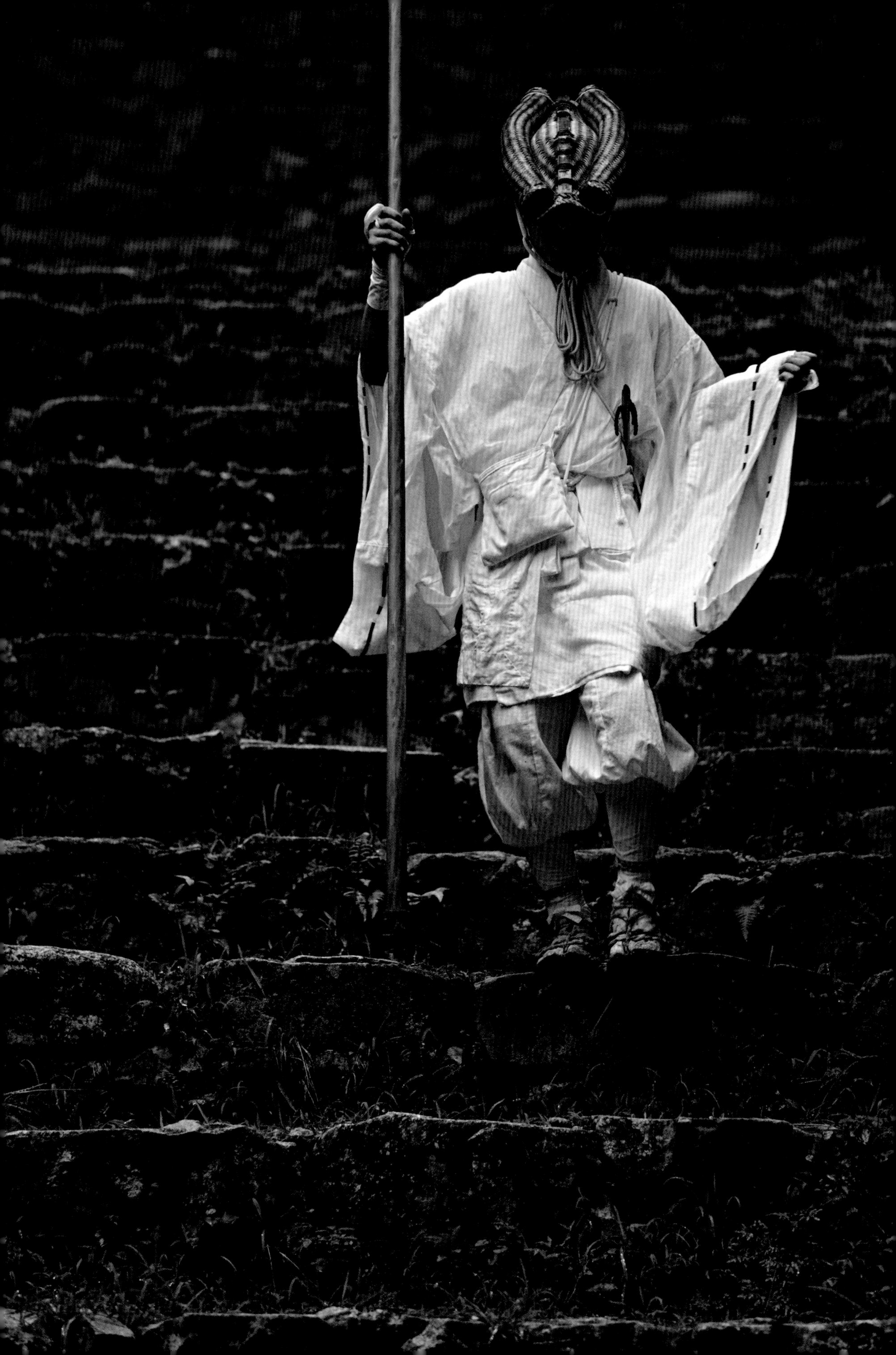

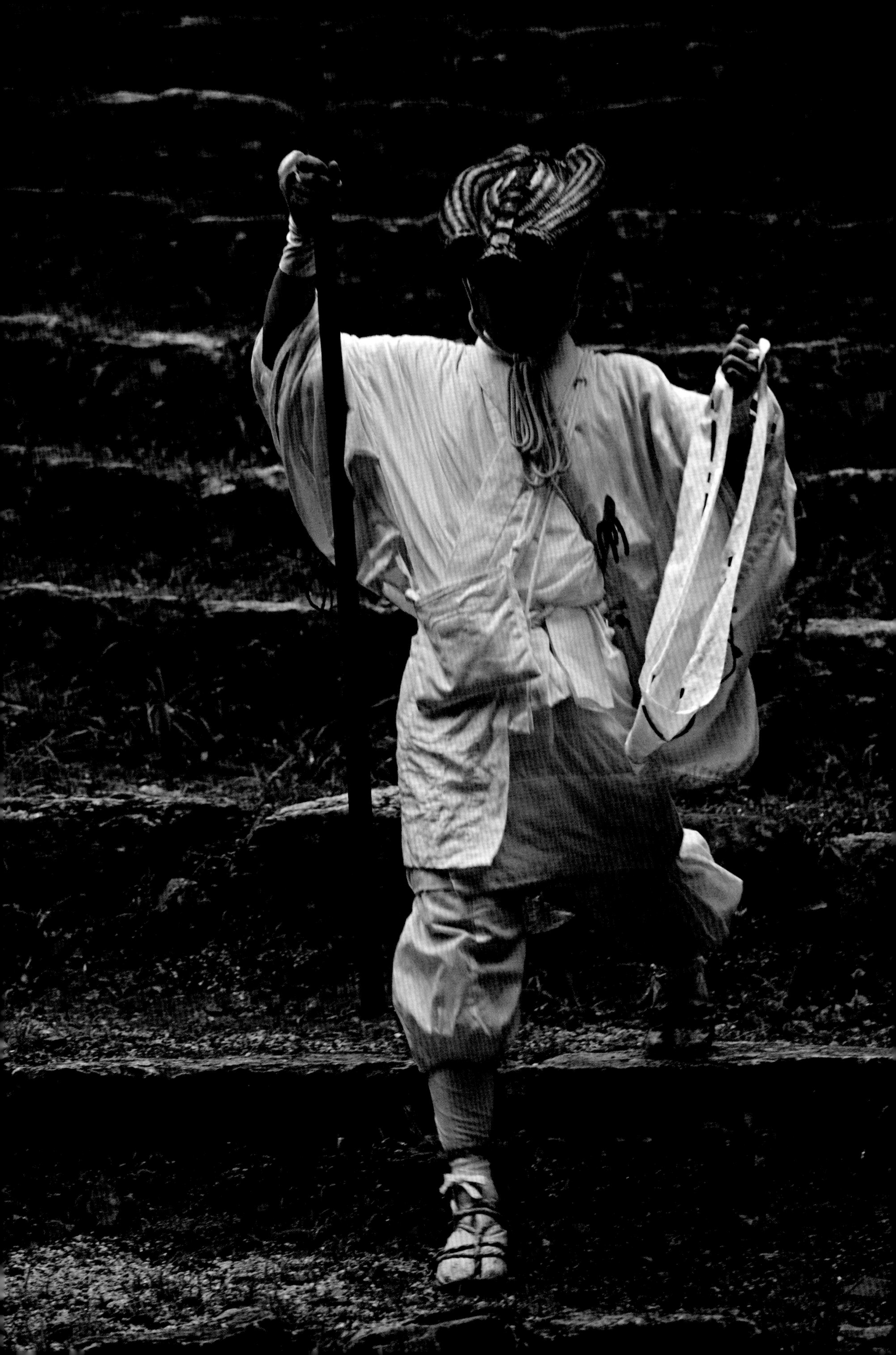

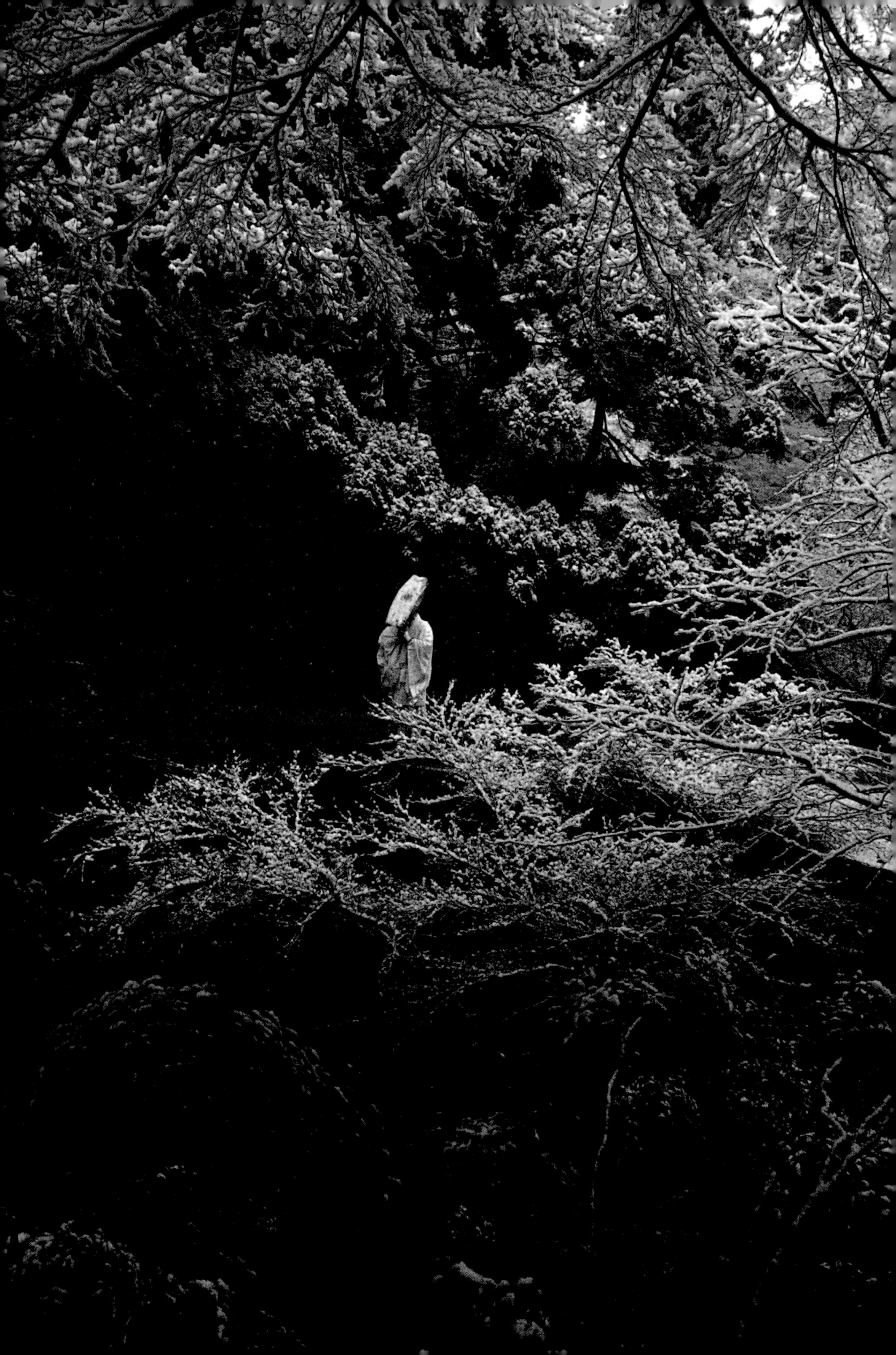

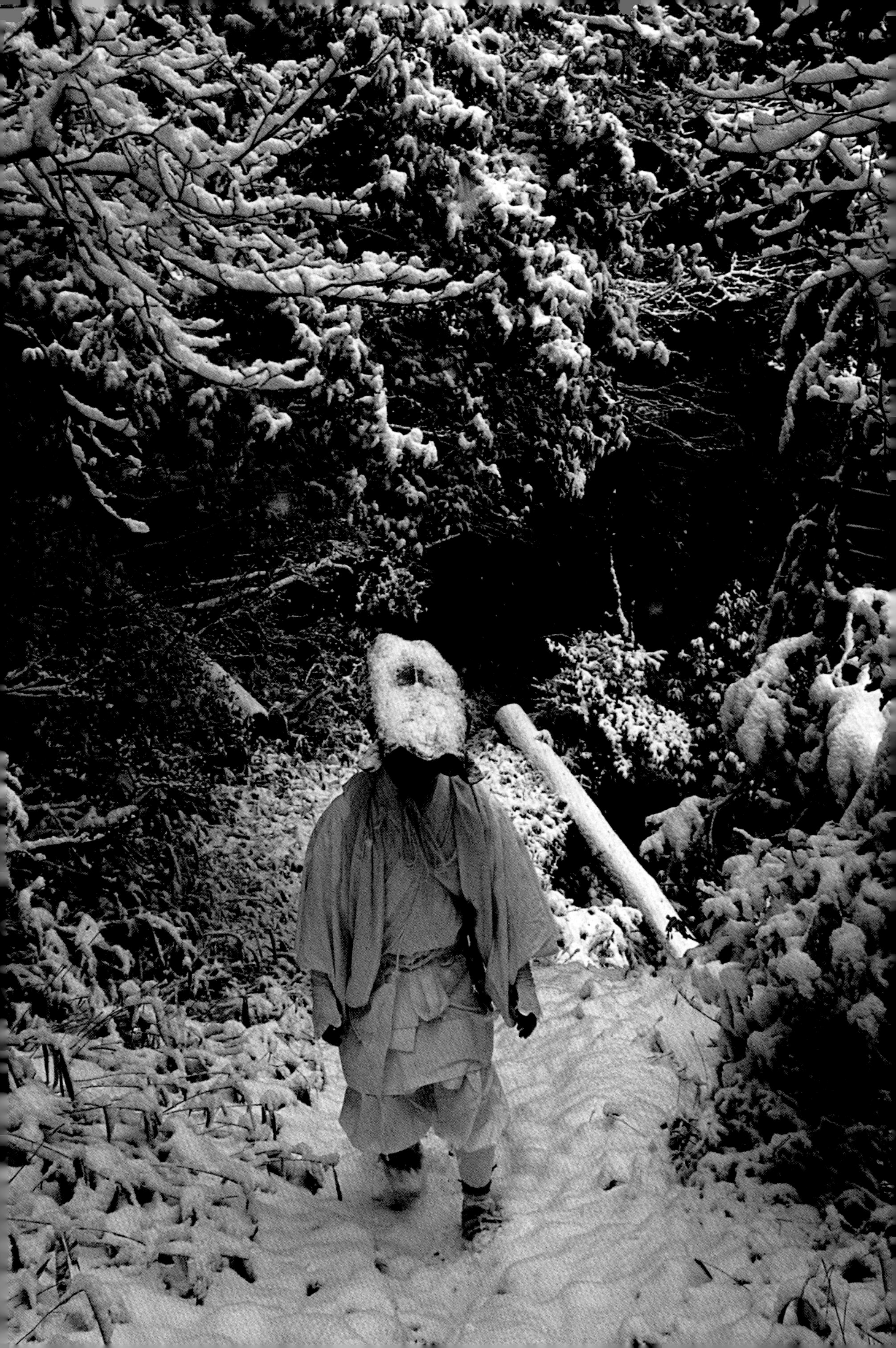

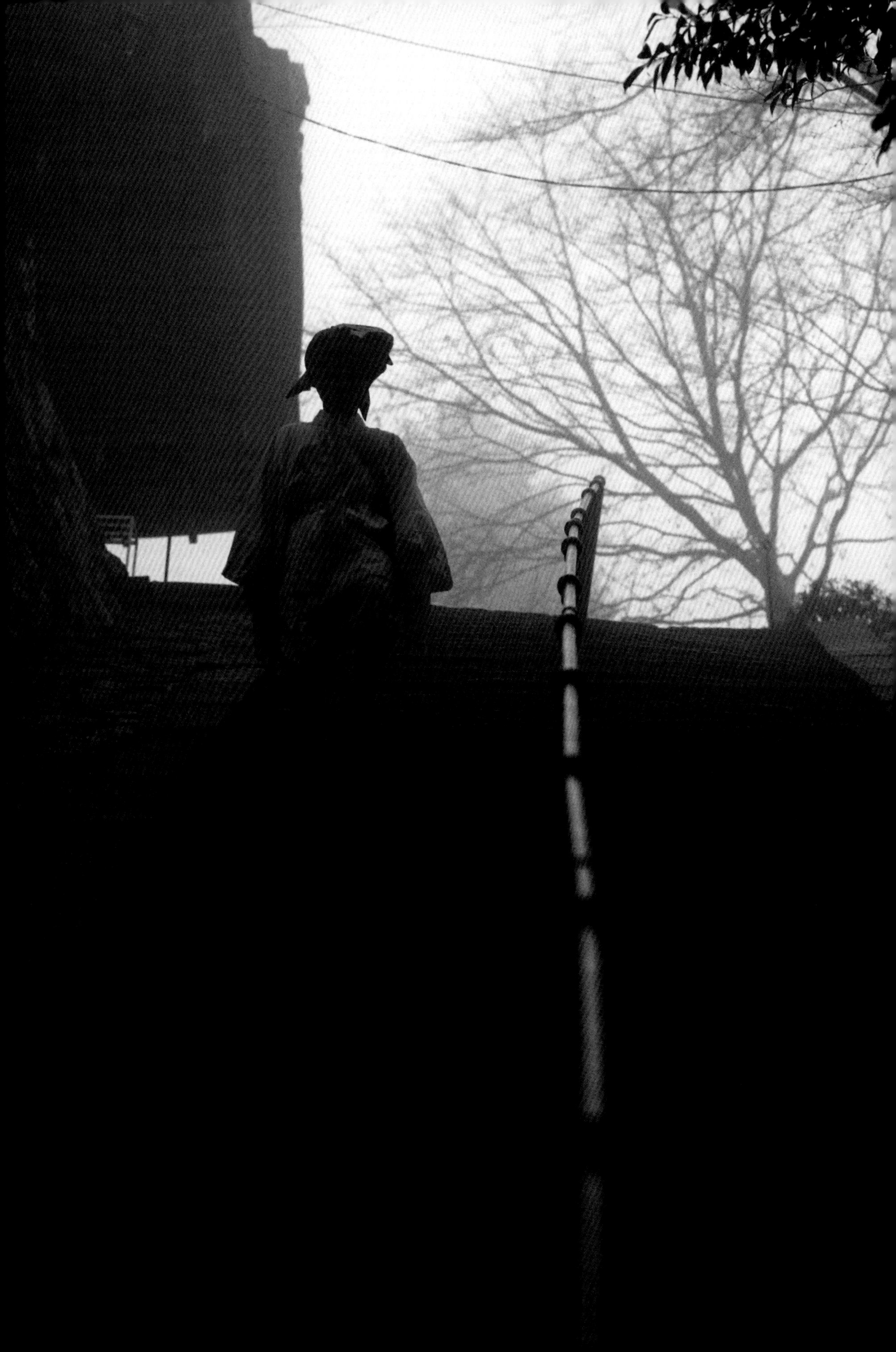

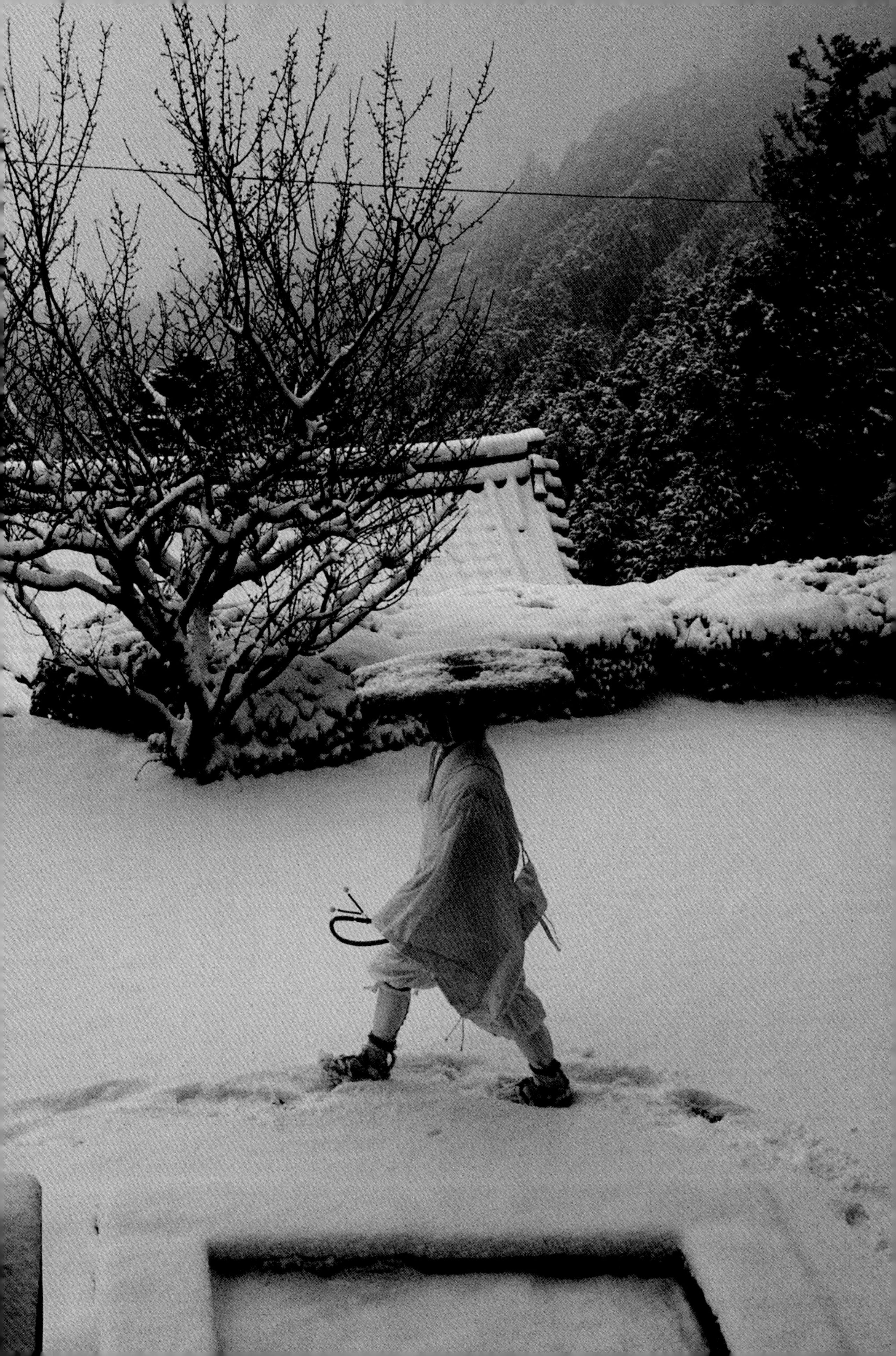

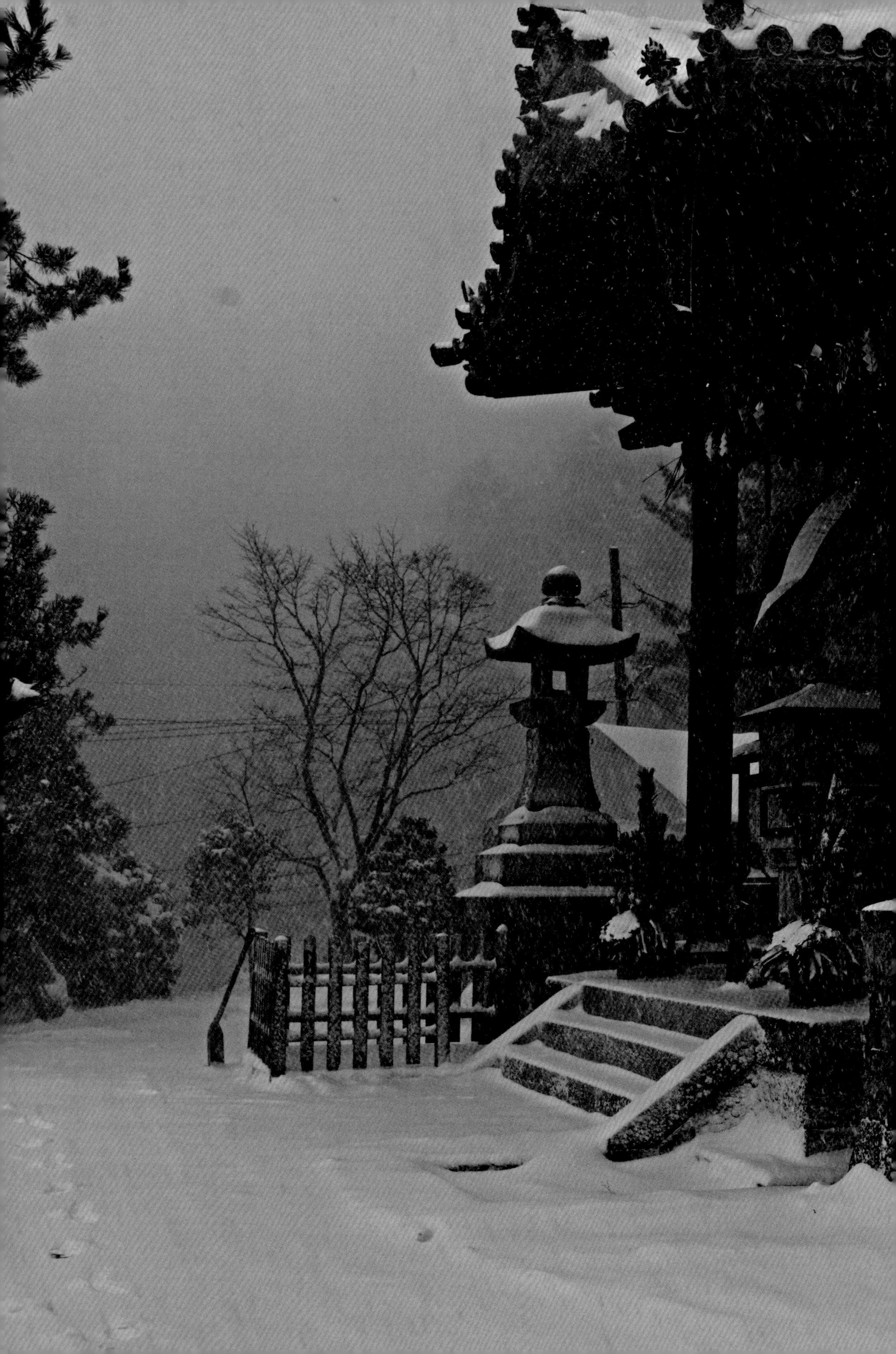

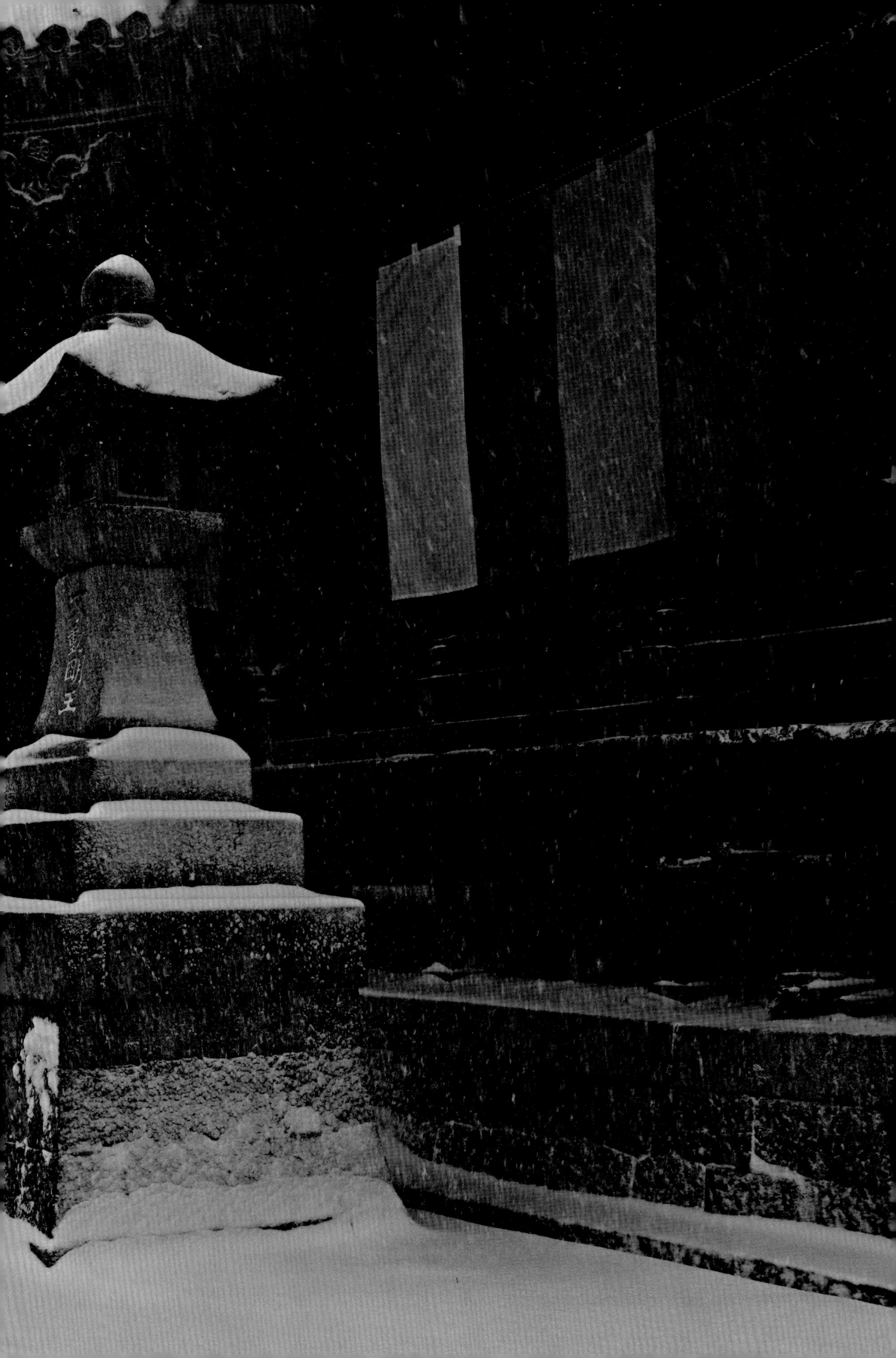
明王

堂入り | *Dōiri*

「明王堂参籠」(堂入り)は、九日間、食べ物も水も一切口にしない常識を逸脱した厳しい行である。入堂に先立つ斎食儀では、圓道師は食前の祈りを捧げただけで箸をとらず、ただ、一点を見つめて、じっと座っているだけであった。出堂を控え、明王堂の周囲は溢れんばかりの参拝者で埋め尽くされ、深夜にもかかわらず、無動寺谷に「ナーマク　サーマンダバーサラナンセンダー・・・」と唱える不動真言の声が深く響いていた。
出堂後、目を潤ませながら、「生き仏さんやなあ」と言ったある男性の言葉が、今も思い出される。

Dōiri (Confinement to Myōōdō temple) is a rigorous rite. Over the course of nine days one cannot eat or even drink water, removing oneself from ordinary life and experience. This rite takes place after the first seven hundred days of the *kaihōgyō* has been completed. It is seen as one of the most difficult aspects of the thousand day *kaihōgyō*. Every day the participant must also make a 200m journey to a well to fetch water as an offering. At the lunch ceremony in preparation for entering the temple, Reverend Endō took up no chopsticks. He simply made a pre-lunch prayer, then sat staring.
On the last day of the training when Reverend Endō exited the temple, the building was surrounded by well-wishers and pilgrims. Late into the night the Mudōji Valley resonated with the sound of chanting "*Na-maku Thurman dubber Saranansenda...*".
After Reverend Endō had left the temple, one man said with tears in his eyes, 'He is a living Buddha'. Even now I remember his words.

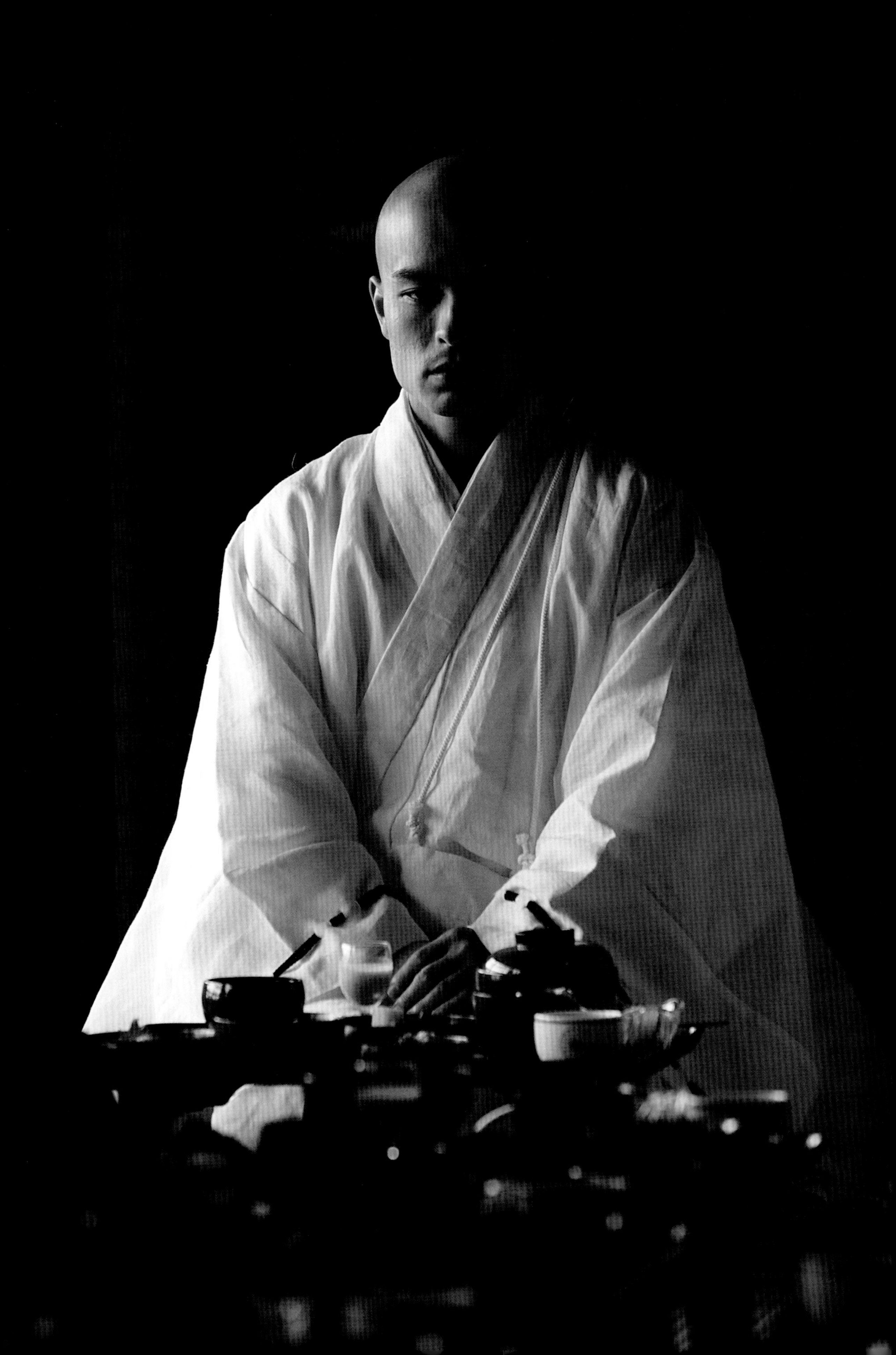

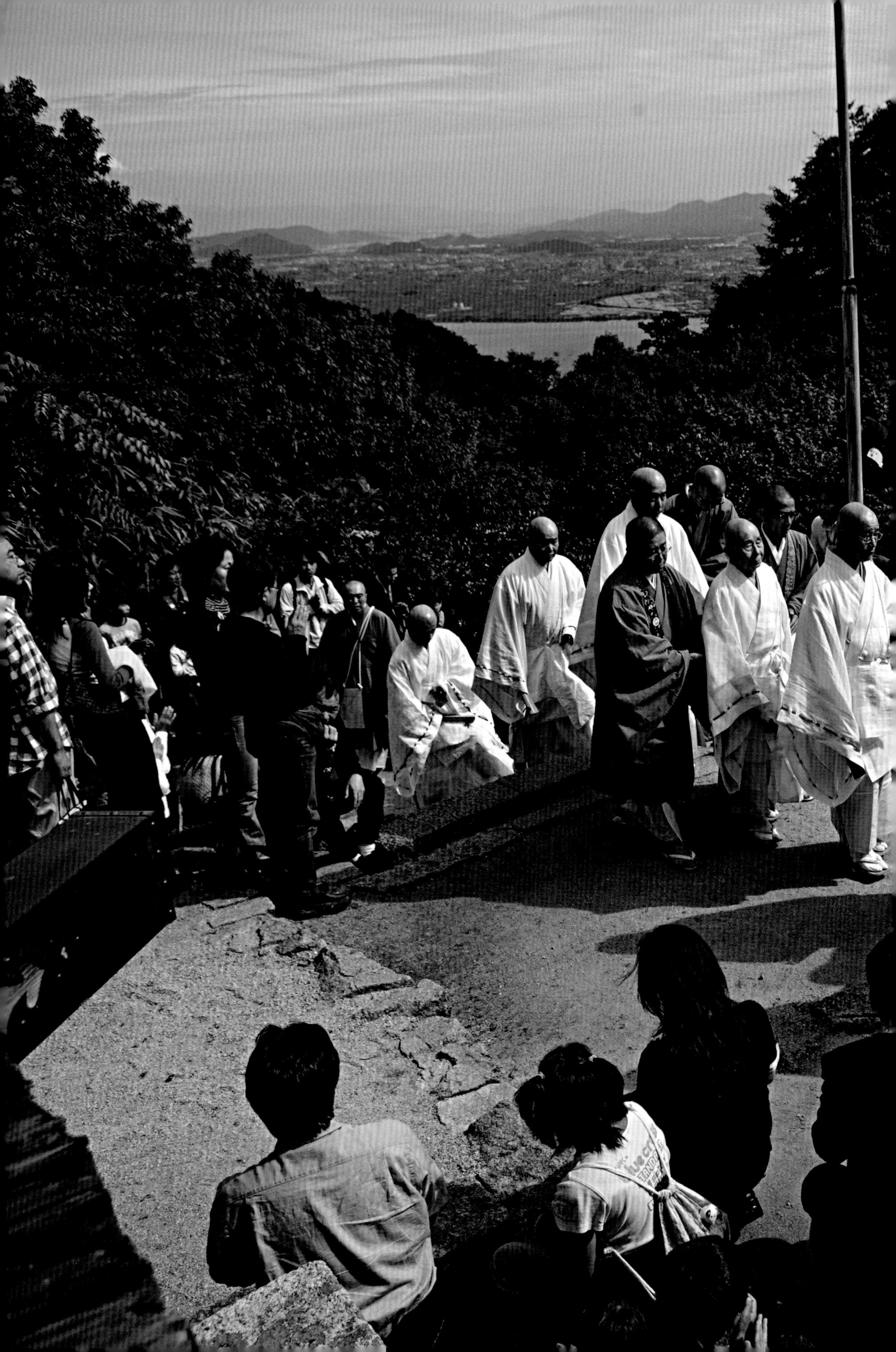

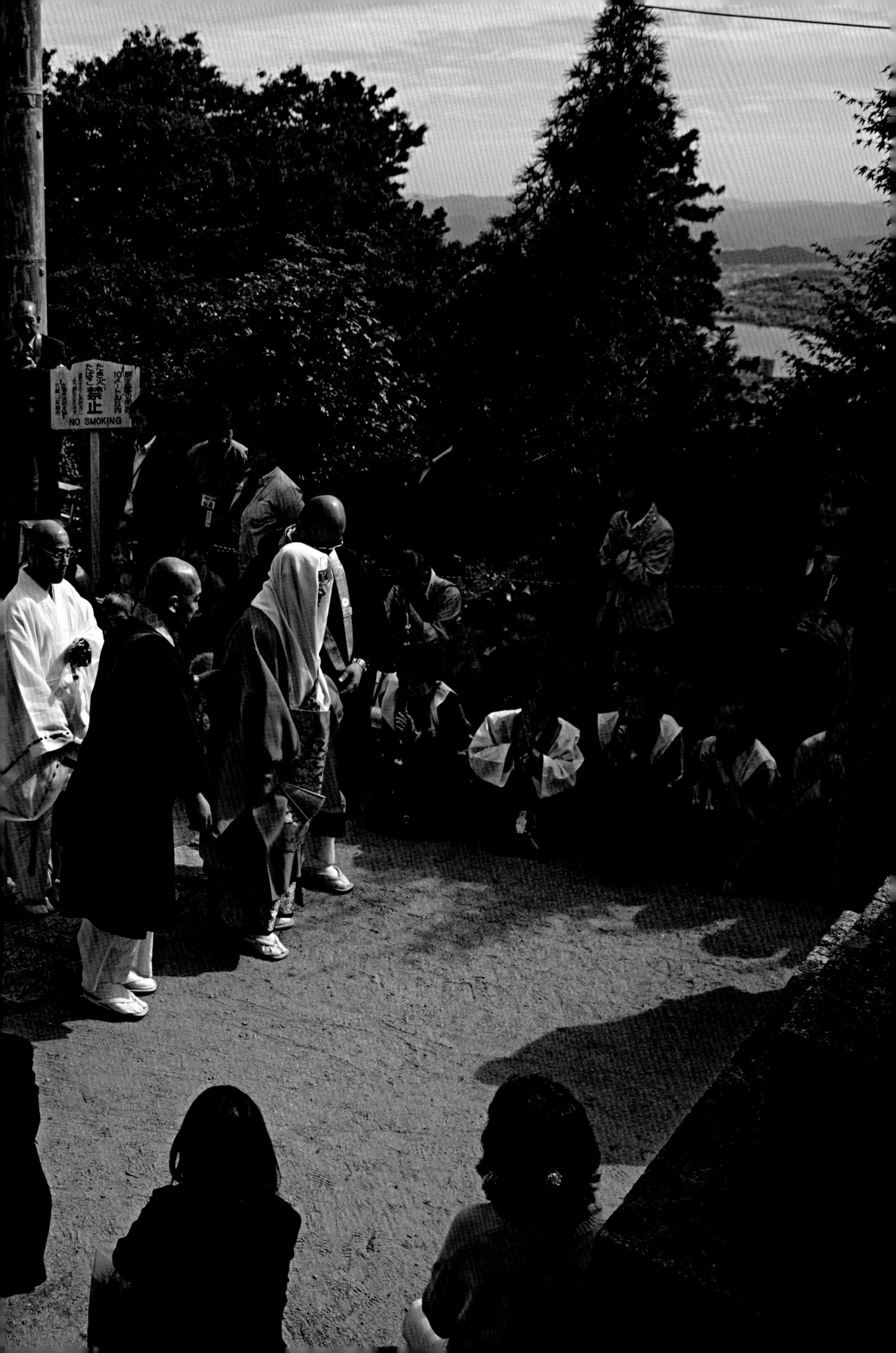
たき火、
たばこ
禁止
NO SMOKING

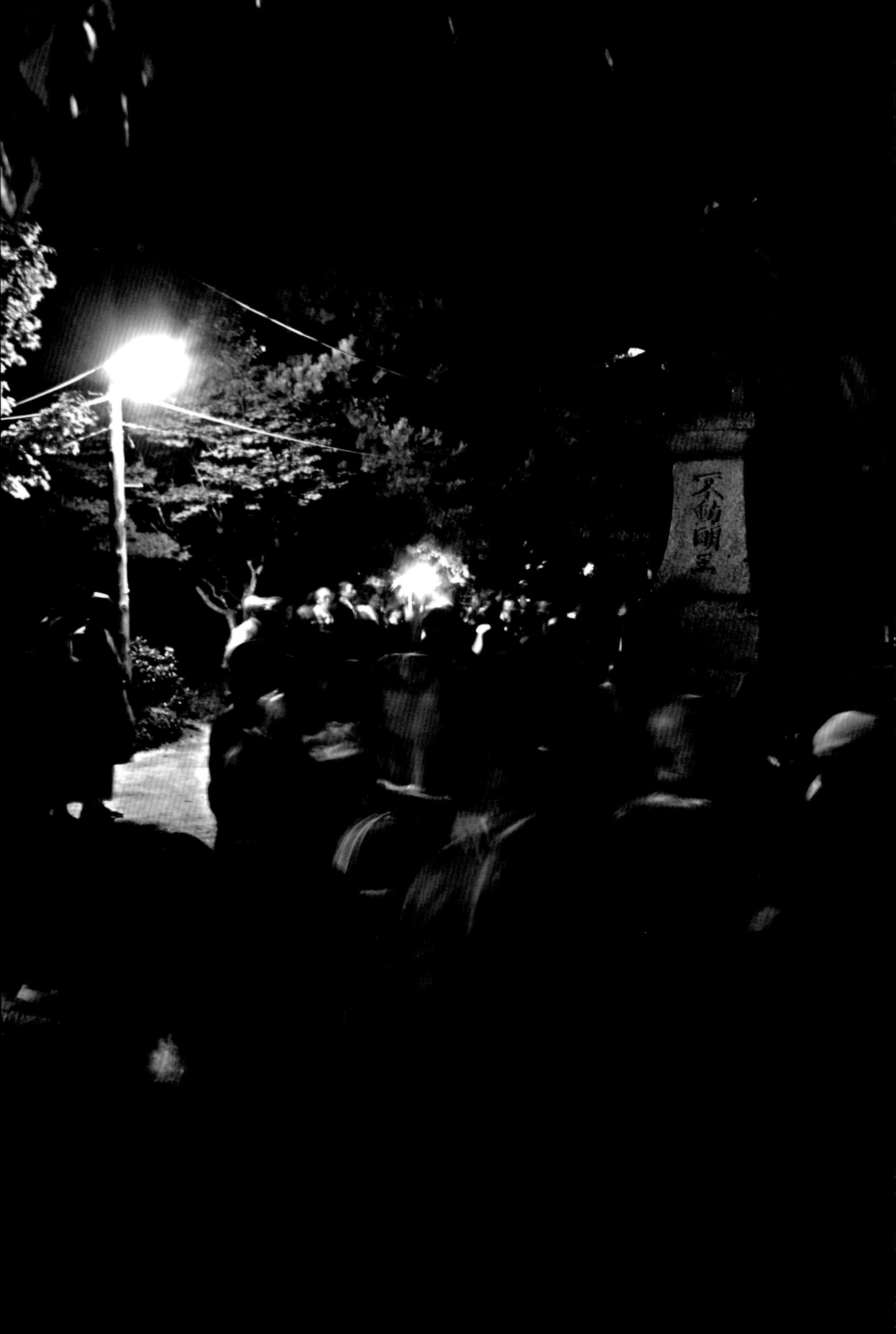
不動明王

大聖不動明王

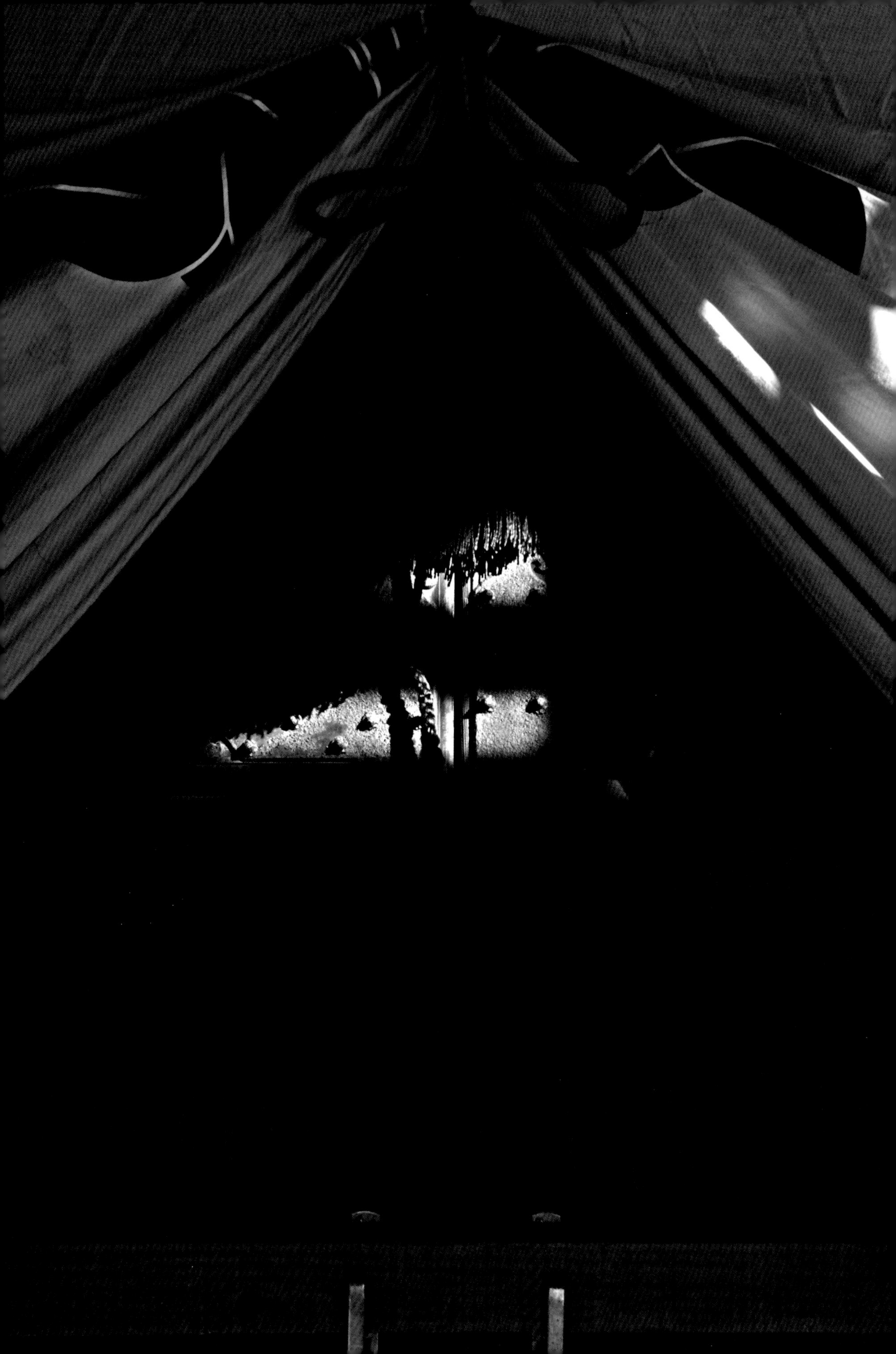

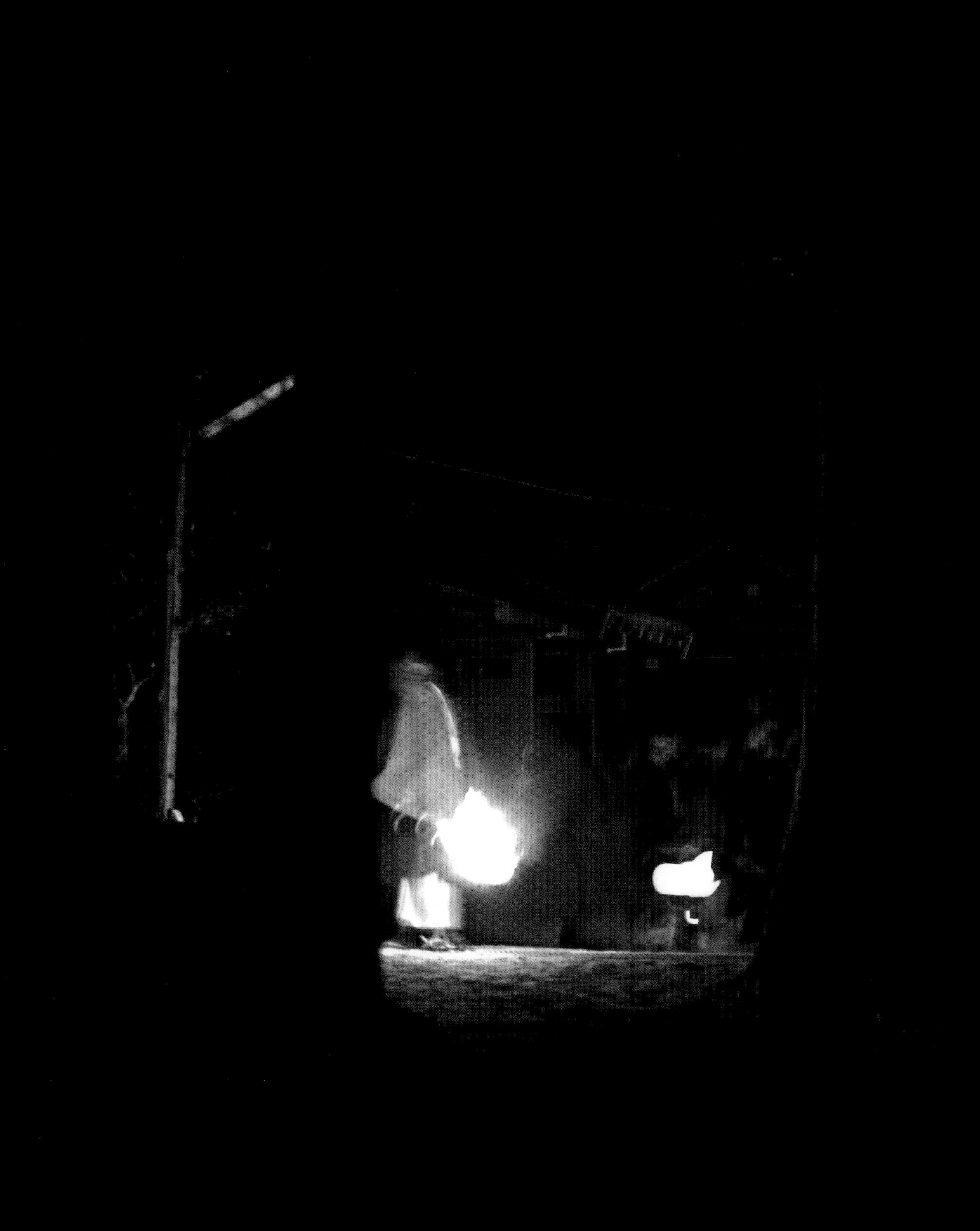

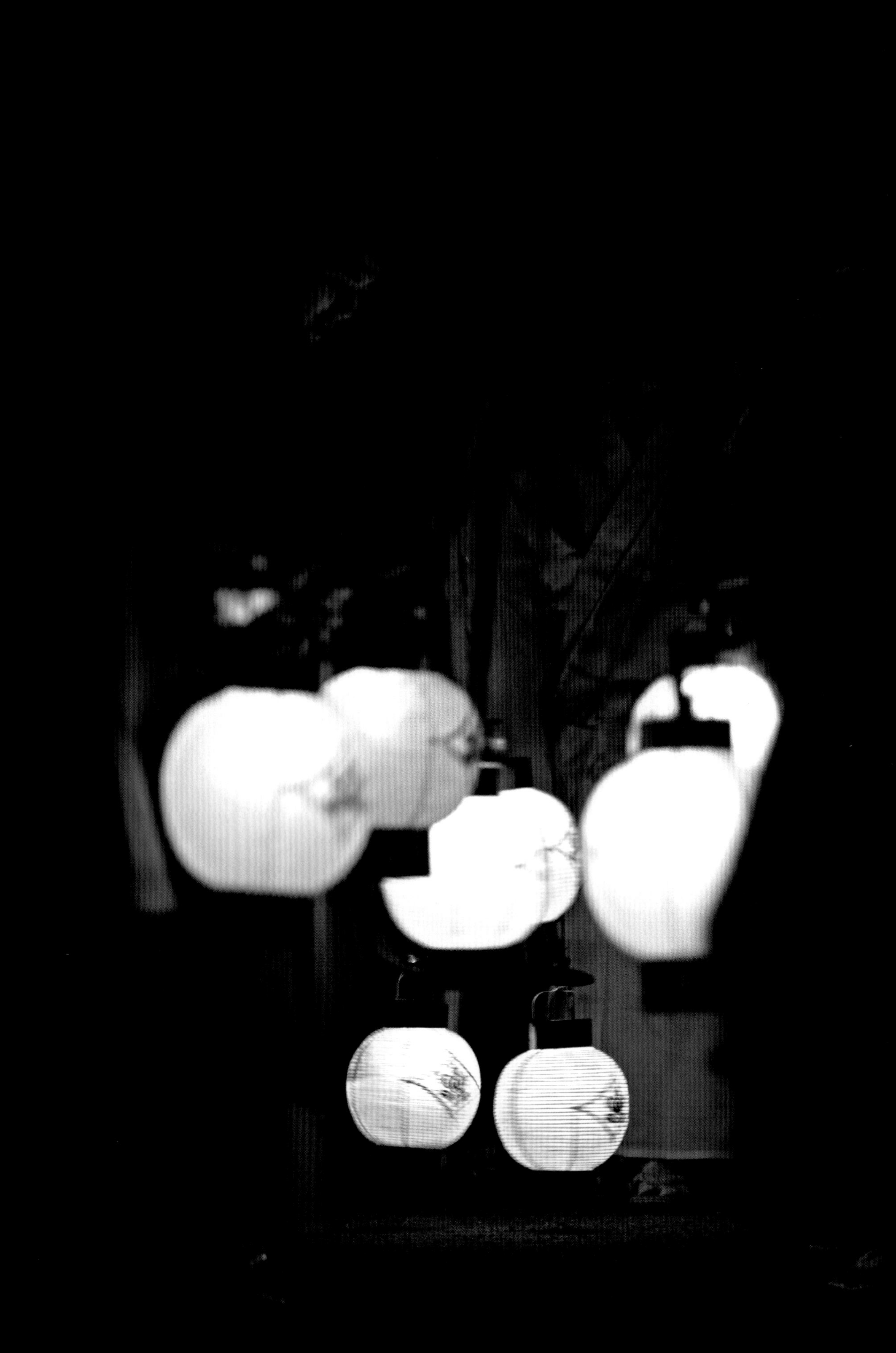

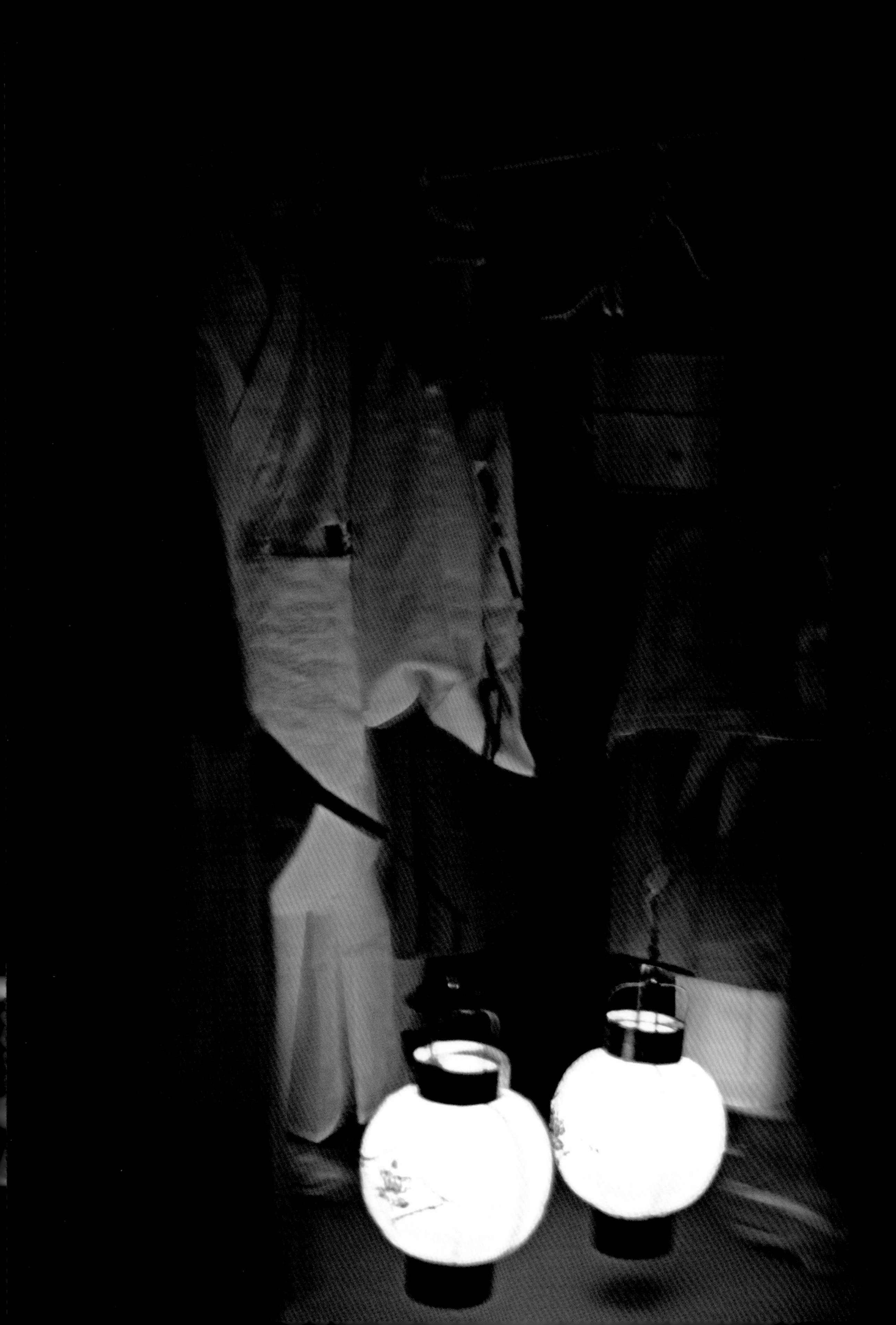

明王堂

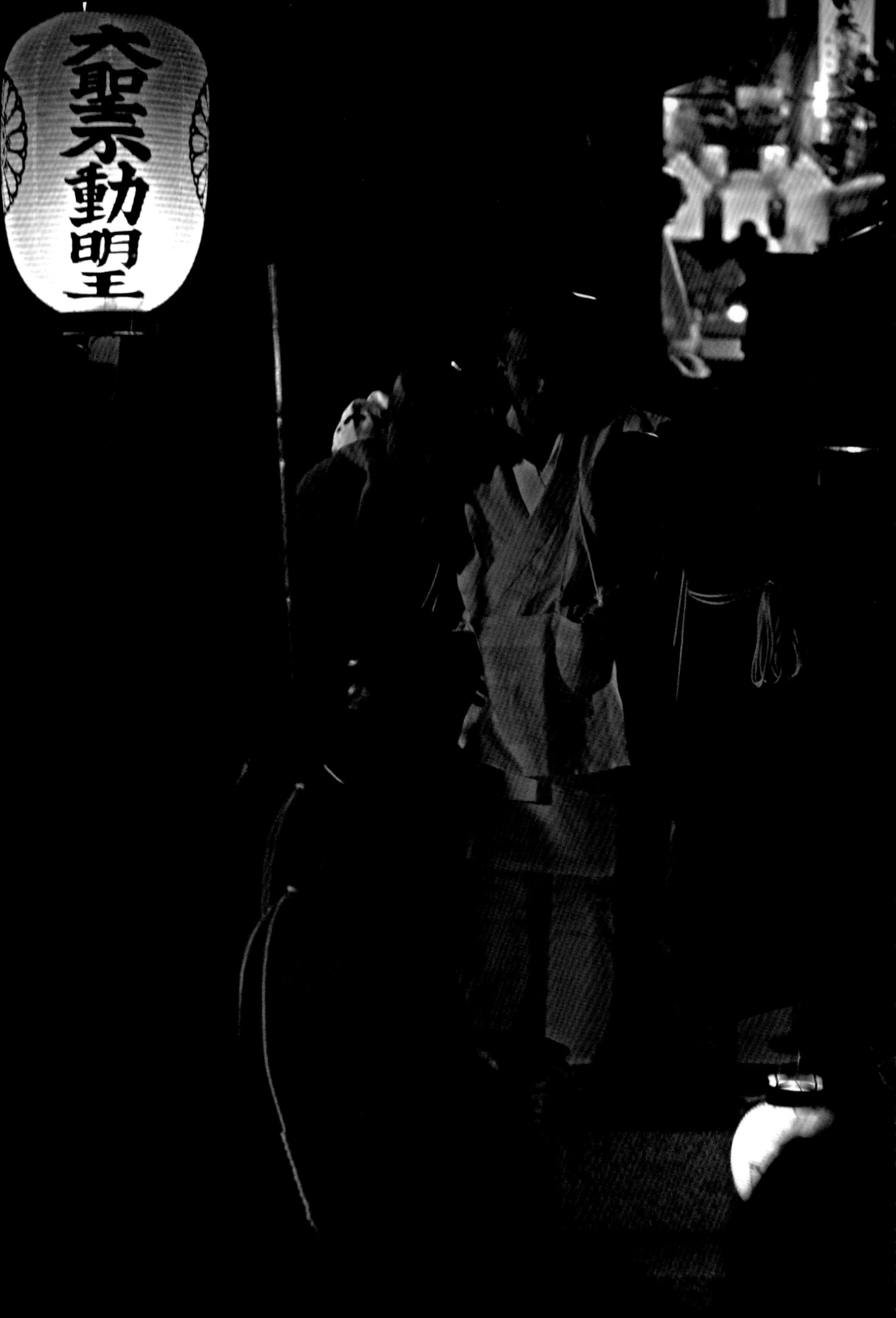
大聖不動明王

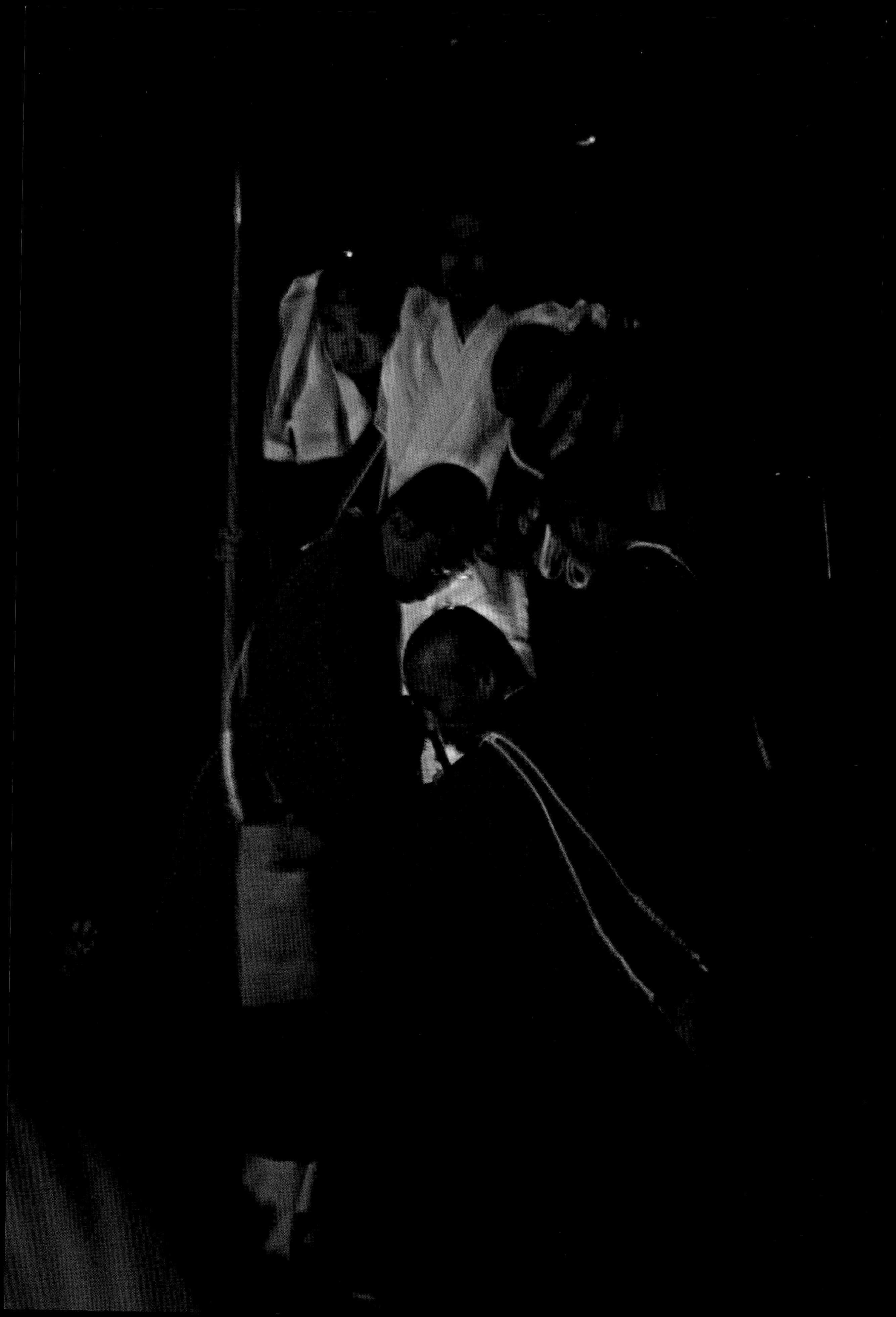

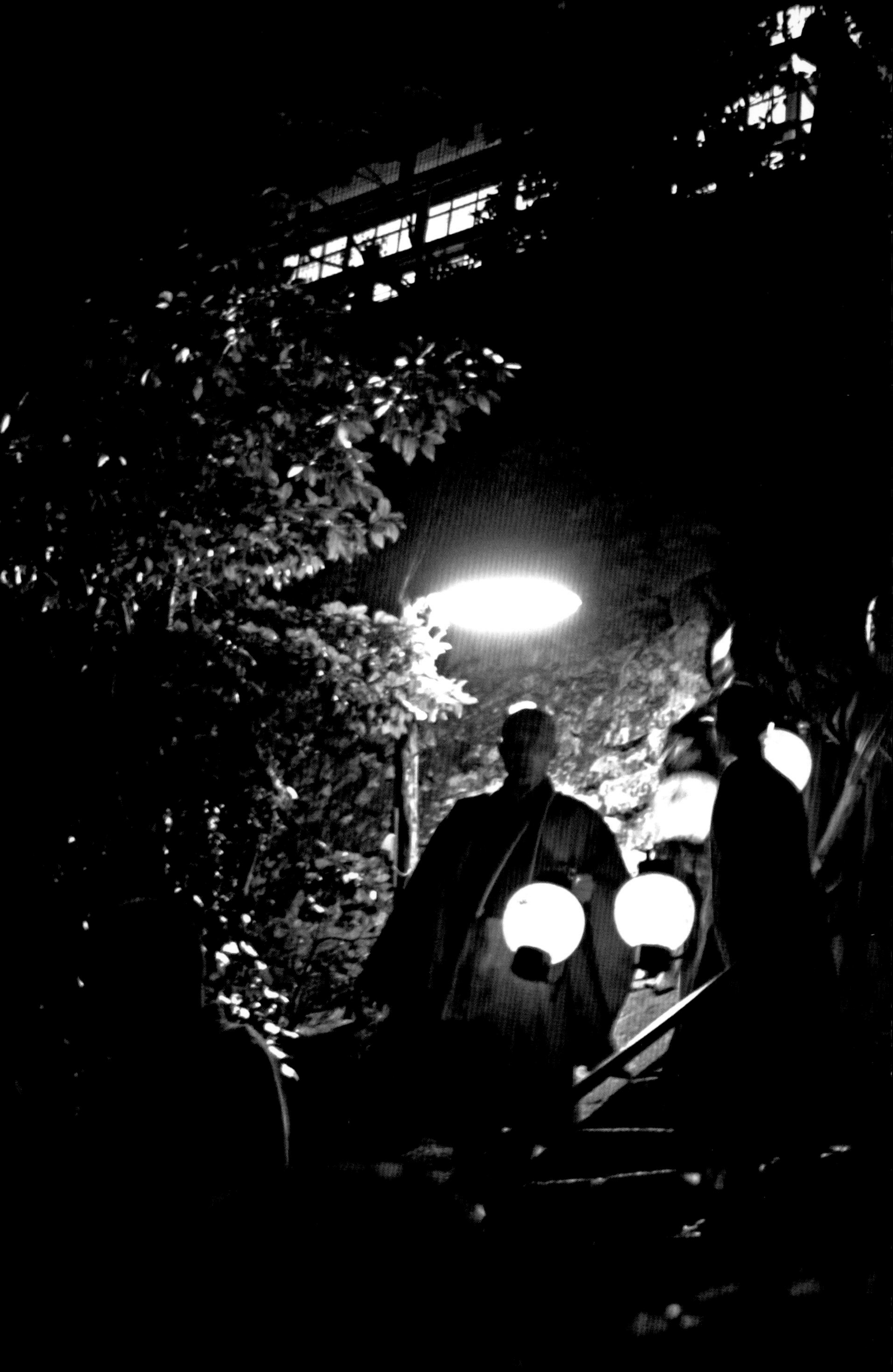

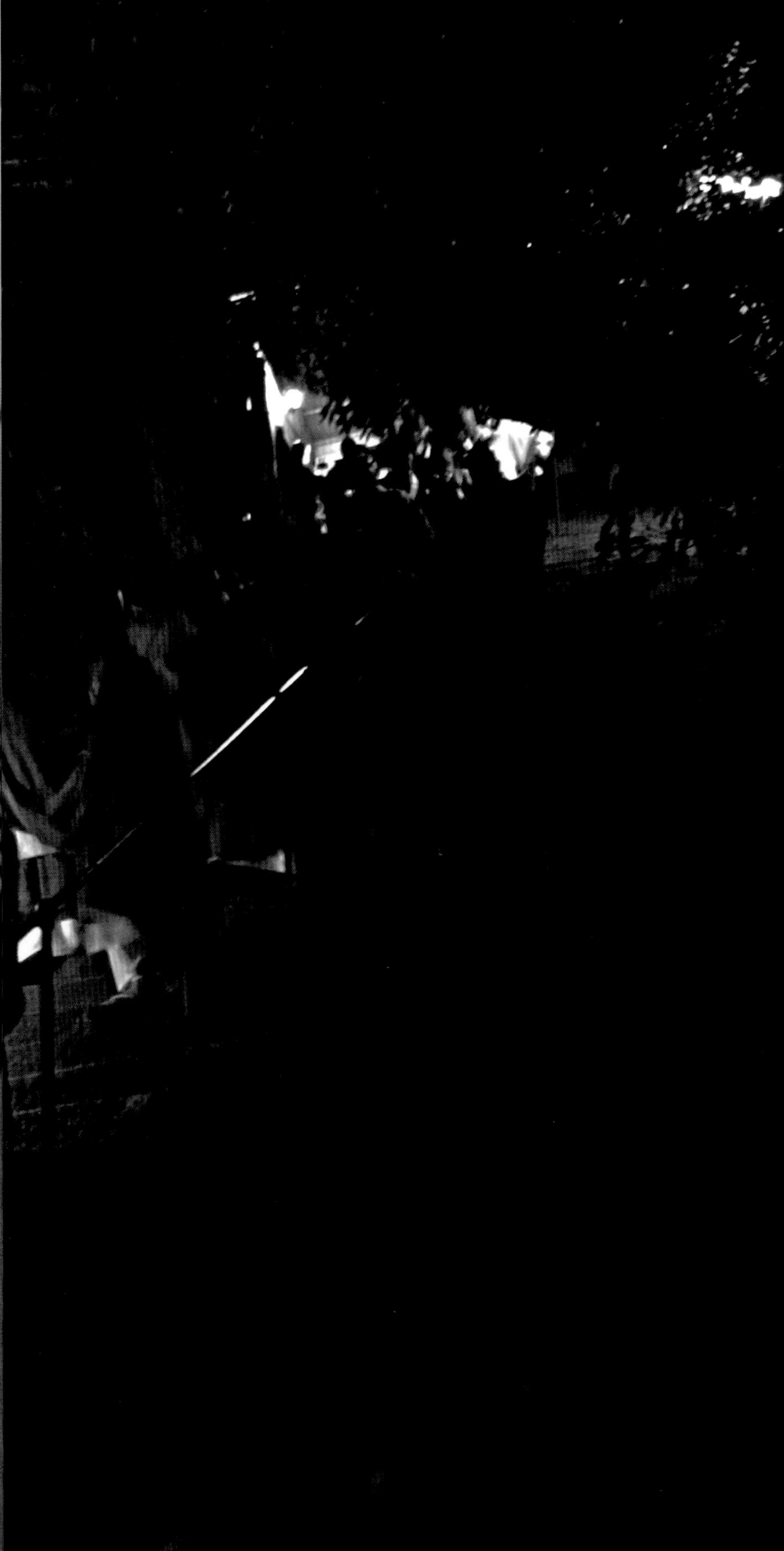

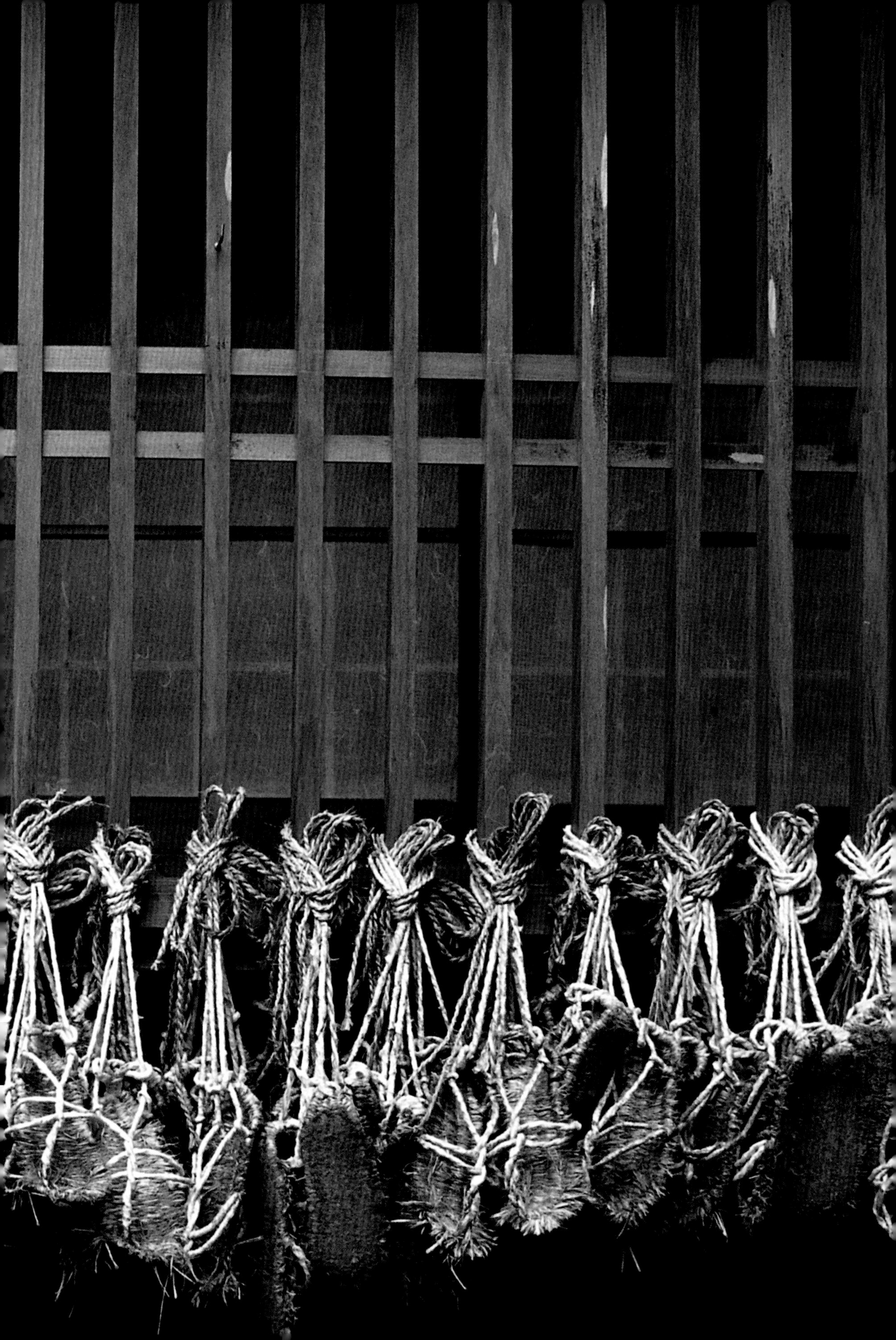

京都大廻り | *Kyoto ōmawari*

赤山苦行からは「化他行」といわれるが、京都大廻りはその最たるものである。
沿道に住んでいる人々は、ずっと昔から「阿闍梨さんが山から下りてこられる」ことを知っている。子供たちには白装束のお坊さんが何をしている人なのか分からないままに、お加持を授けてもらおうと両親や祖父母と一緒に合掌して道端にひざまずいている。
阿闍梨さんの足元が見えるだけで、顔を見ることはない。お加持の数珠が頭に当たると「いたあー!」と口走る子供も少なくない。けれども、不思議なことにこの100日間、子供たちは何度も「痛い」と言いながらも、お加持を受けている。沿道近くに住んでいること自体が奇縁であり、受け継がれる地域性ともいえるのだろう。
出峰から一月ほど経った頃から圓道師の右足がみるみるうちに腫れ上がり、化膿していった。両足は太さが歴然と違うまでになったが、行を中断するわけにはいかない。それでも、不思議なことに草履を履くと歩ける。そして、沿道ではお加持を待っていてくれる人がいる。これが圓道師の心の支えだったのではないだろうか。大廻りを支えているのは実はこの人たちなのだと。

Starting with the *Sekizan kugyō* there are many types of spiritual practice called k*etagyō*. *Ketagyō* practices are done for the sake of others, as opposed to *jirigyō* which are practices done for personal development. *Kyoto ōmawari* is one of the most extreme *ketagyō* practices.
People living along the route, have always known when Ajari was coming down from the mountain. To the children, Endō was a white robe wearing monk doing something they didn't quite understand, however they would clasp their hands in prayer and kneel along with their parents and grandparents as they received blessings. They only ever saw his feet as he walked past, they never saw his face kneeling as they were.
Some of the children, would cry out '*itai!*' (ouch!) as he tapped his prayer beads to their heads. Even so the children who would gather every day, despite their lack of understanding, were receiving prayers and healing. To be living near the route in itself is unusual, these children will go on to uphold the local custom.
During the course of the first month of the *Kyoto ōmawari*, Reverend Endō's foot swelled before my eyes and had become infected. Before long it was unmistakable that that both of his feet were thickened by swelling, however it was impossible for him to suspend his training to recover. Nevertheless, it was a mystery how he was still able to walk in his straw sandals. I think it was the people waiting to receive blessings along the route which gave him the will to continue.

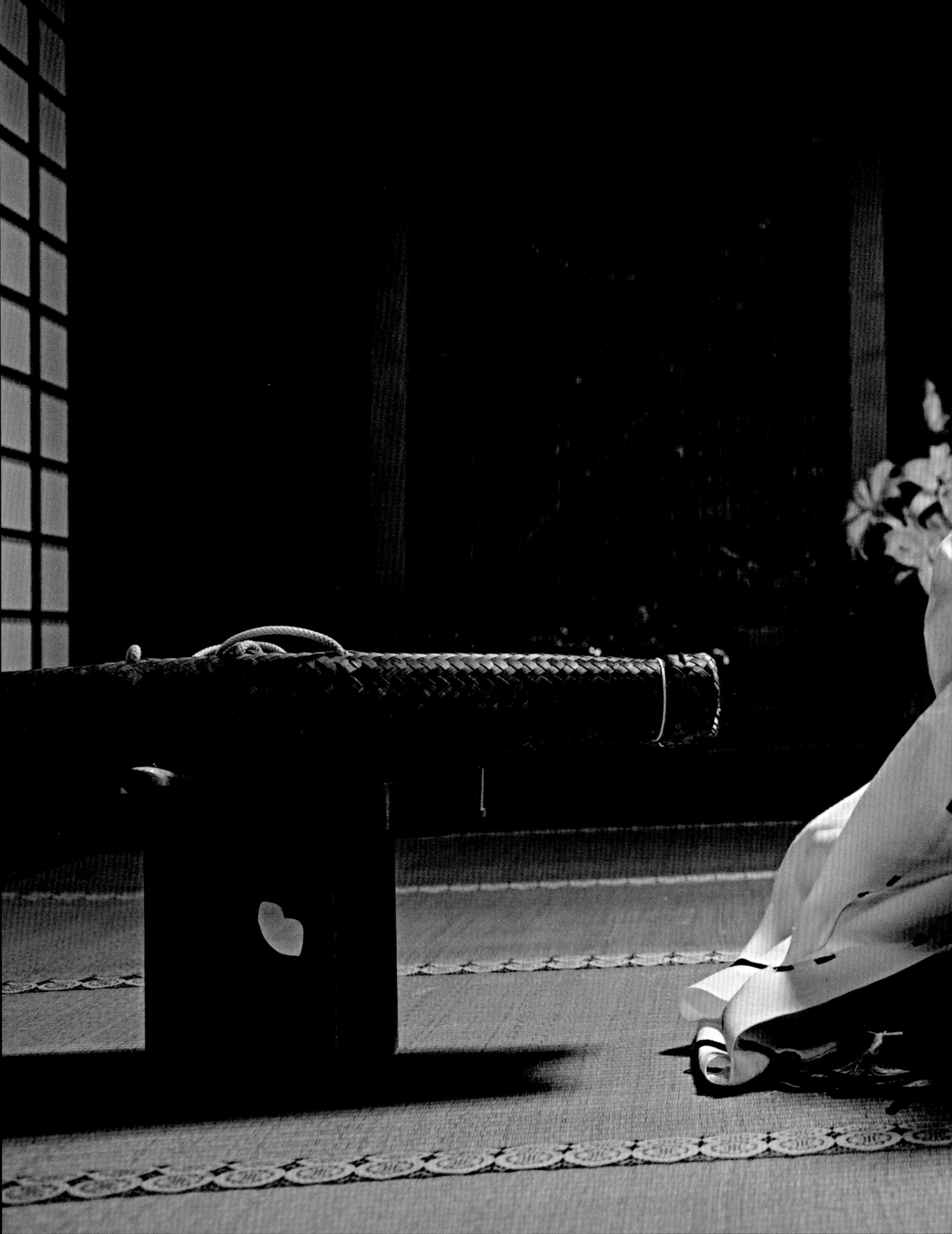

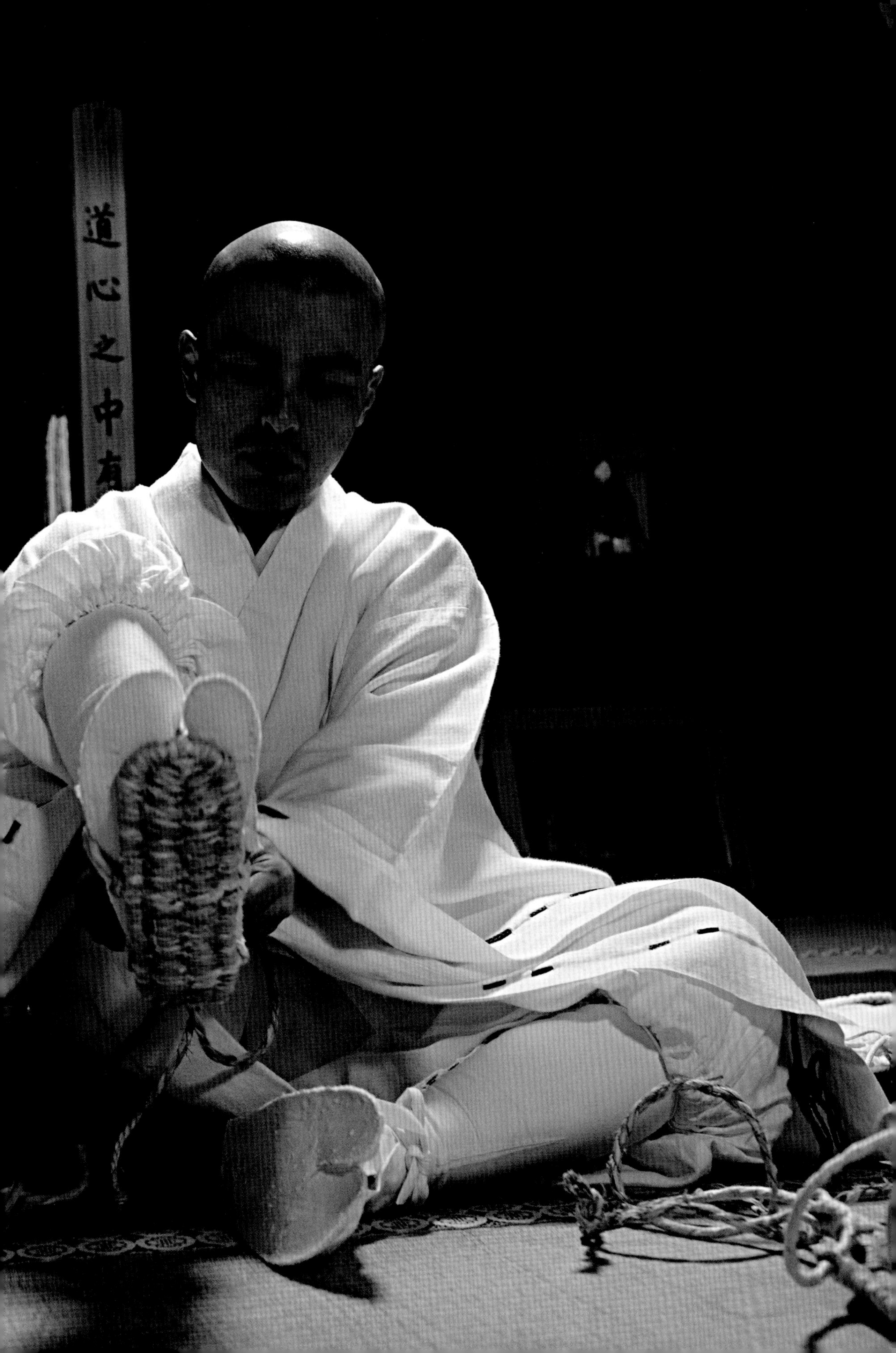
道心之中有

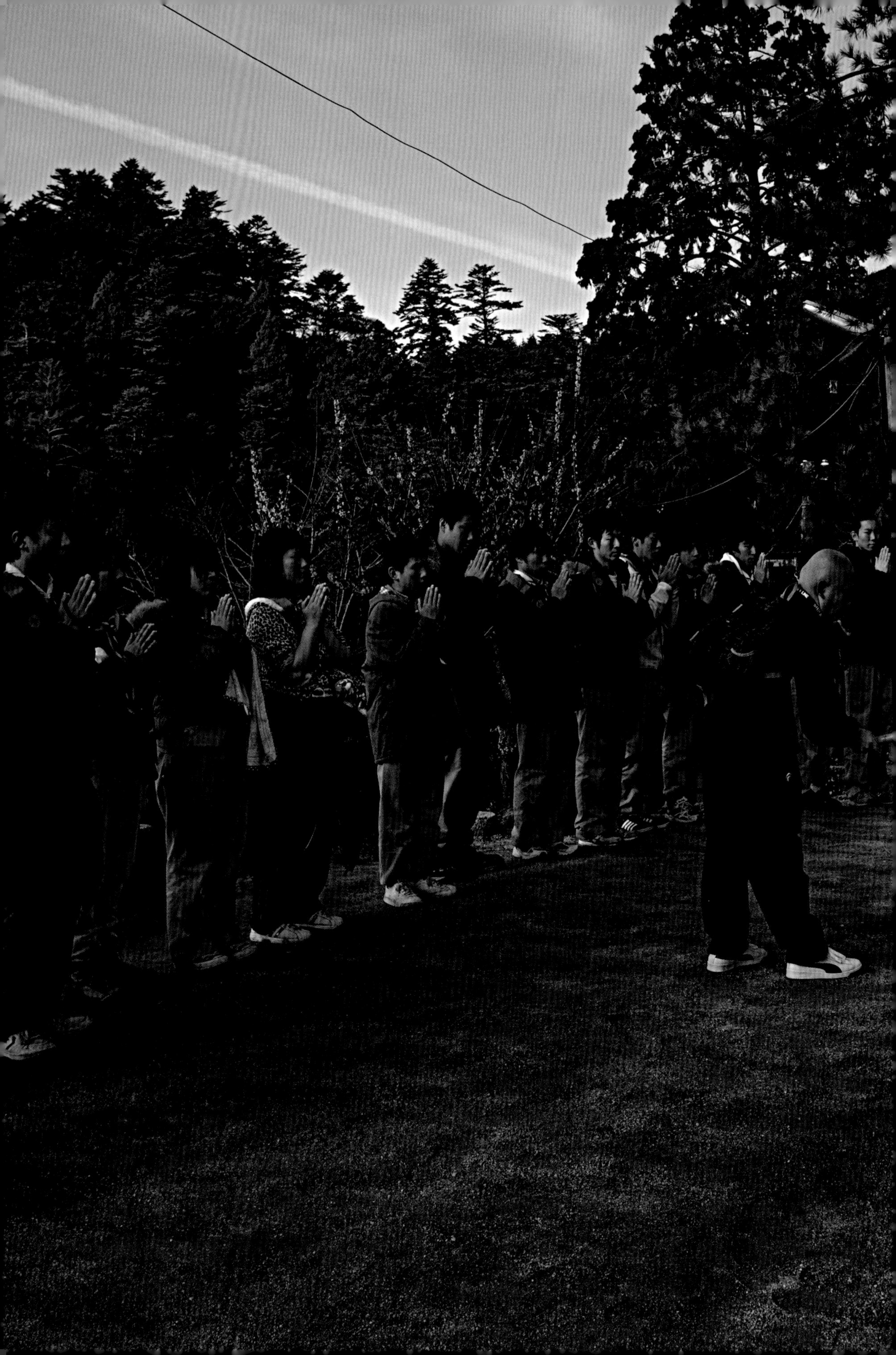

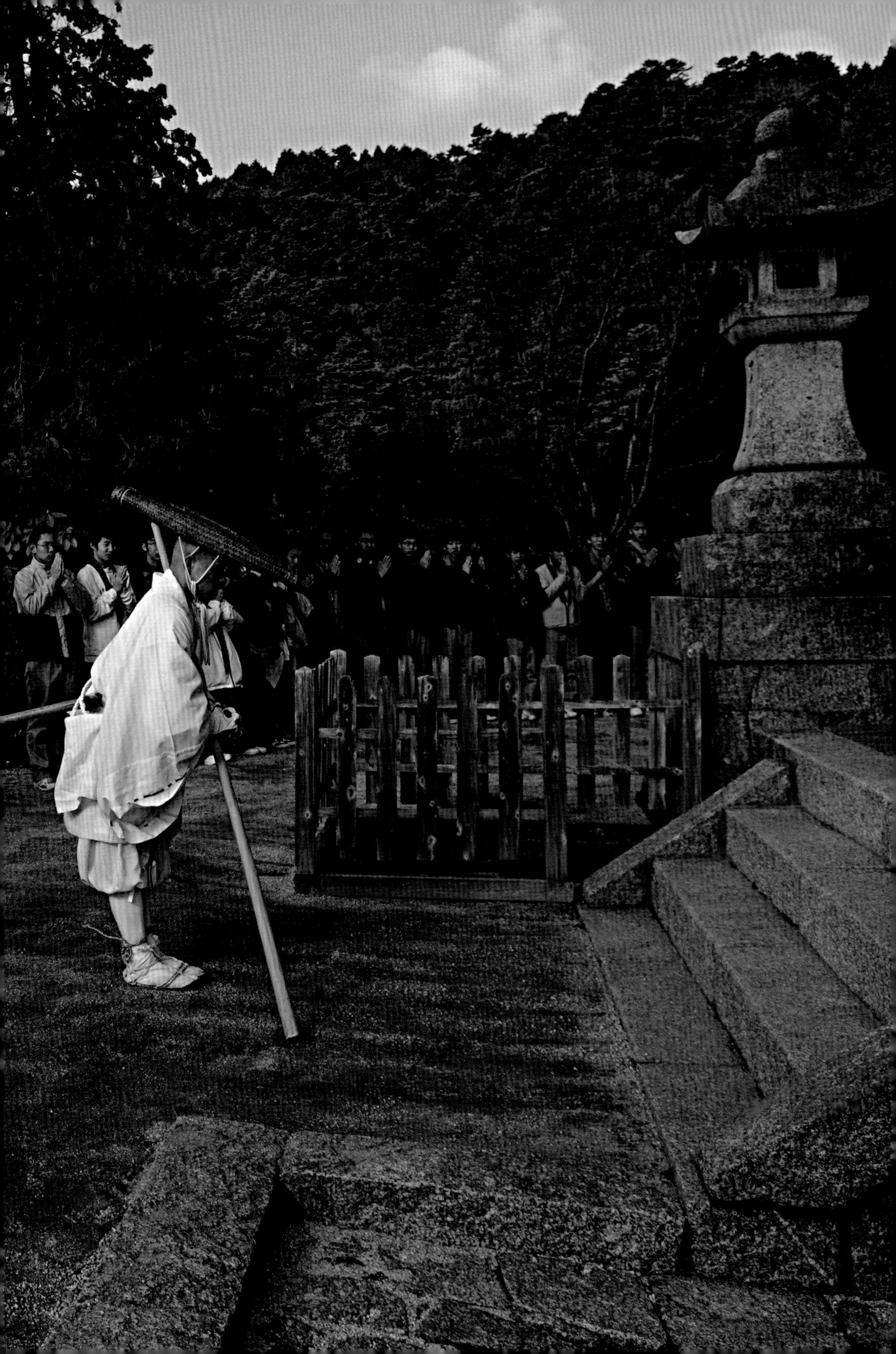

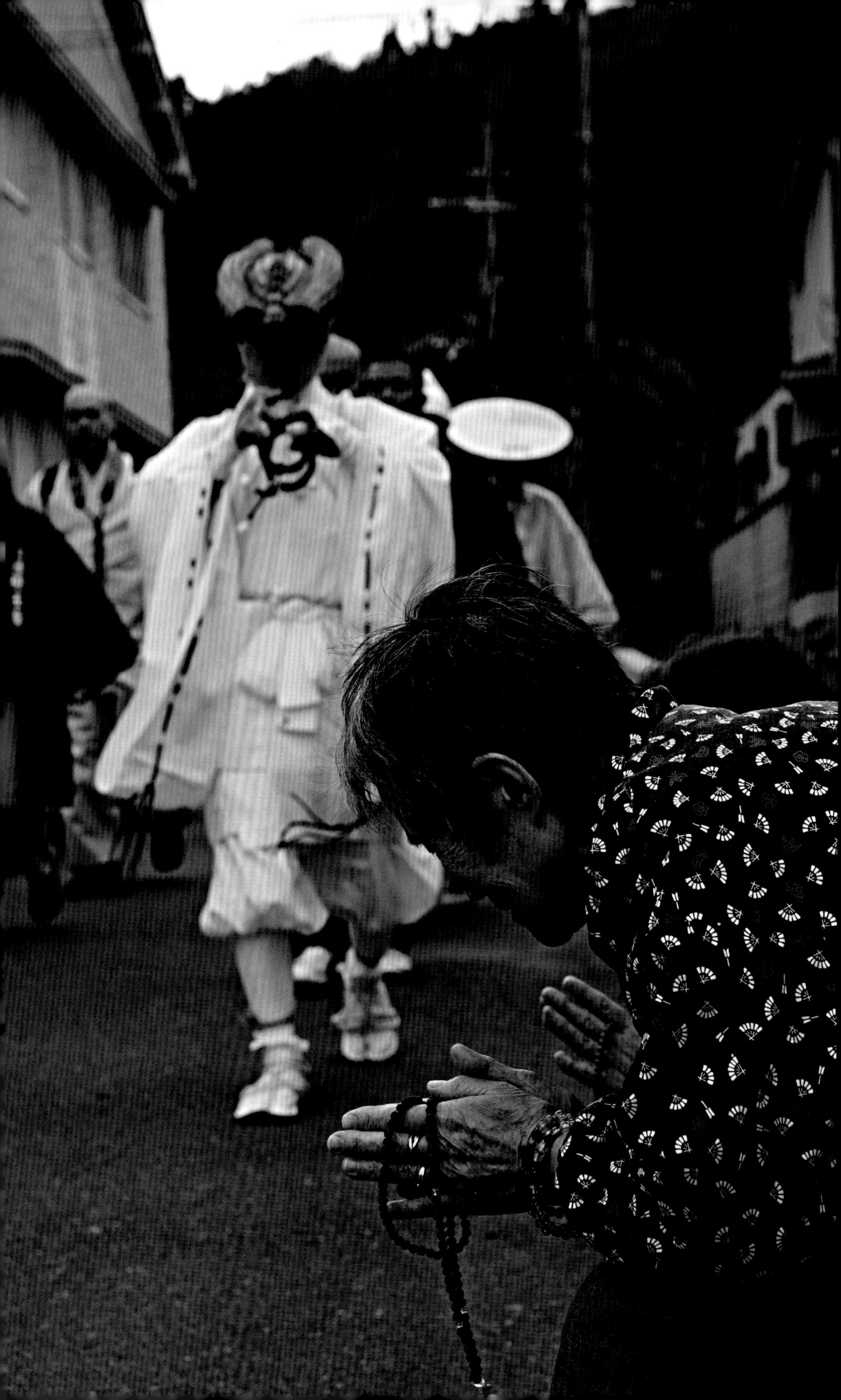

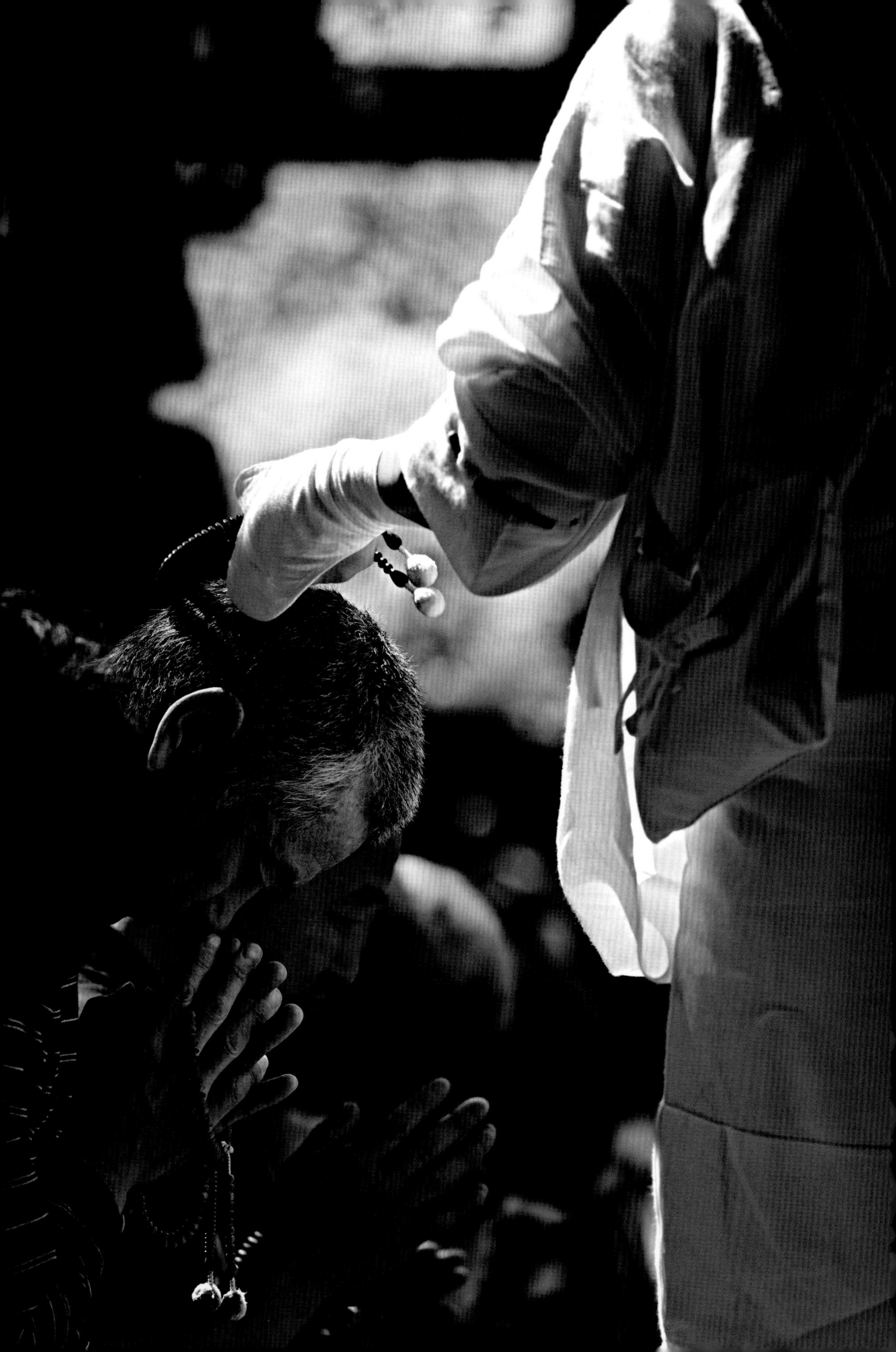

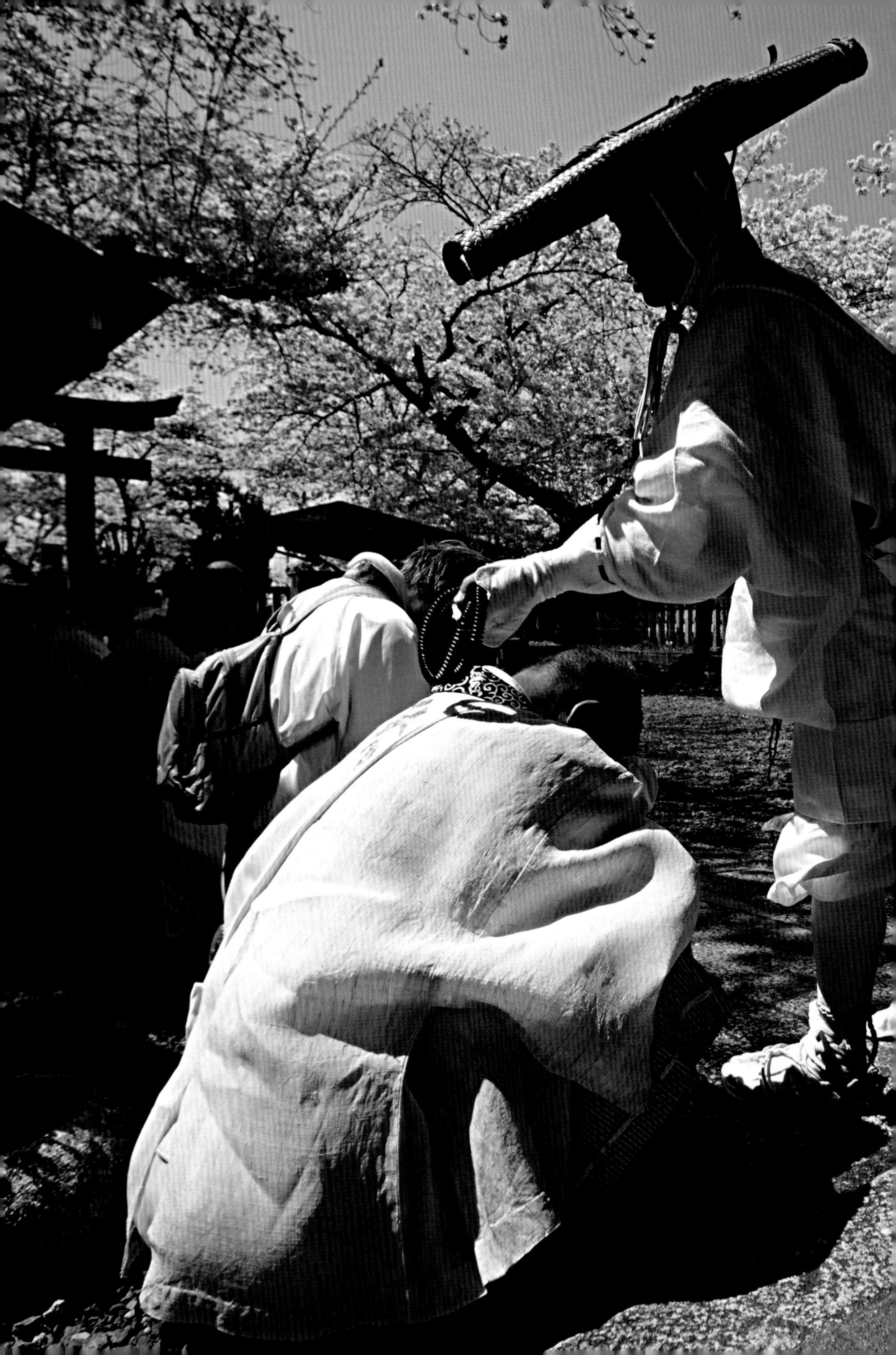

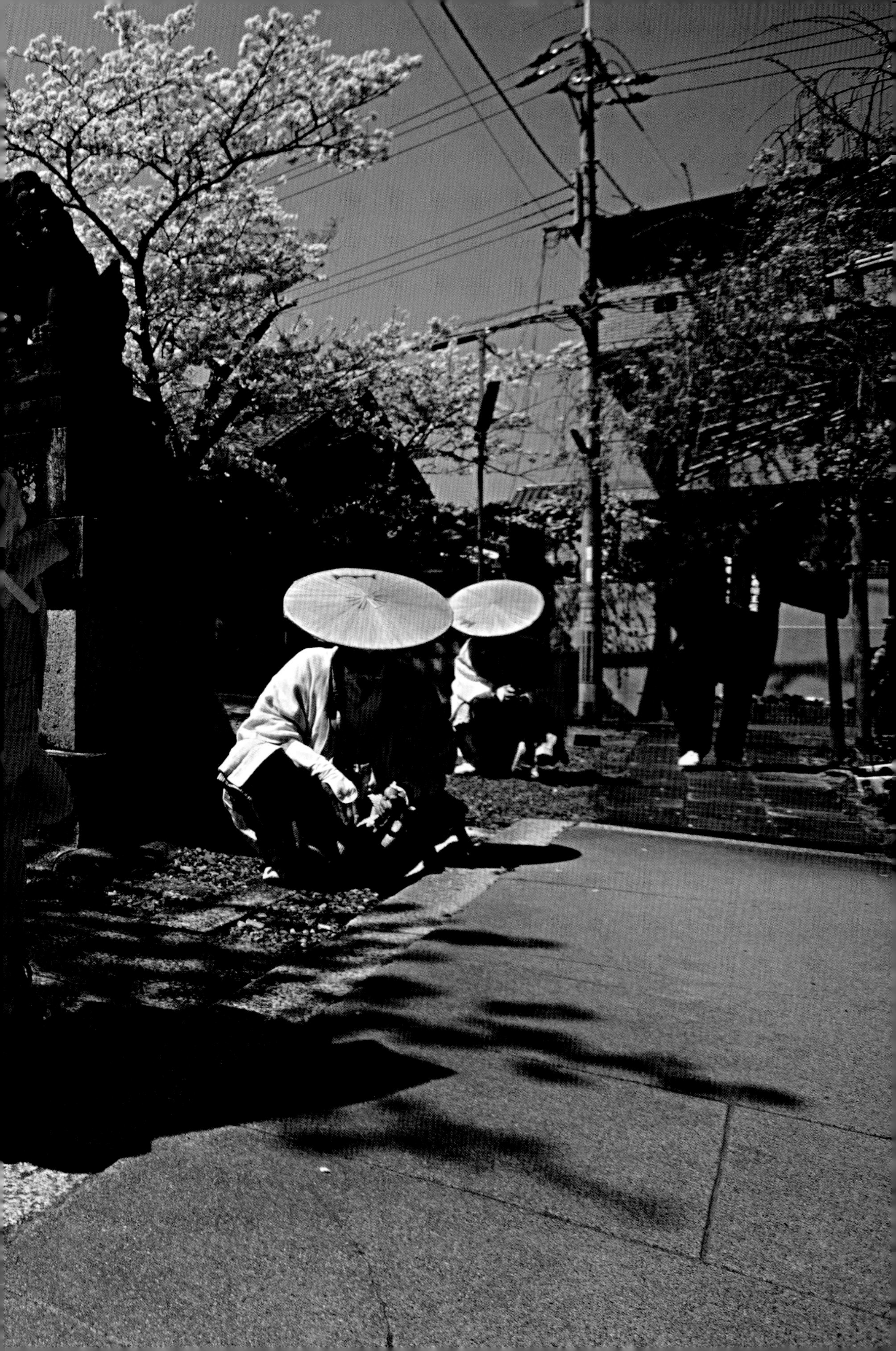

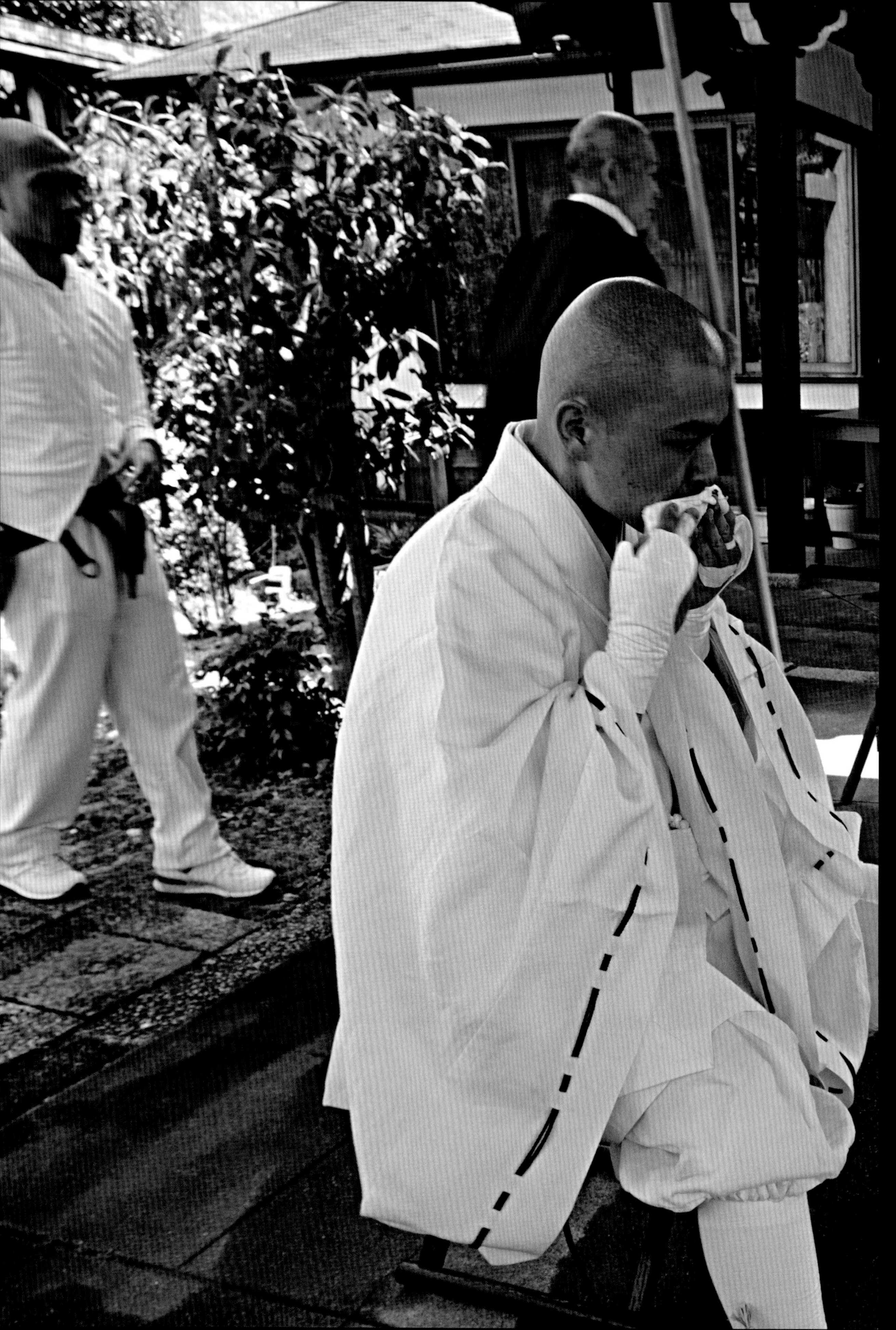

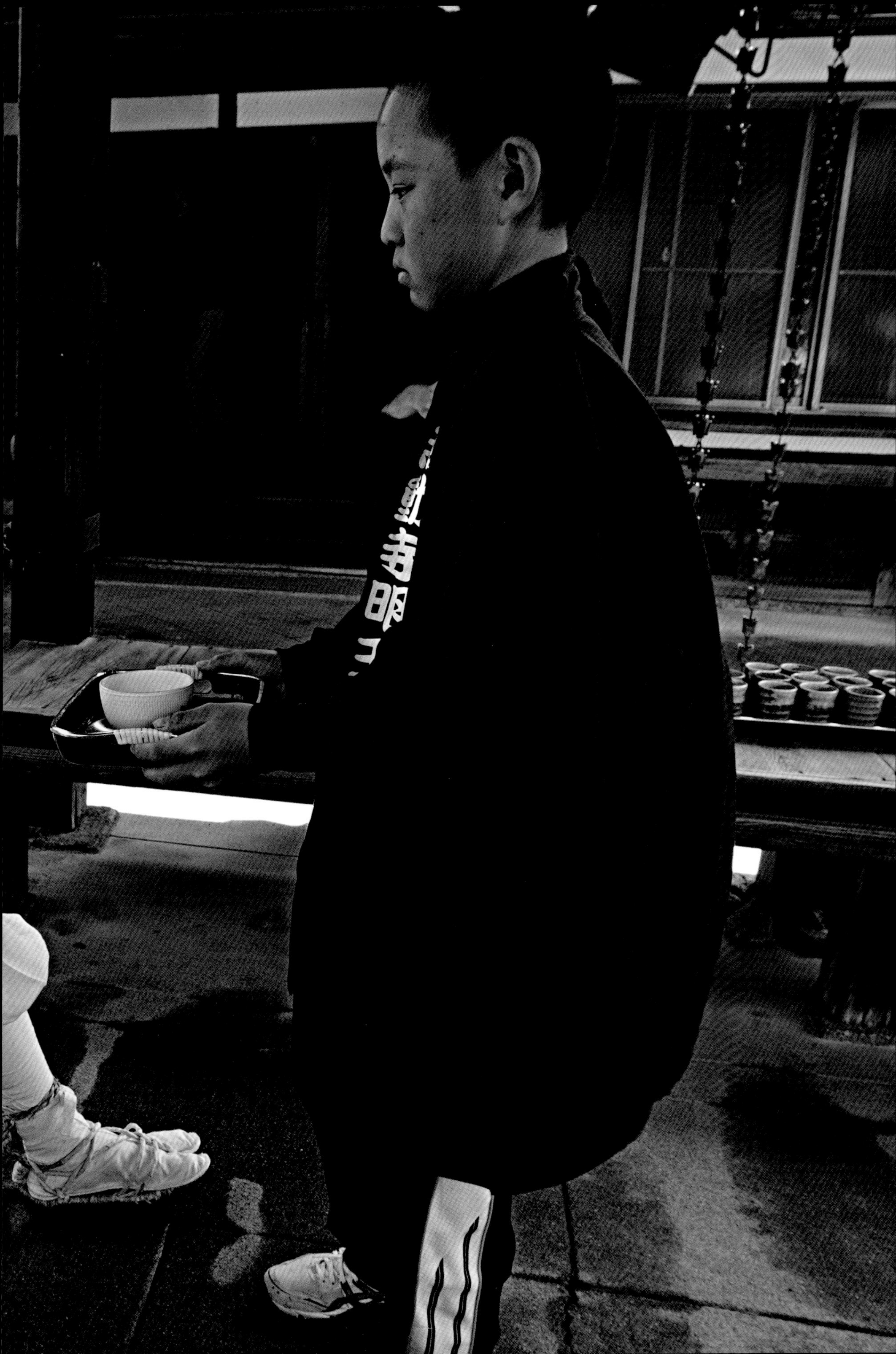

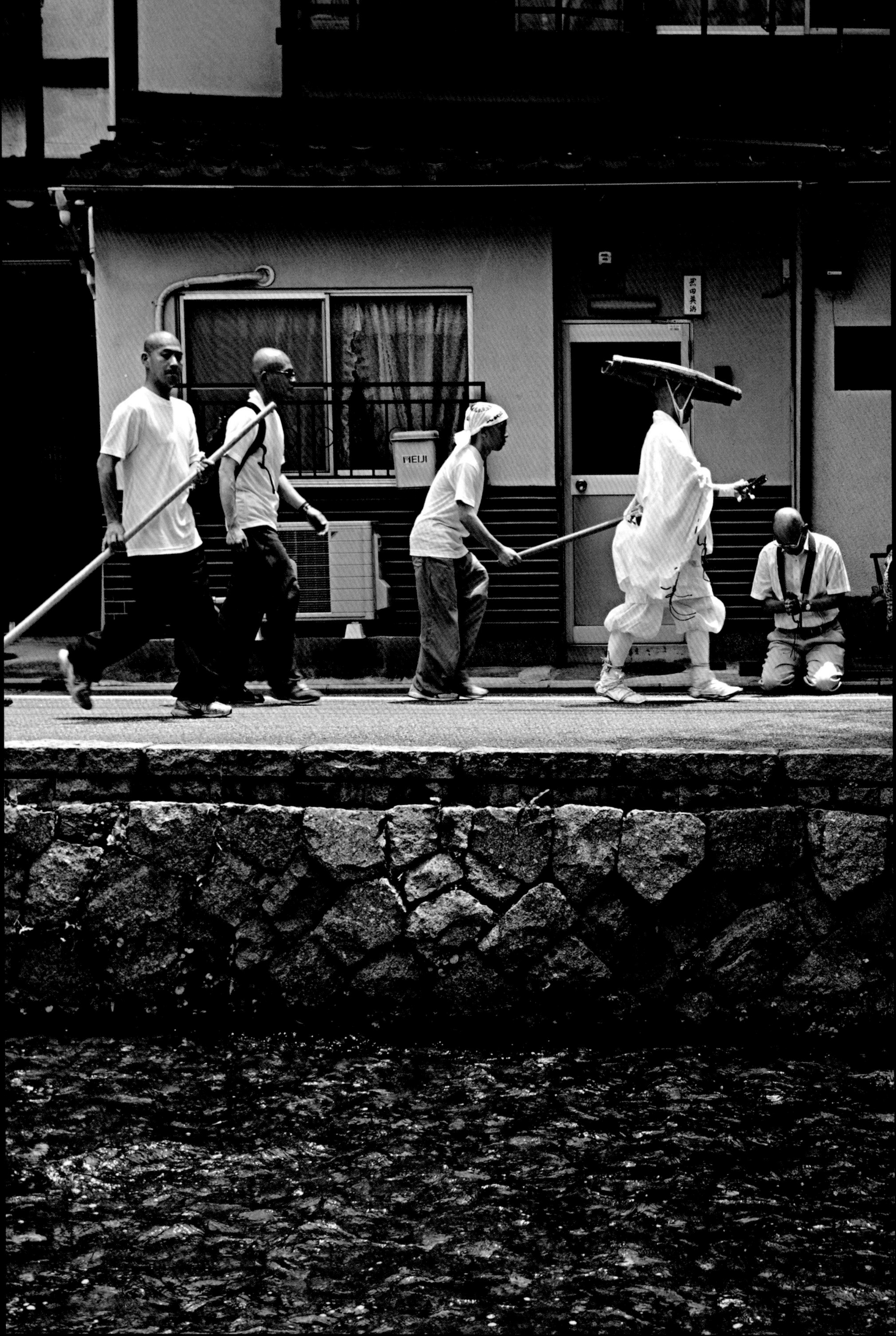
MEIJI

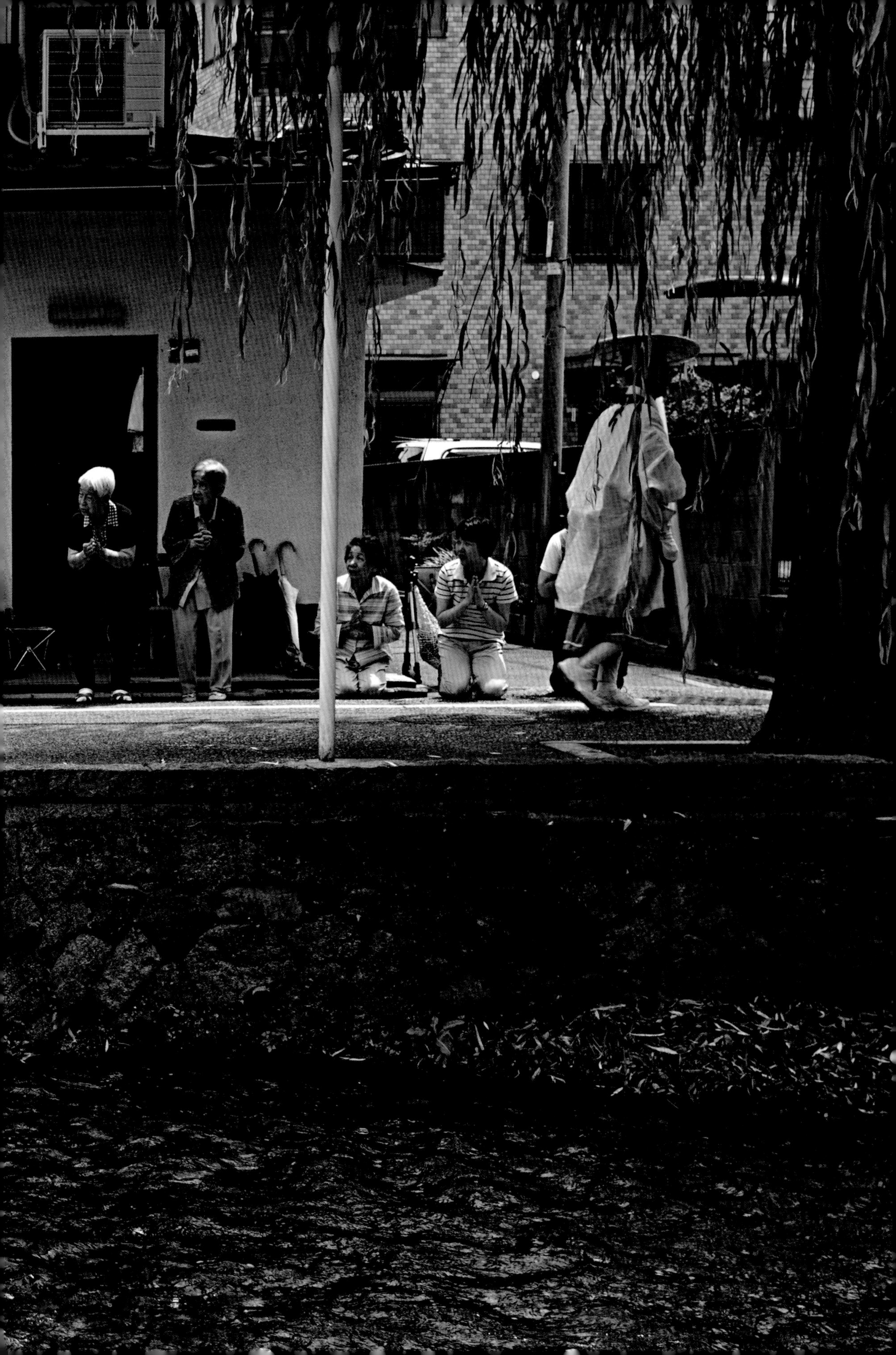

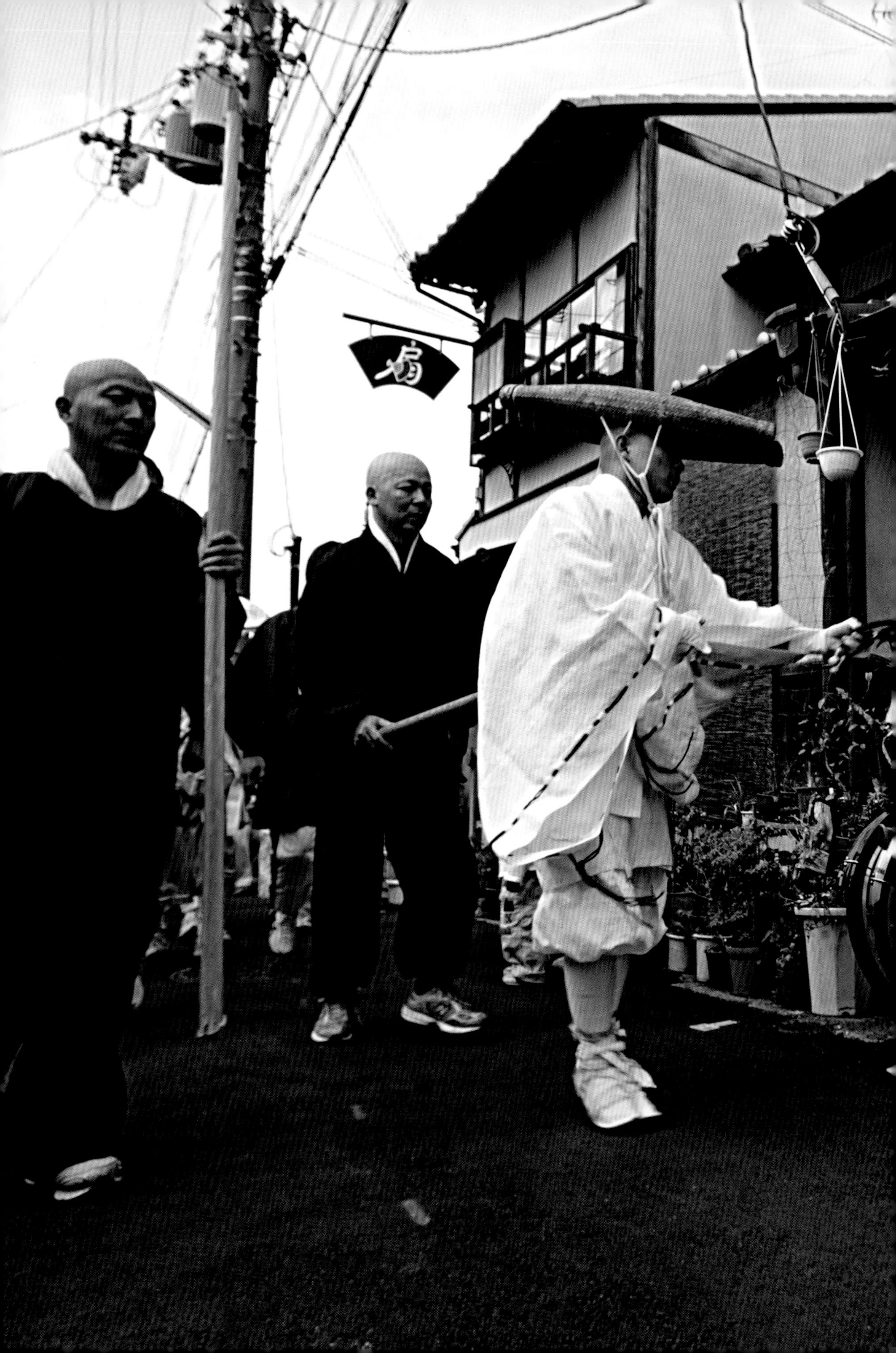

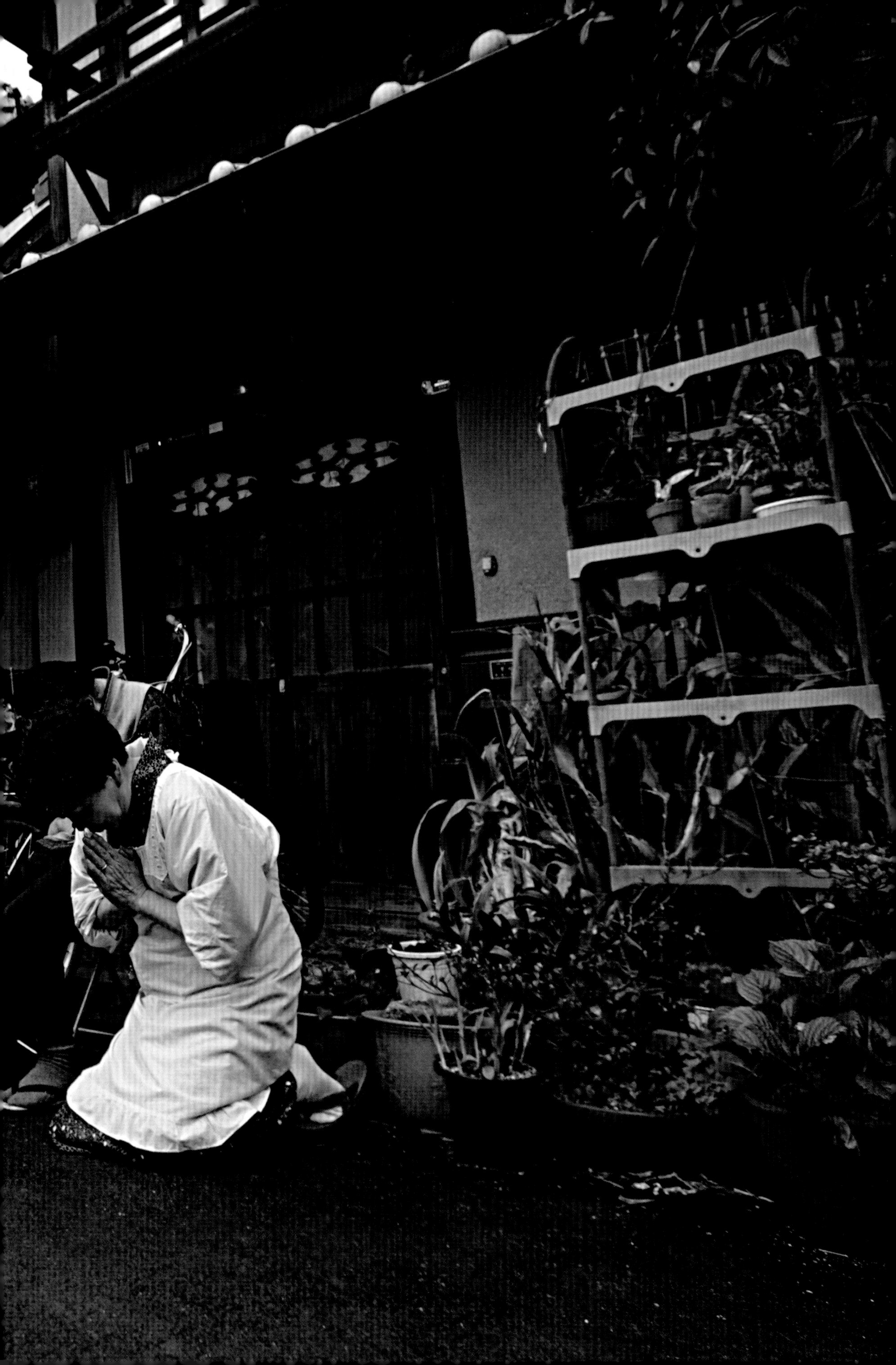

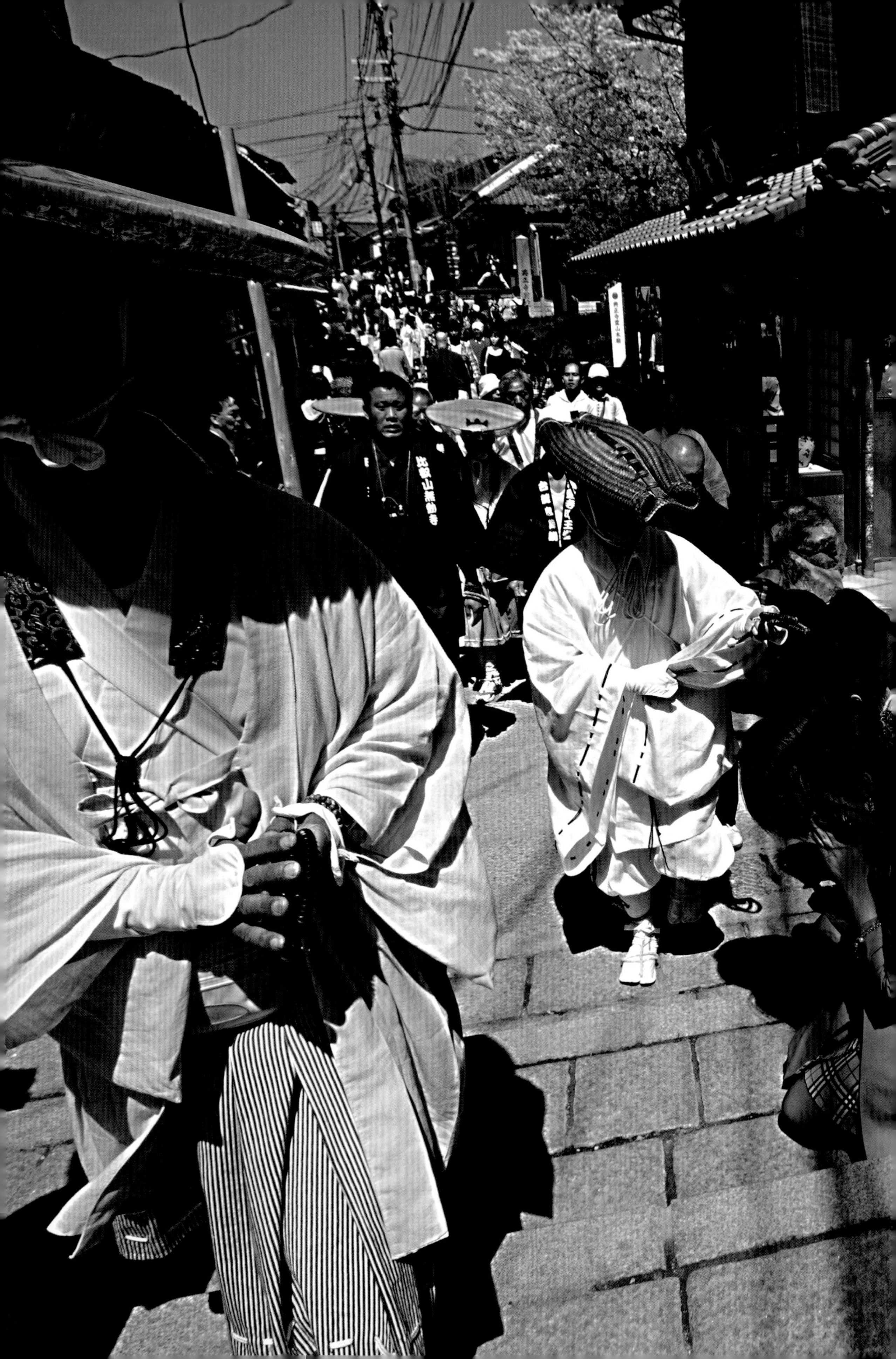
比叡山無動寺

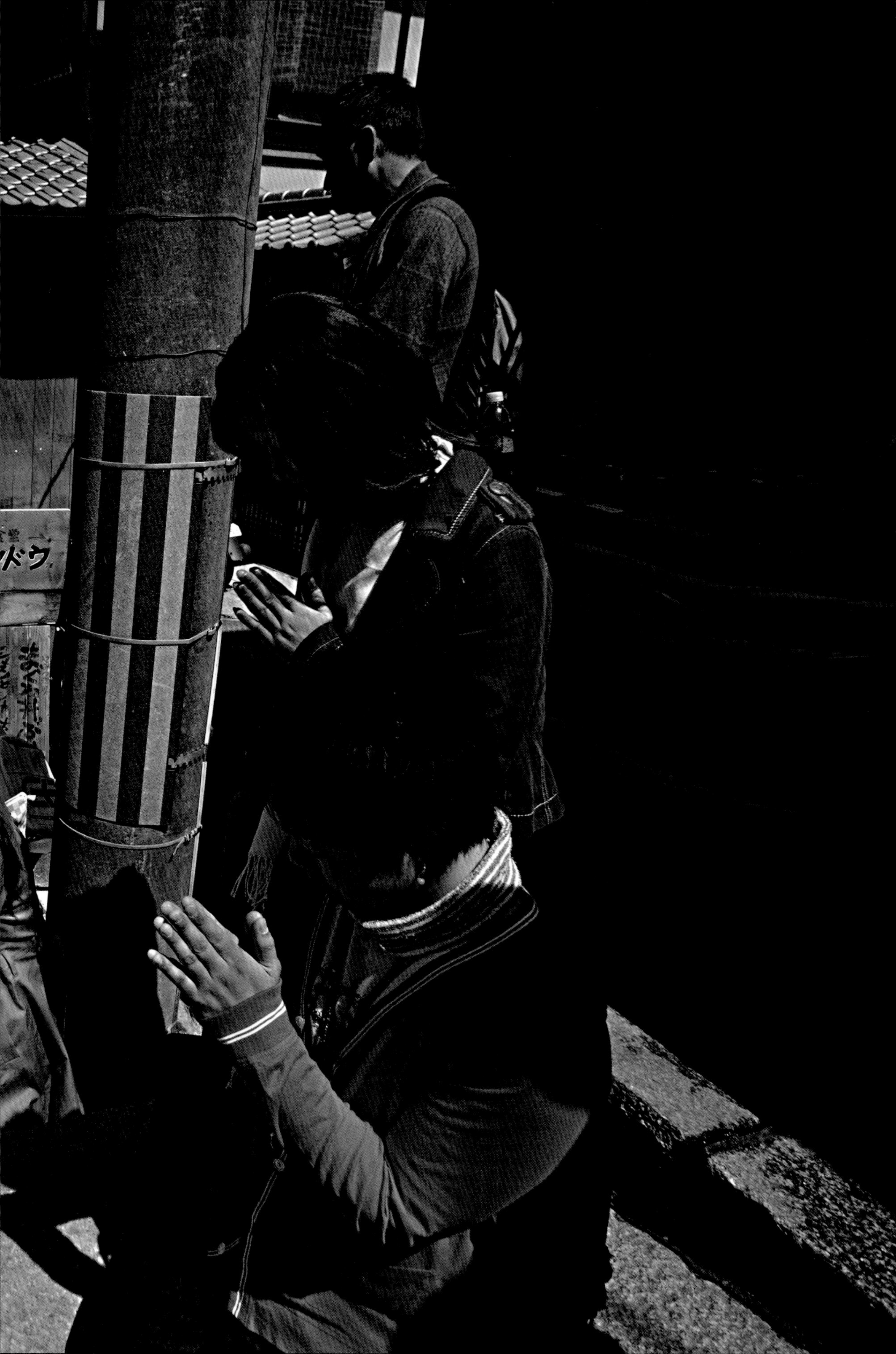

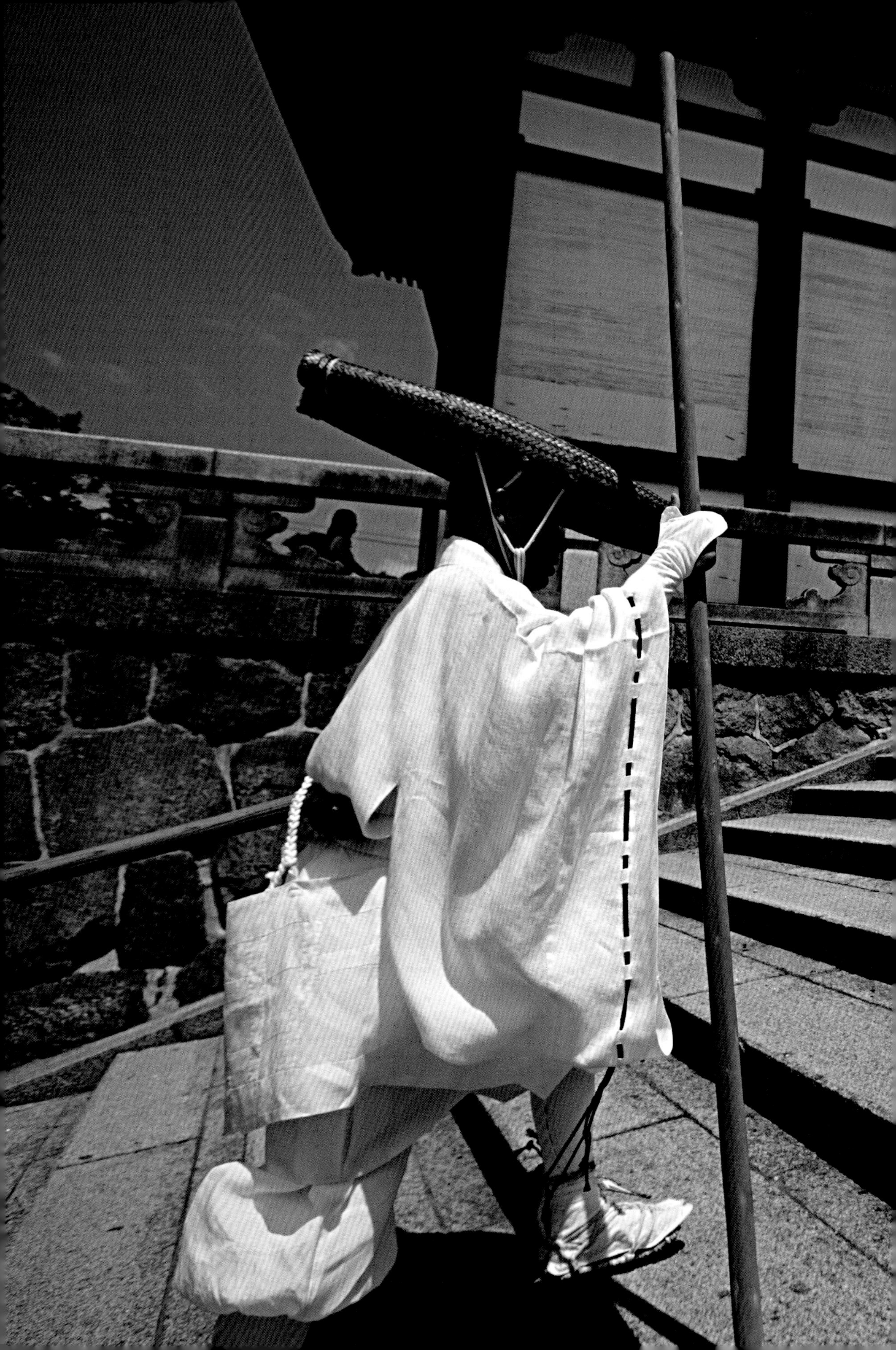

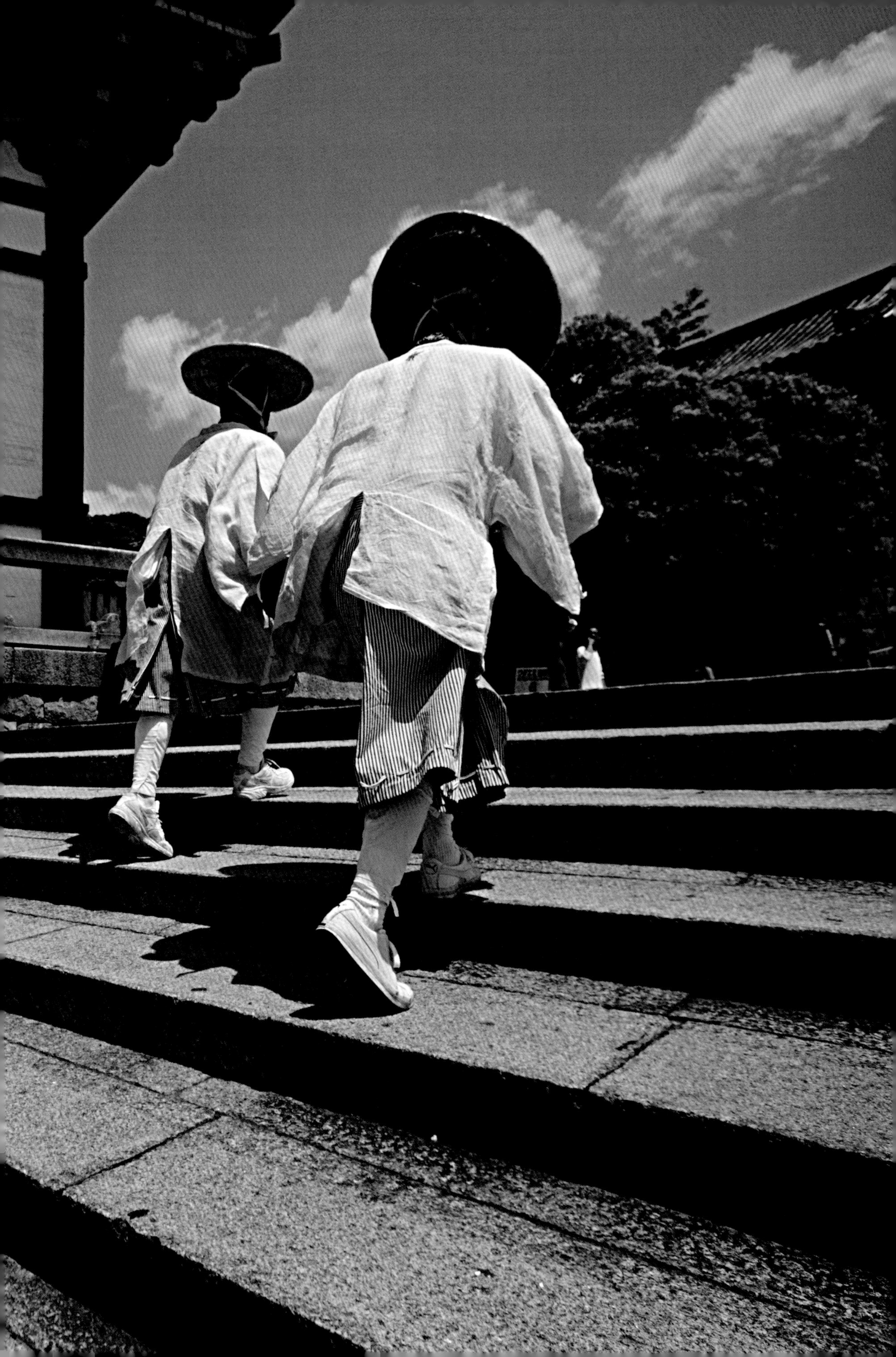

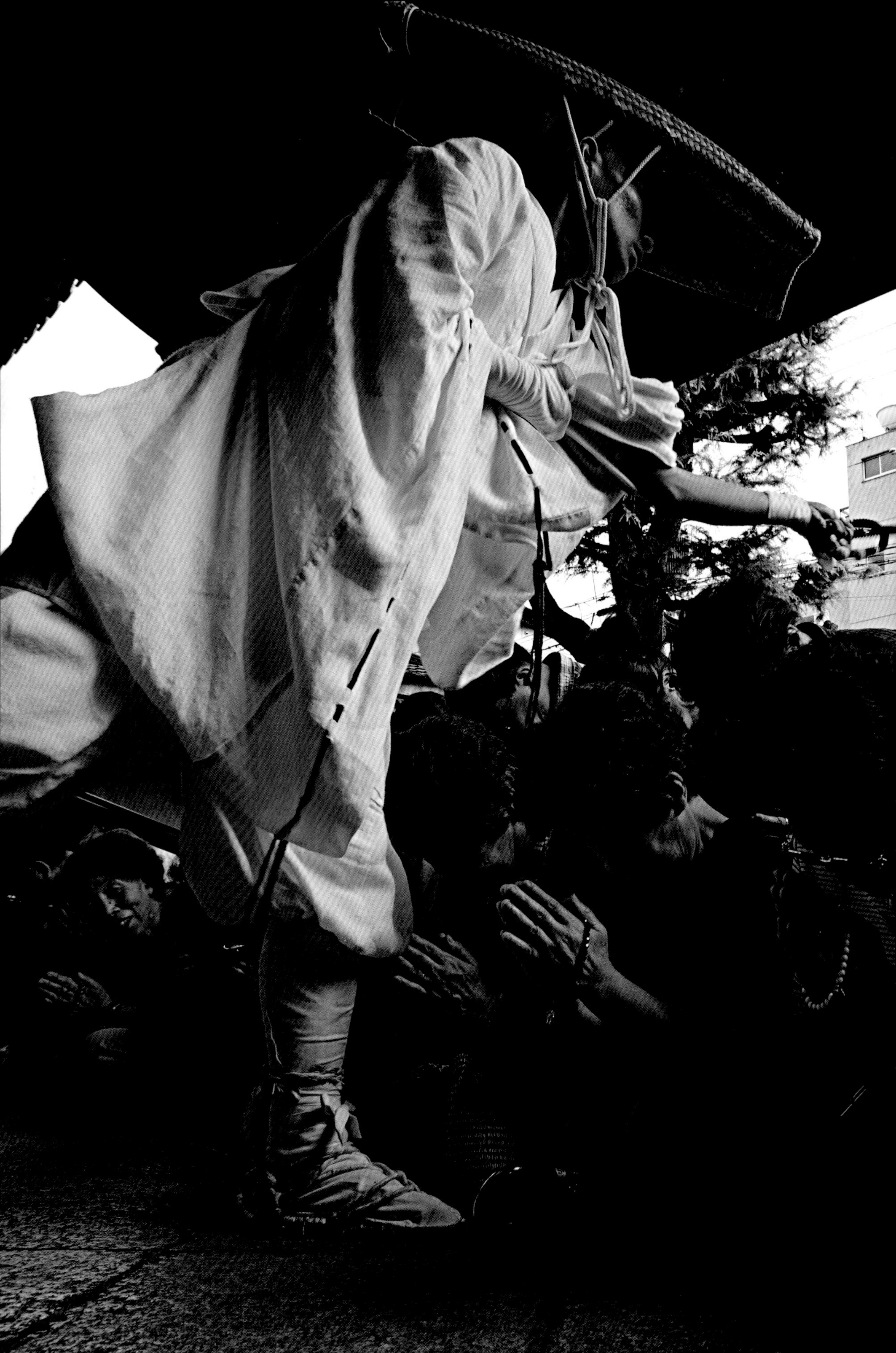

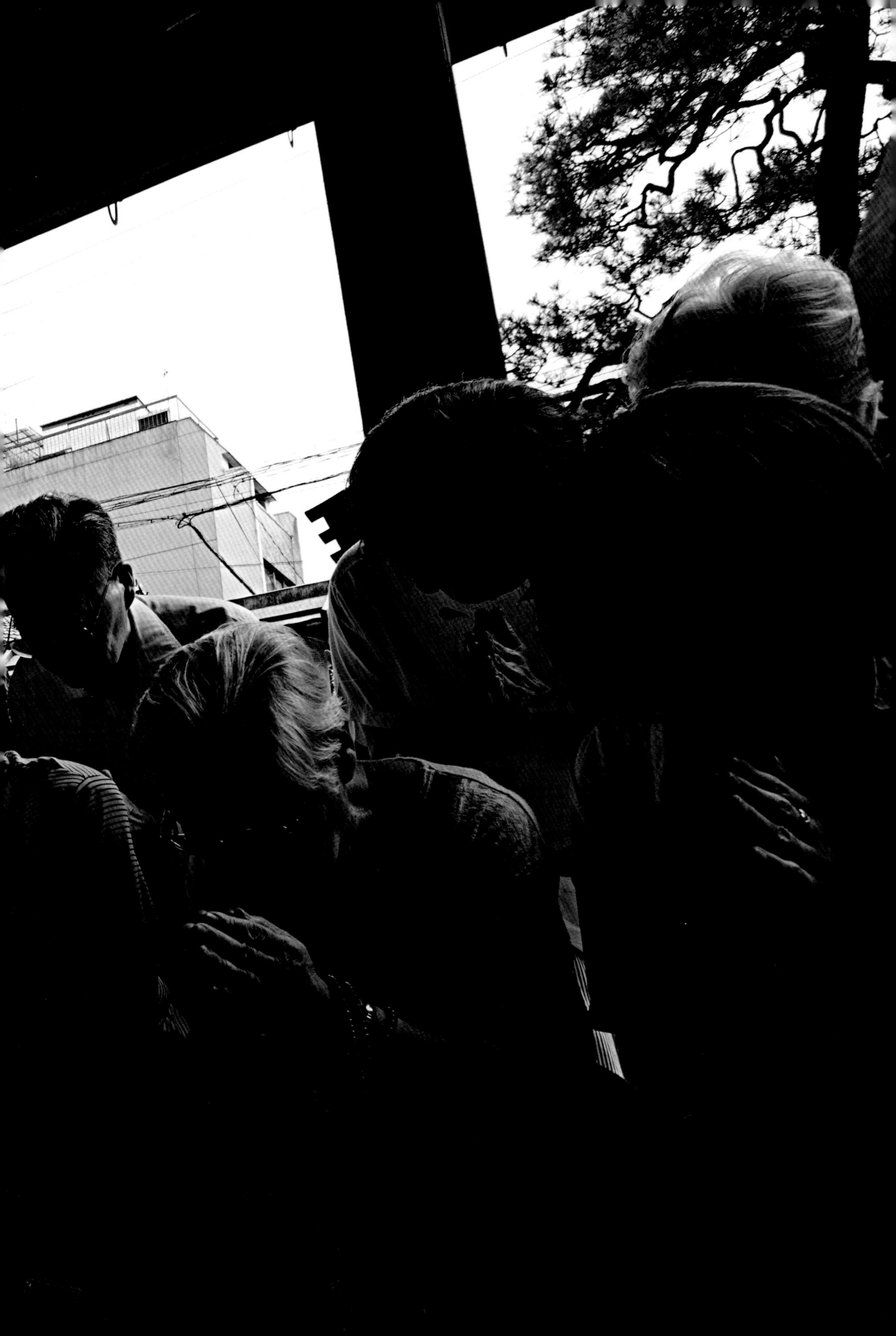

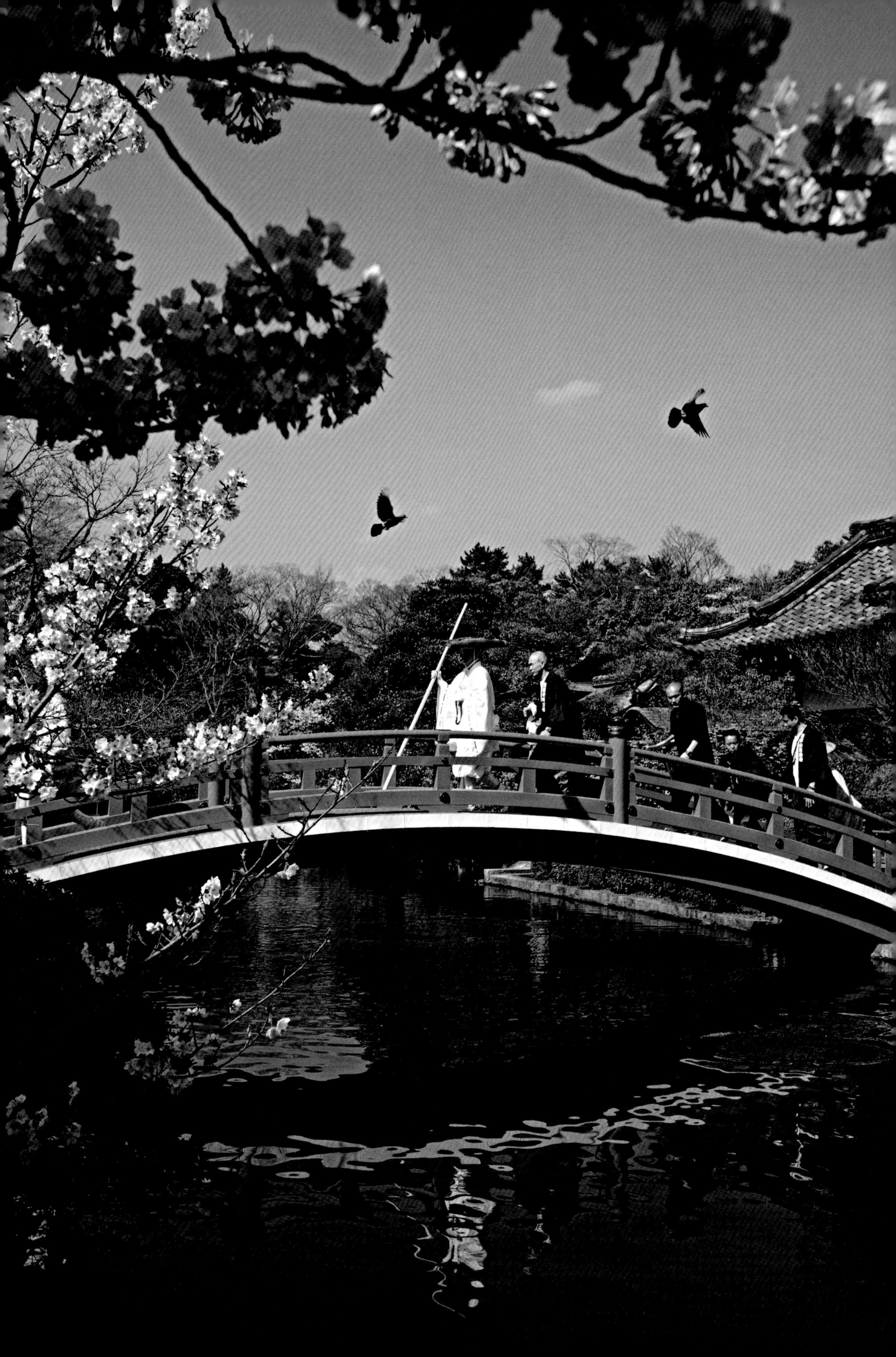

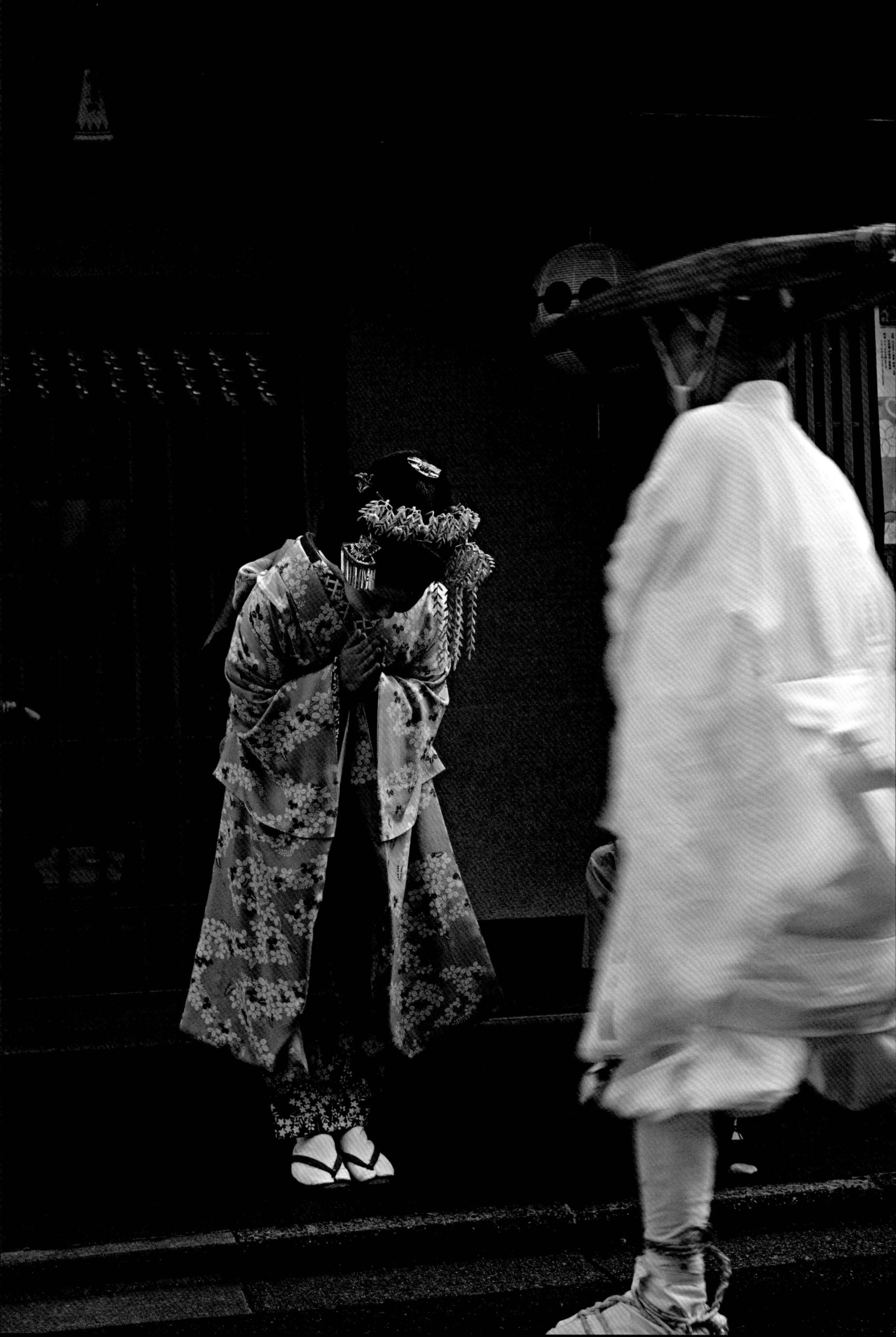

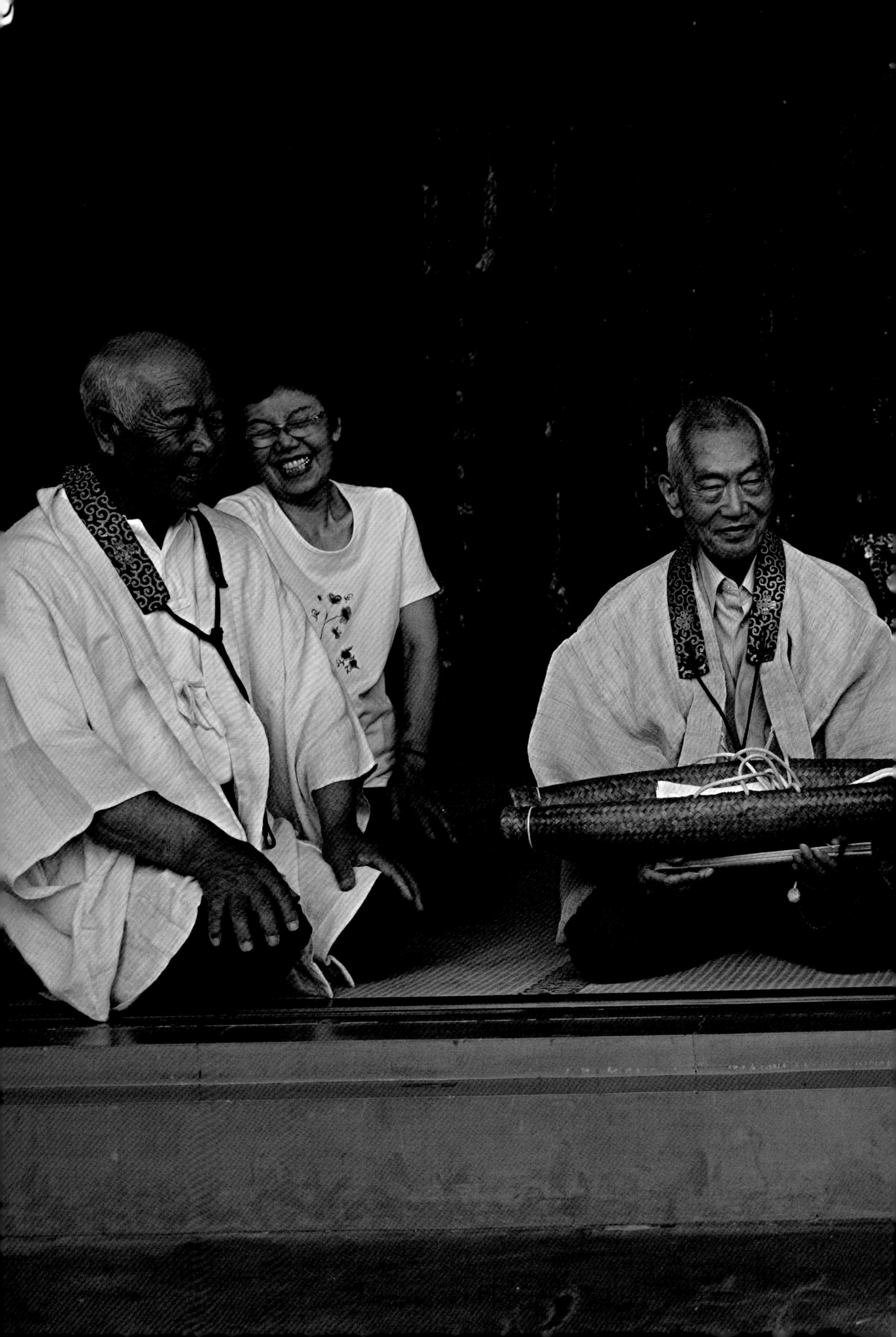

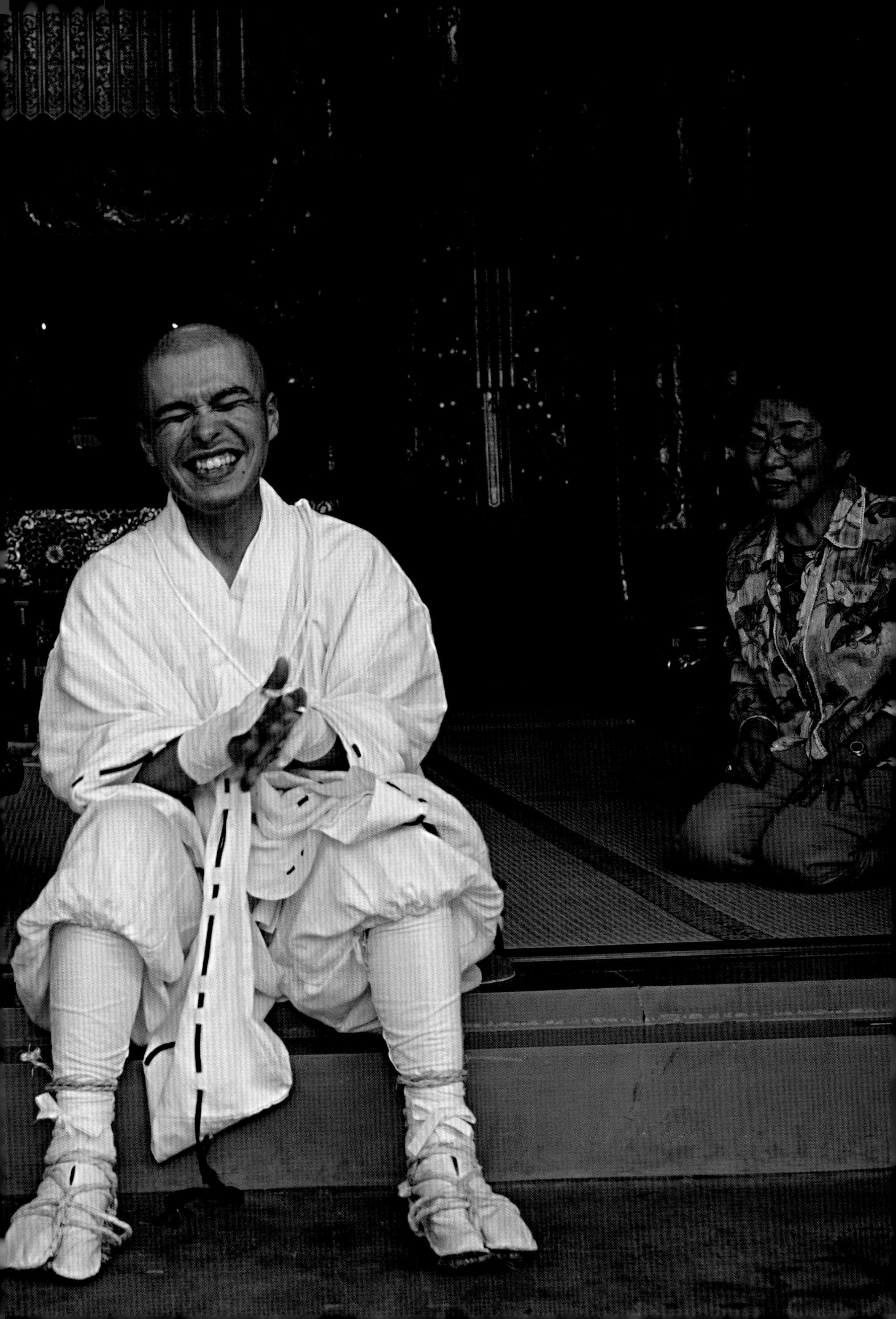

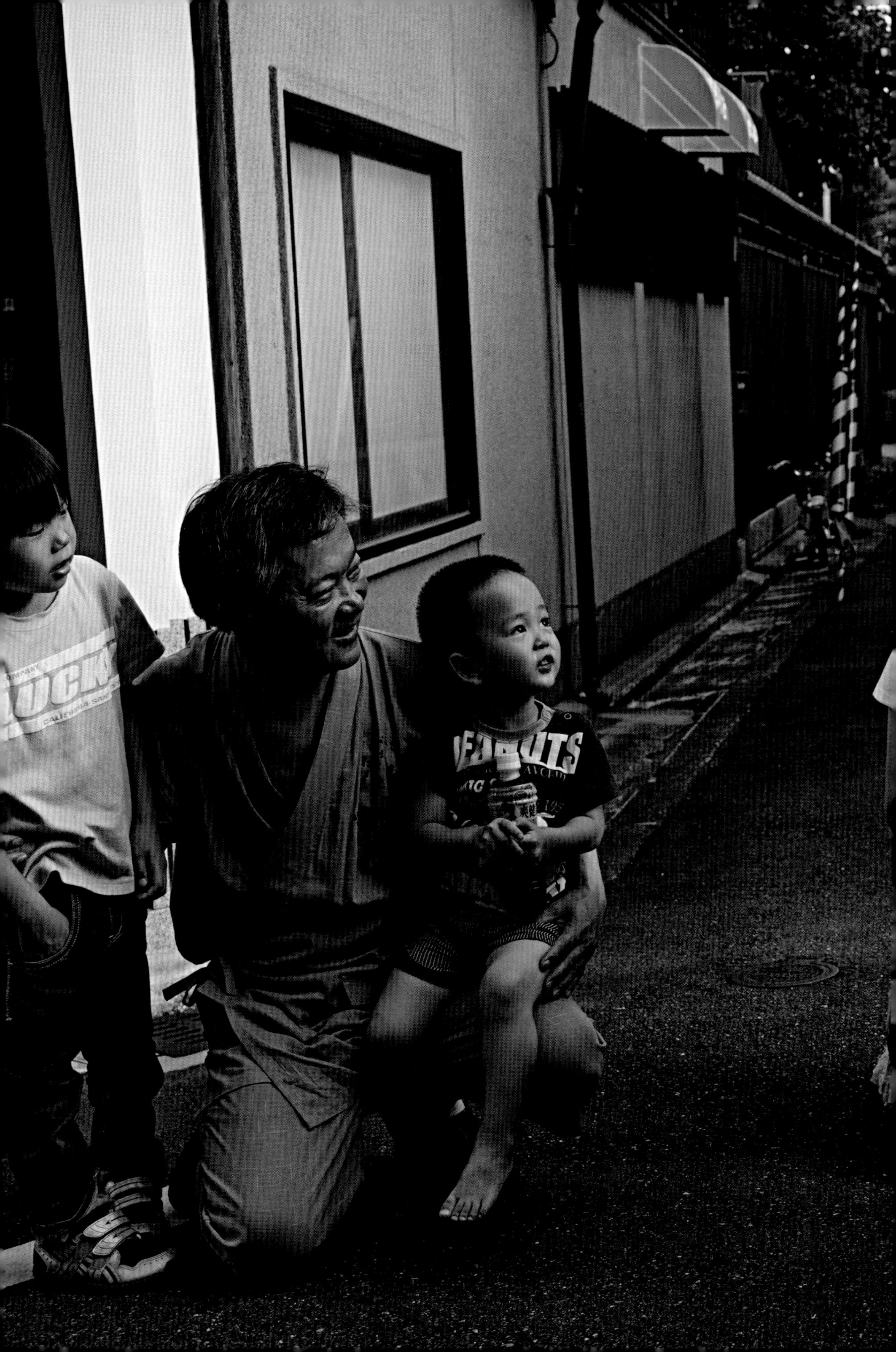

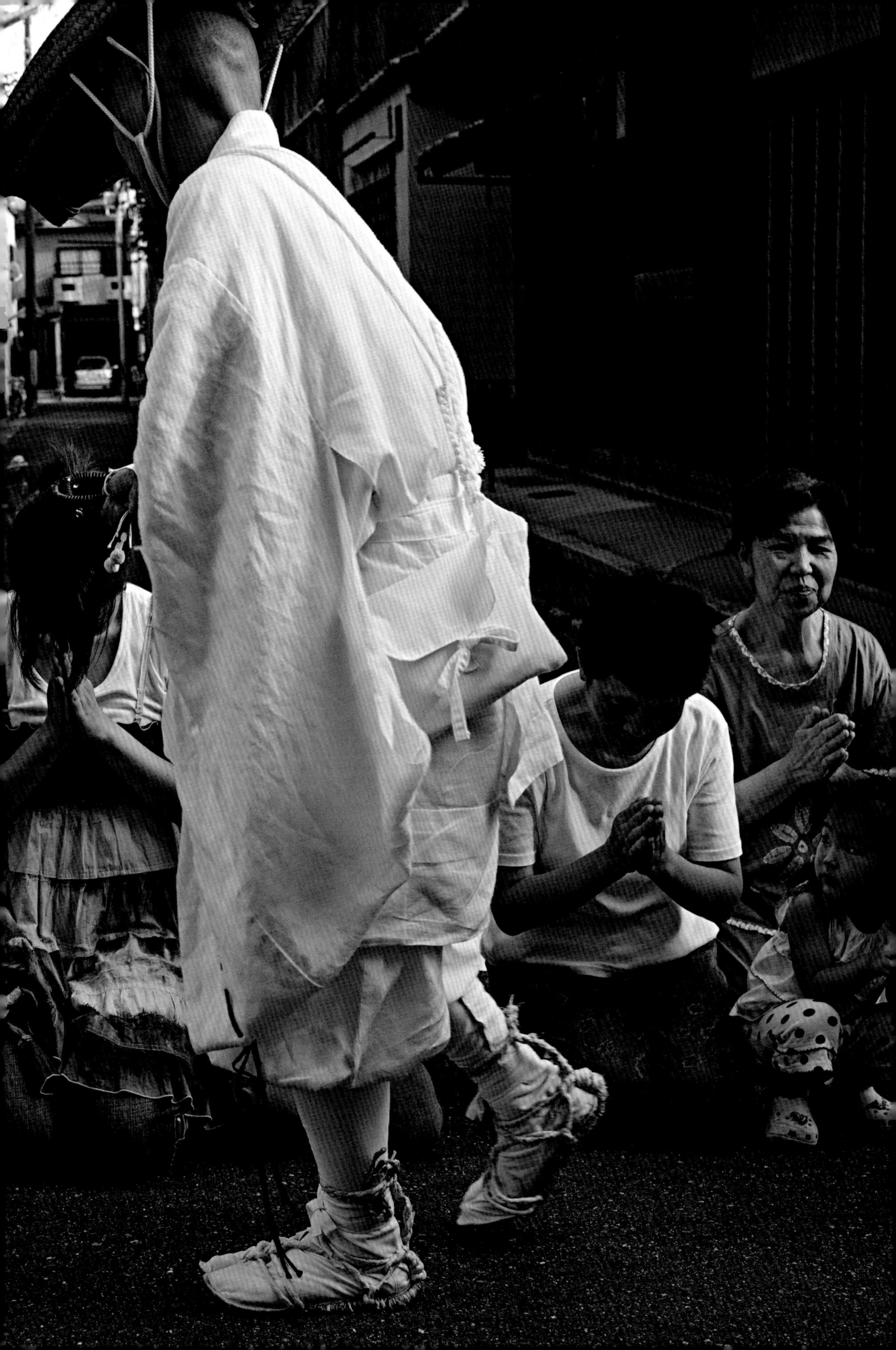

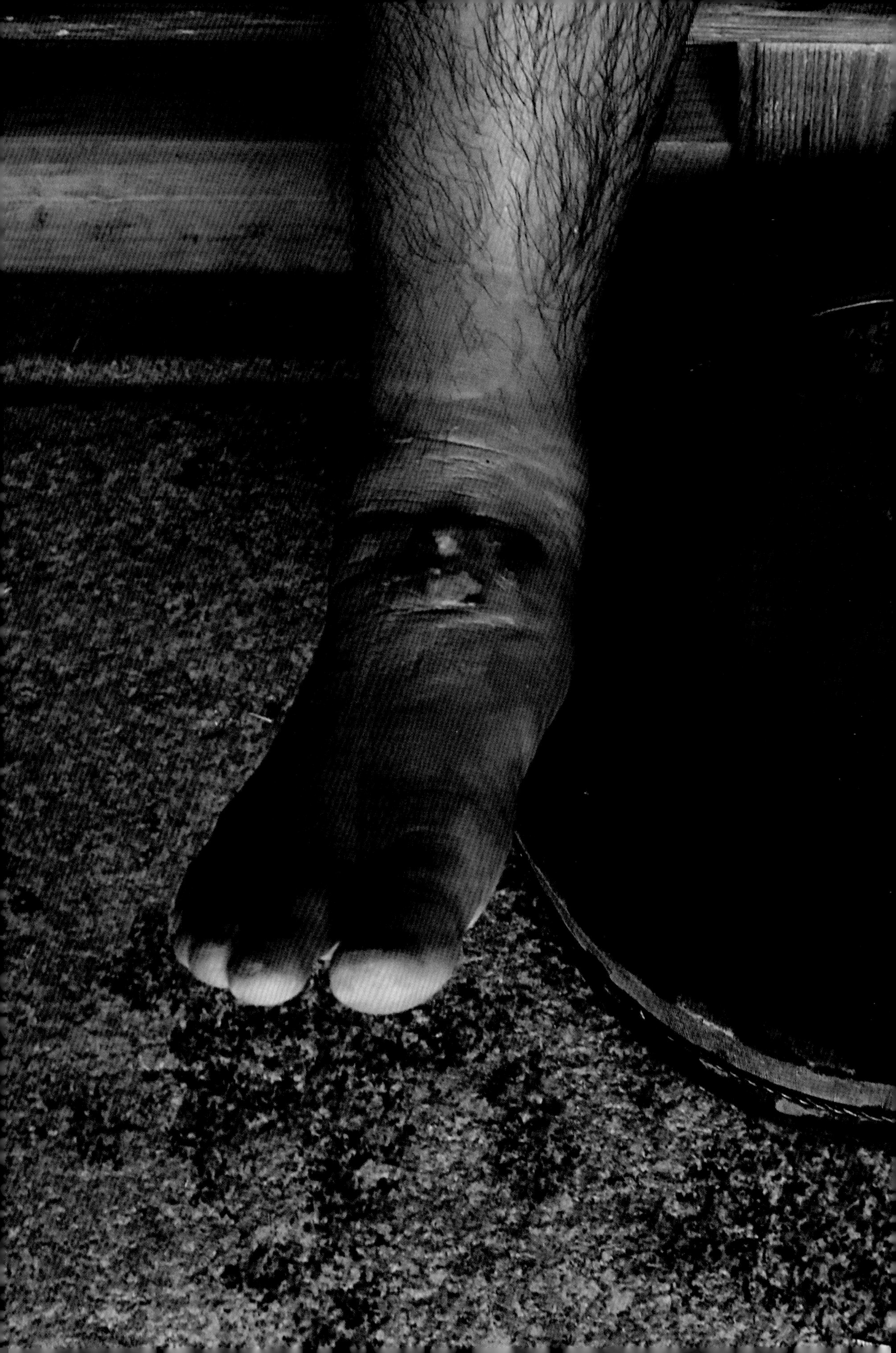

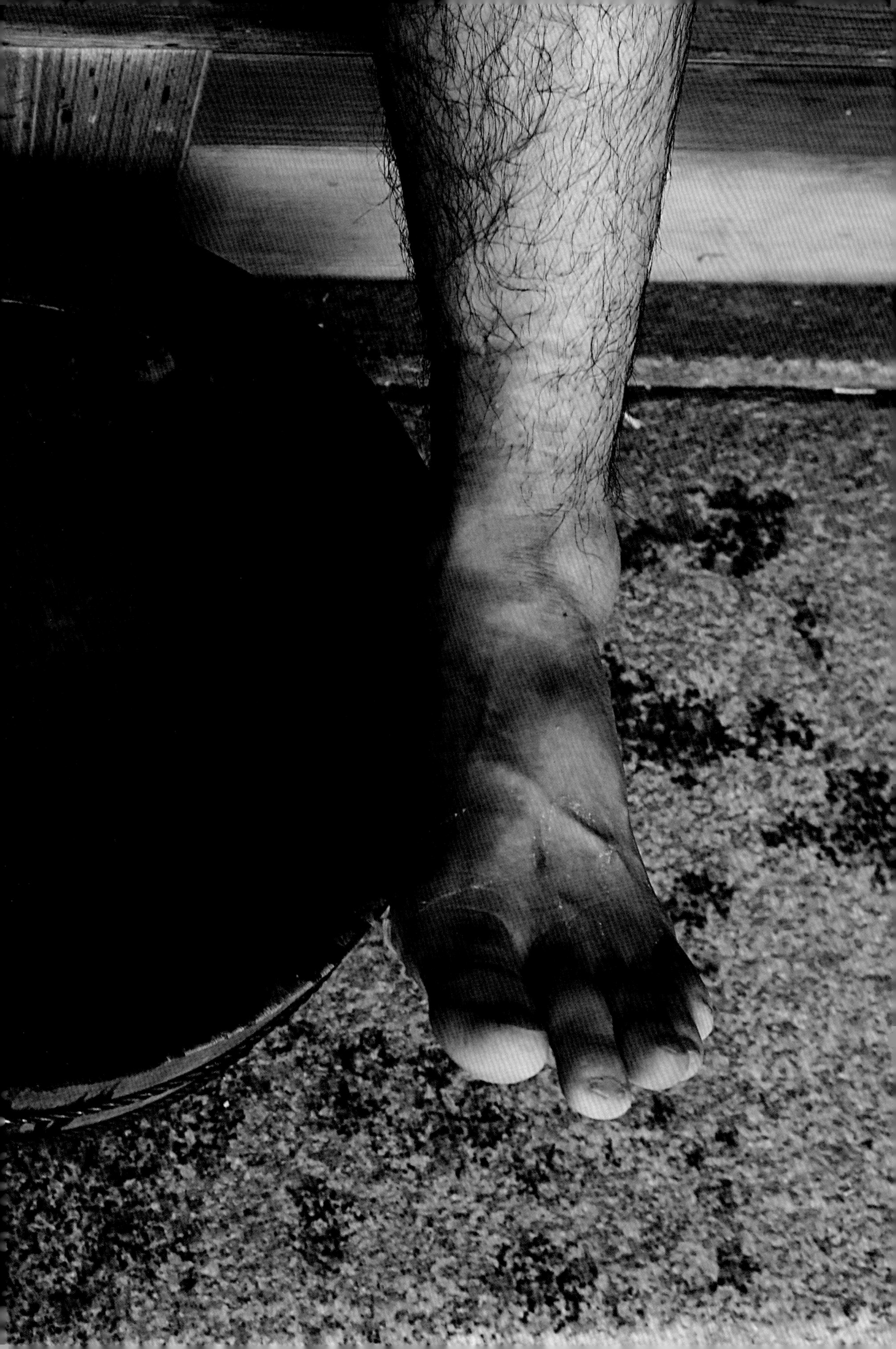

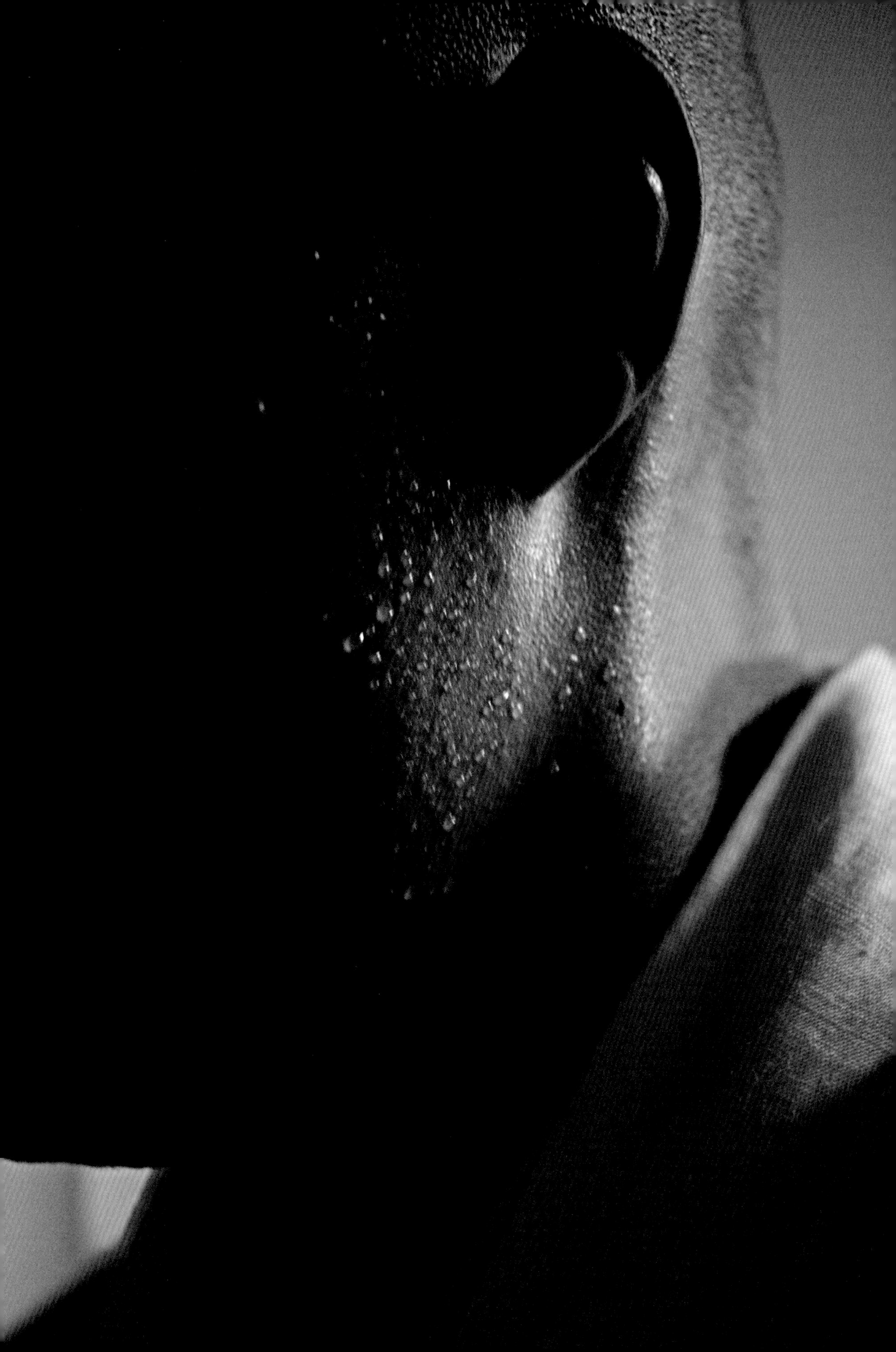

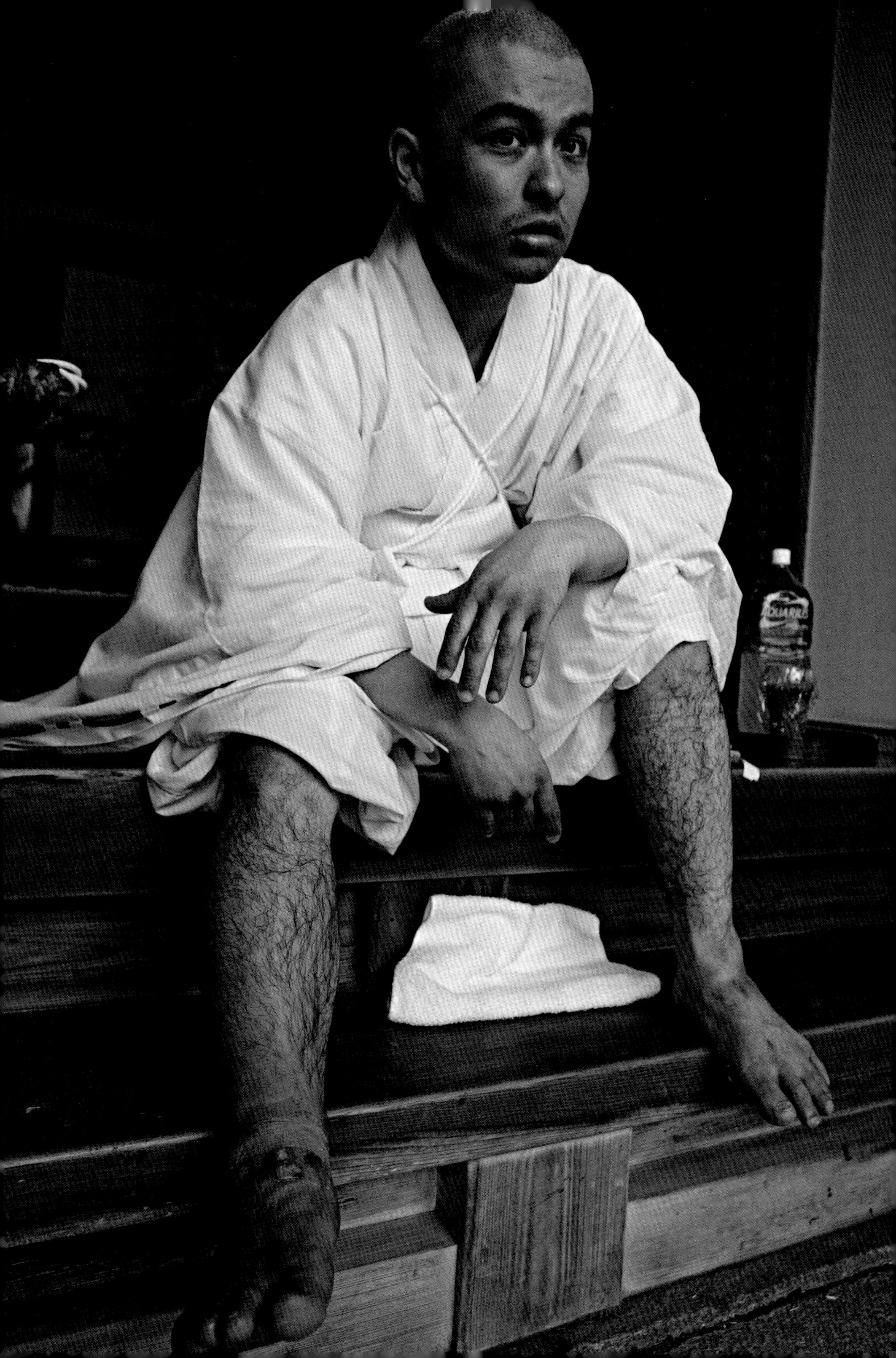

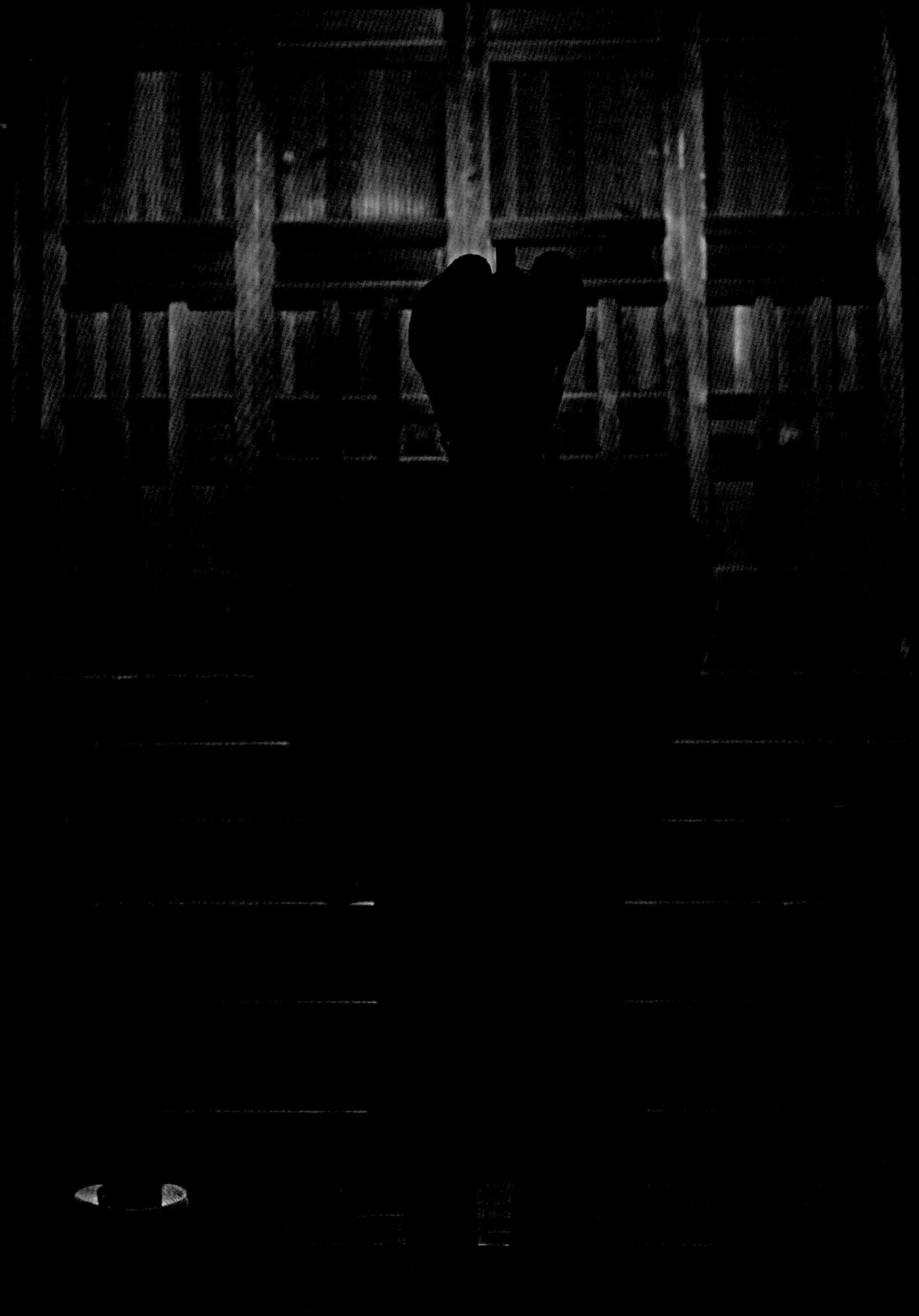

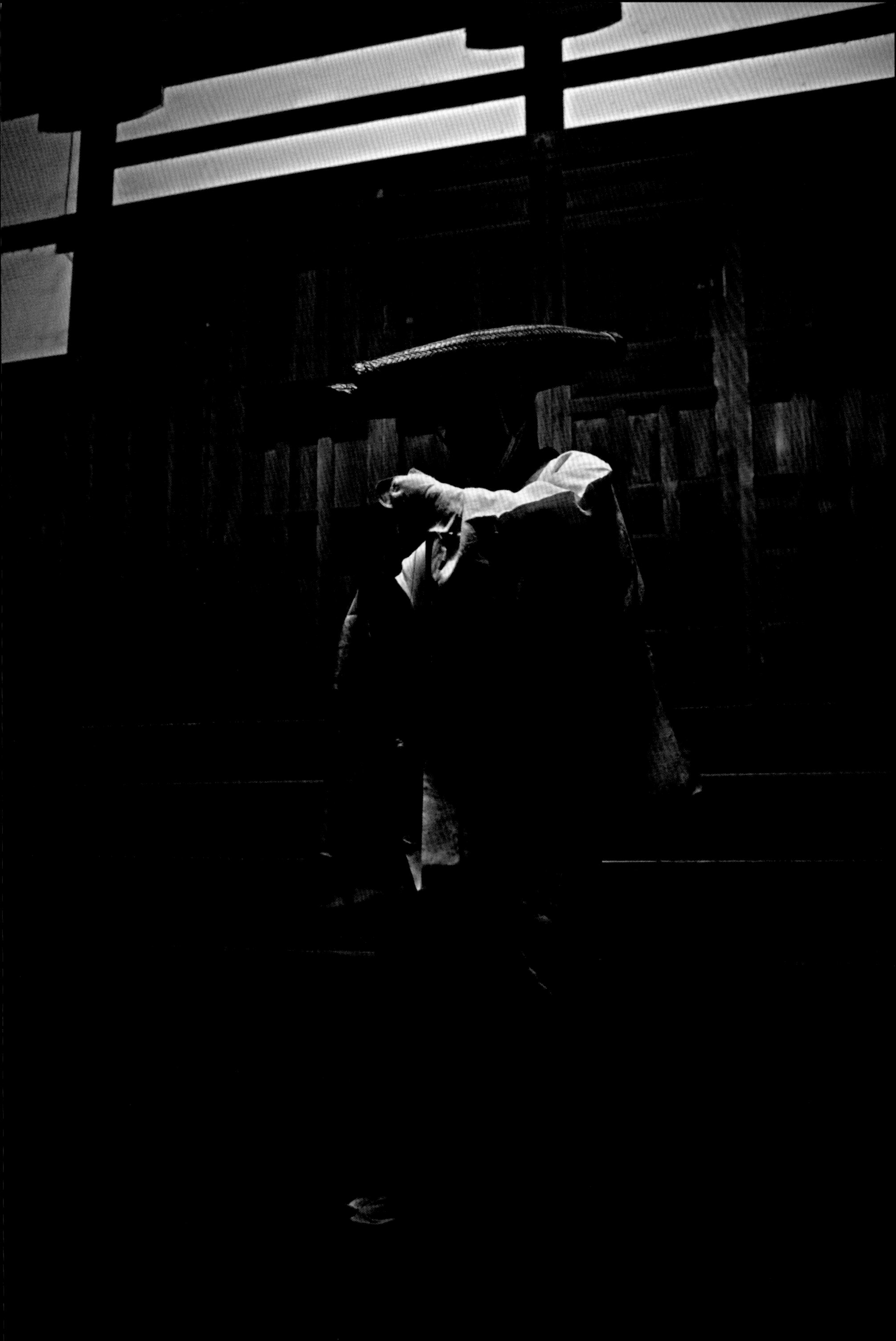

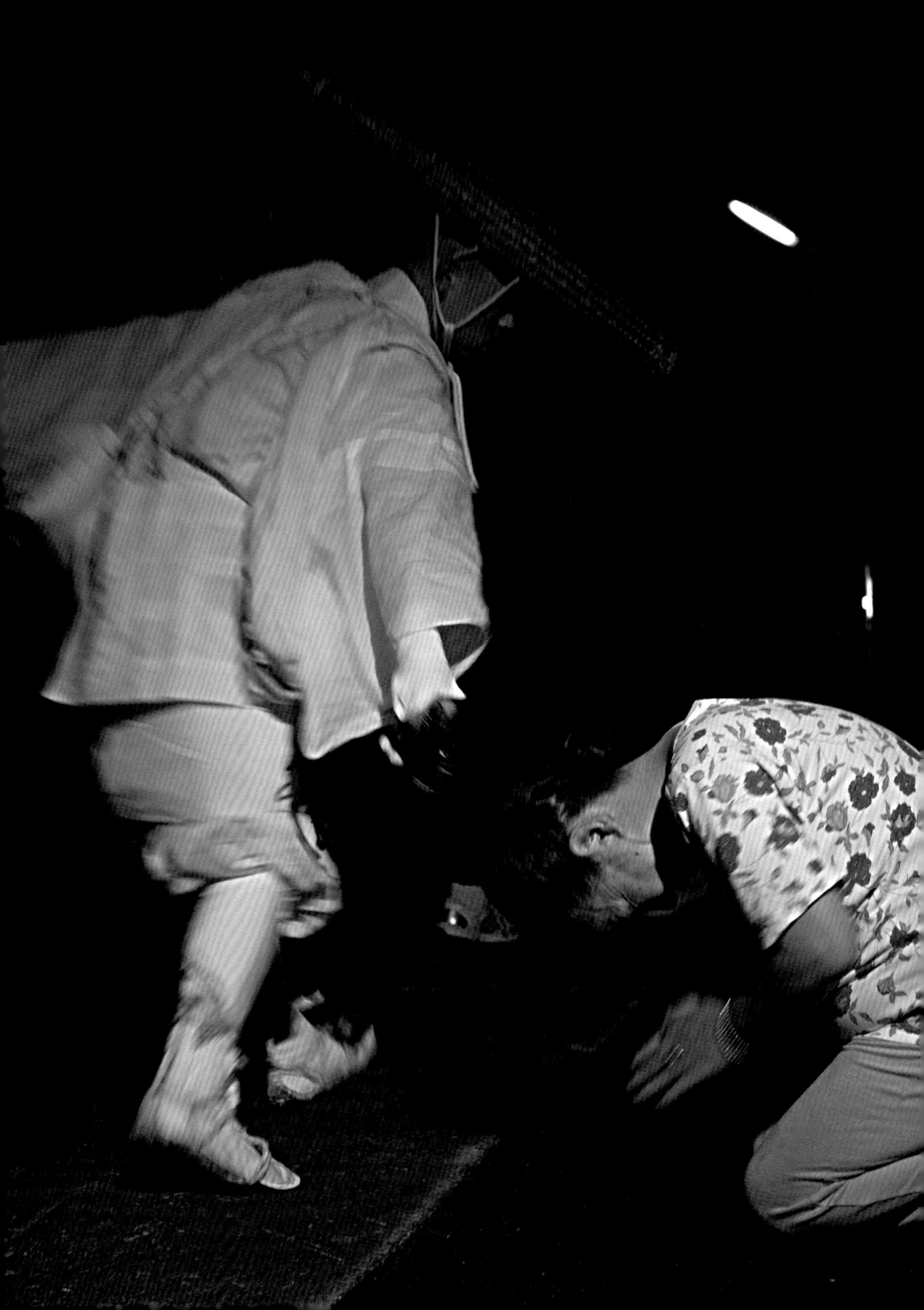

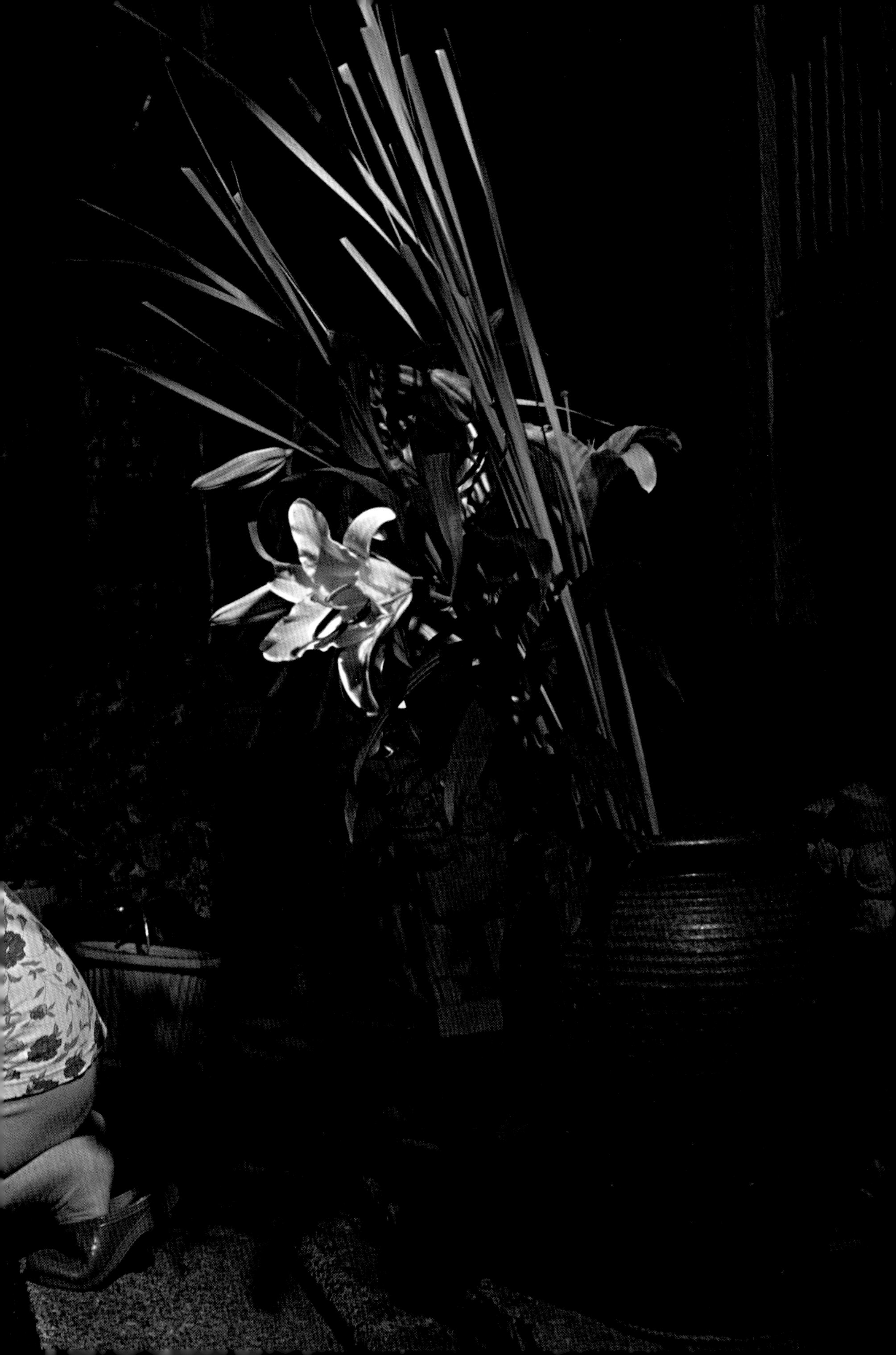

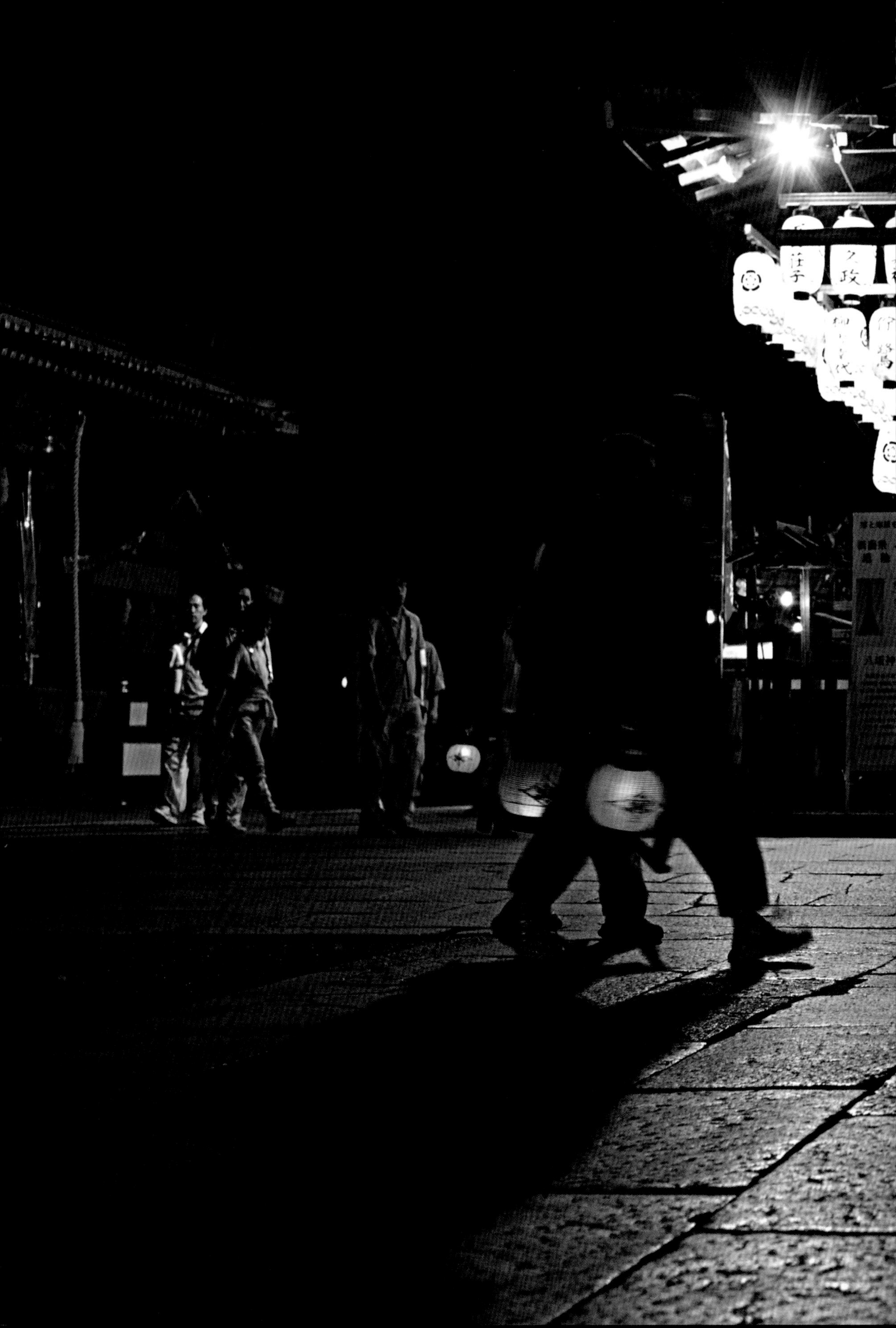

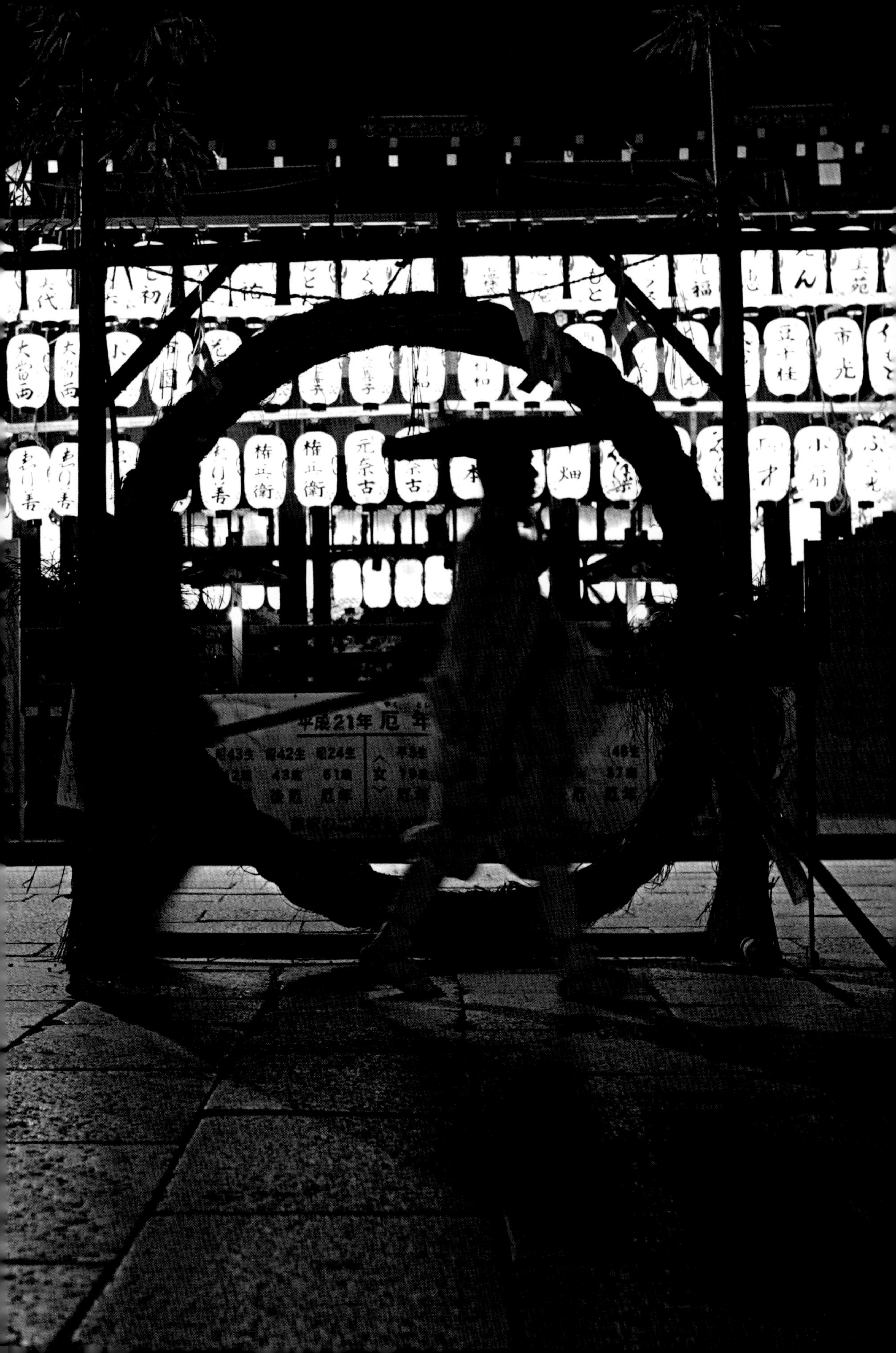
平成21年 厄年

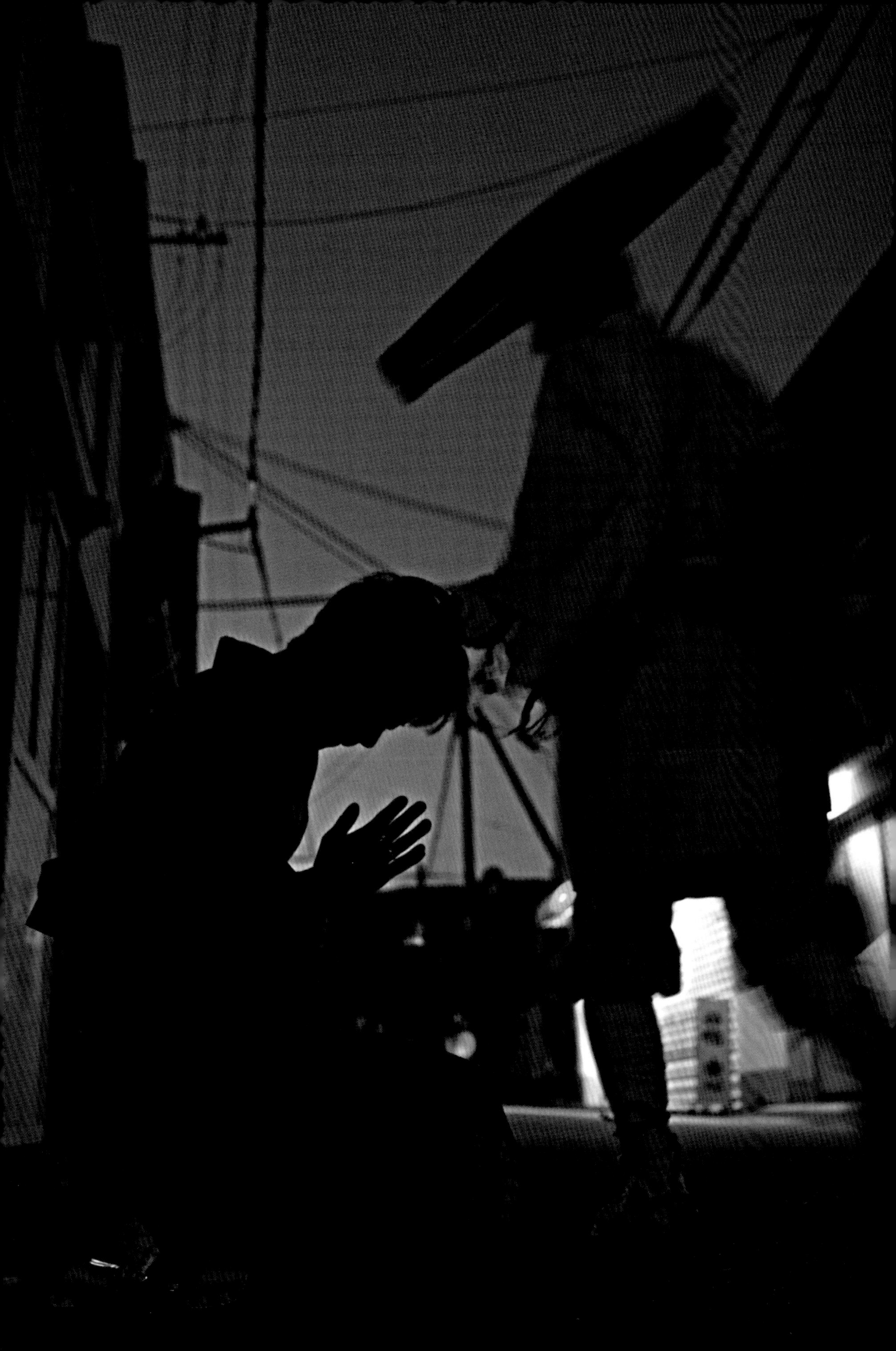

土足参内 | *Dosokusandai*

2009年10月12日、雲一つない青空が広がり、汗ばむほどの陽気だった。
数百人の僧侶と大人数の随喜者が、京都御所に敷き詰められた玉砂利の上を歩く足音が千日分の足音に聞こえた。
千日回峰行では、日々、西塔にある「玉体杉」という場所で、「国家安寧・玉体安穏」を祈願される。この日は相応和尚の加持力によって、染殿皇后の病気が平癒した故事にならって、京都御所のなかにある小御所において「玉体加持」が行われた。
小御所の上段の間には玉座が設えられ、圓道師は中段の間に進んで力強い声で「玉体加持」をされた。
小御所の外に列立した随喜の人たちも頭を垂れていたのが印象的で、「御池庭」の池の水を波立たせるかのような圓道師の大きな声だった。

October 12, 2009 was a day with not even a single cloud in the clear blue sky, it was warm to the point where one would sweat. Several hundred priests and pilgrims had gathered at the Imperial Palace in Kyoto. The sound of thousands of footsteps on gravel could be heard. Every day during his thousand day *kaihōgyō* training, at 'The Emperor's Cedar' at the West Pagoda, Reverend Endō had made prayers for peace for the country, and peace for the Emperor. On that day there was a special healing to be performed by Reverend Endō known as 'the Emperor's Healing'. Its origin comes from when Sōō (the priest who founded *kaihōgyō* training practices), healed the Emperor of his sickness using a powerful incantation.
Reverend Endō sat in the throne room, and performed 'the Emperor's Healing'. His voice was so powerful and impressive that the water in the pond in the garden rippled, and the pilgrims outside lowered their heads.

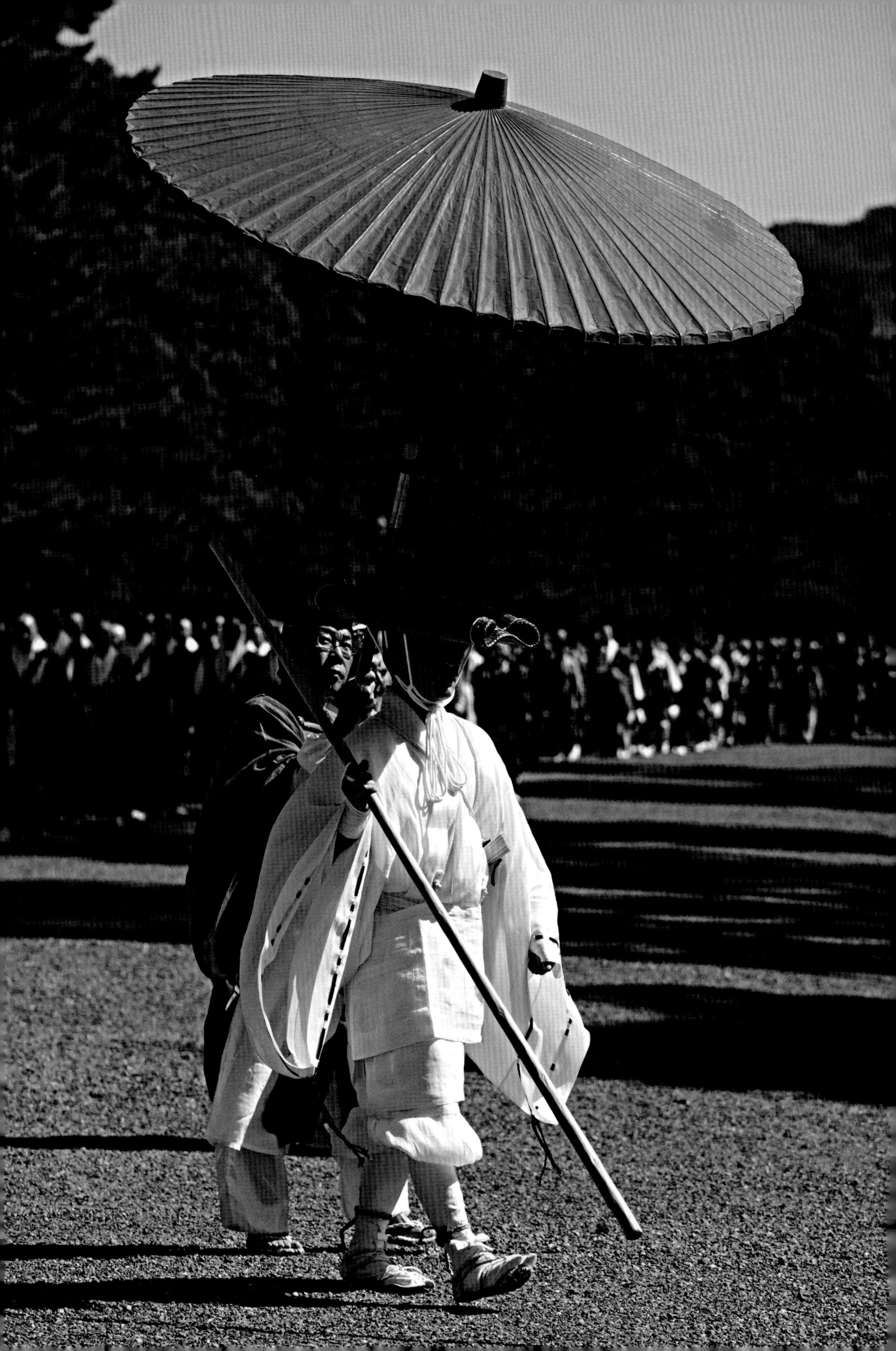

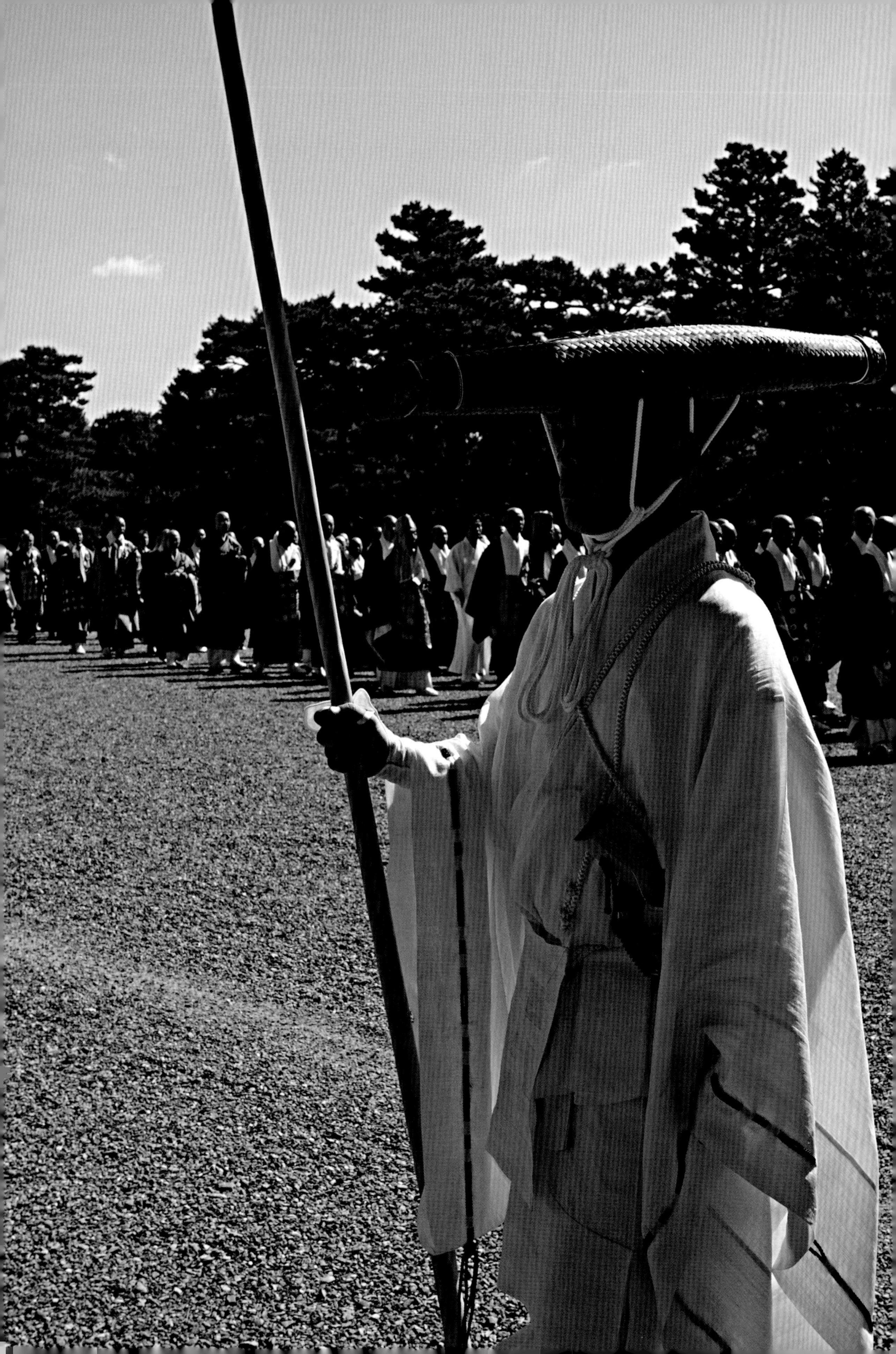

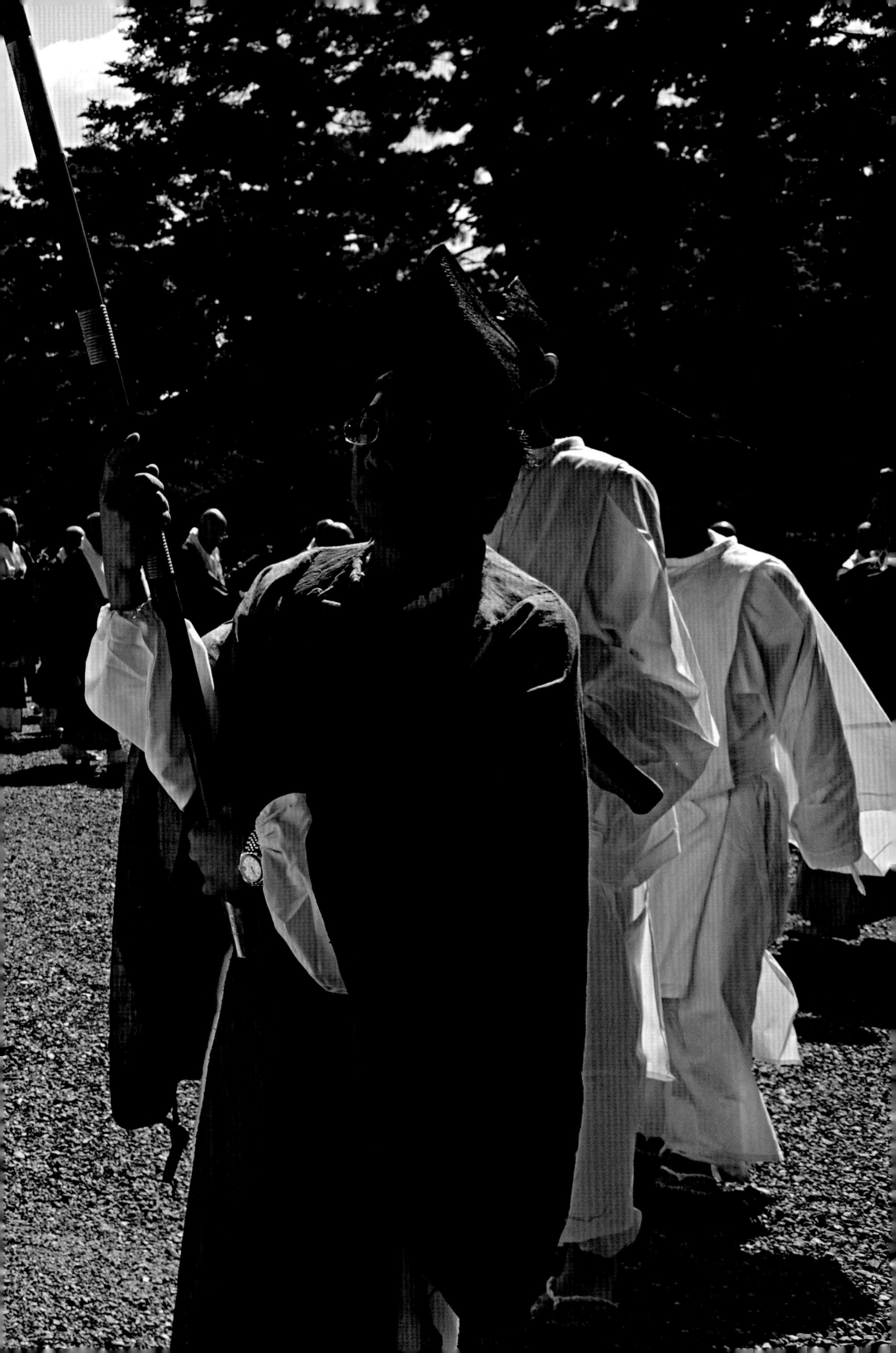

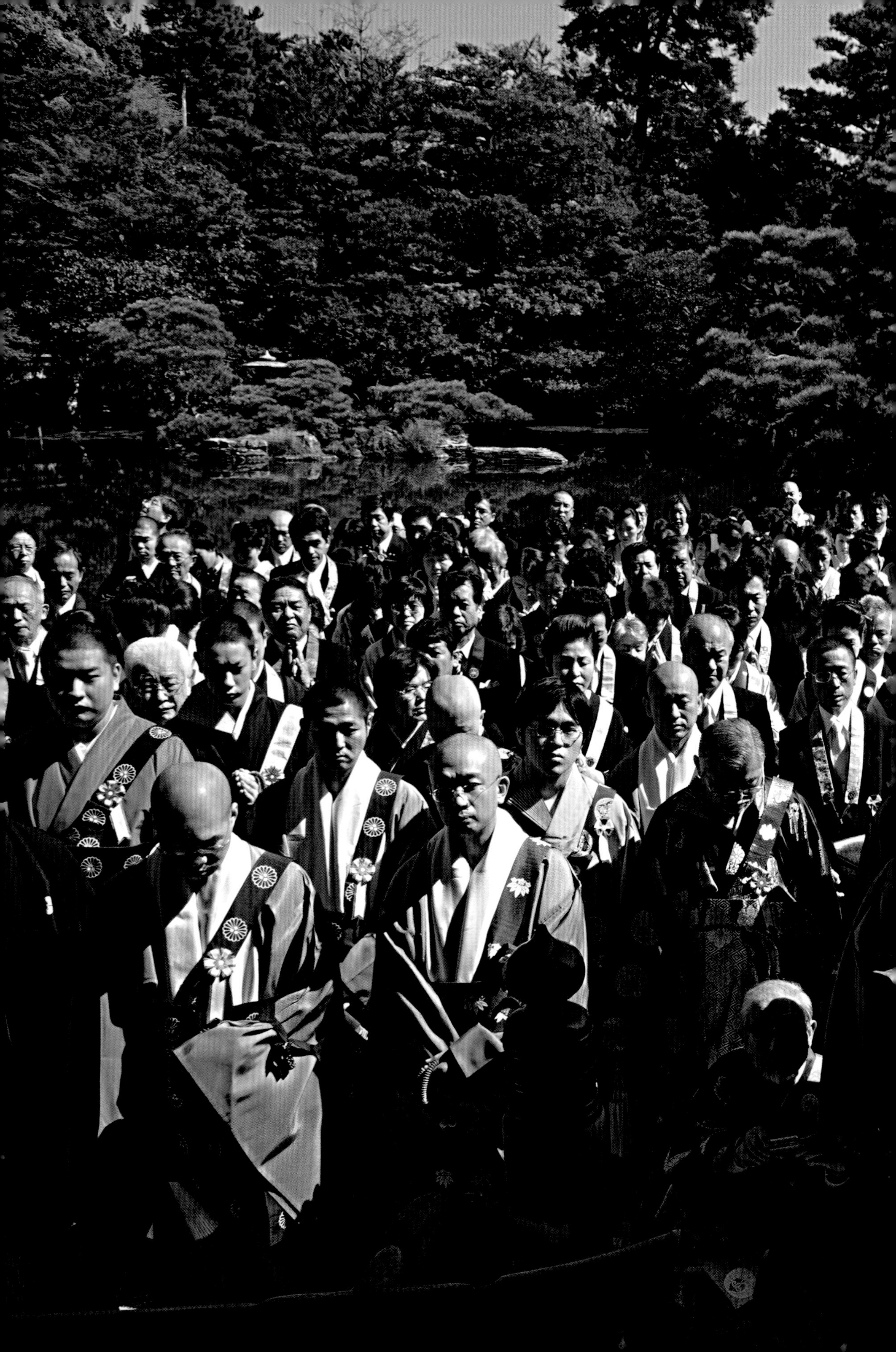

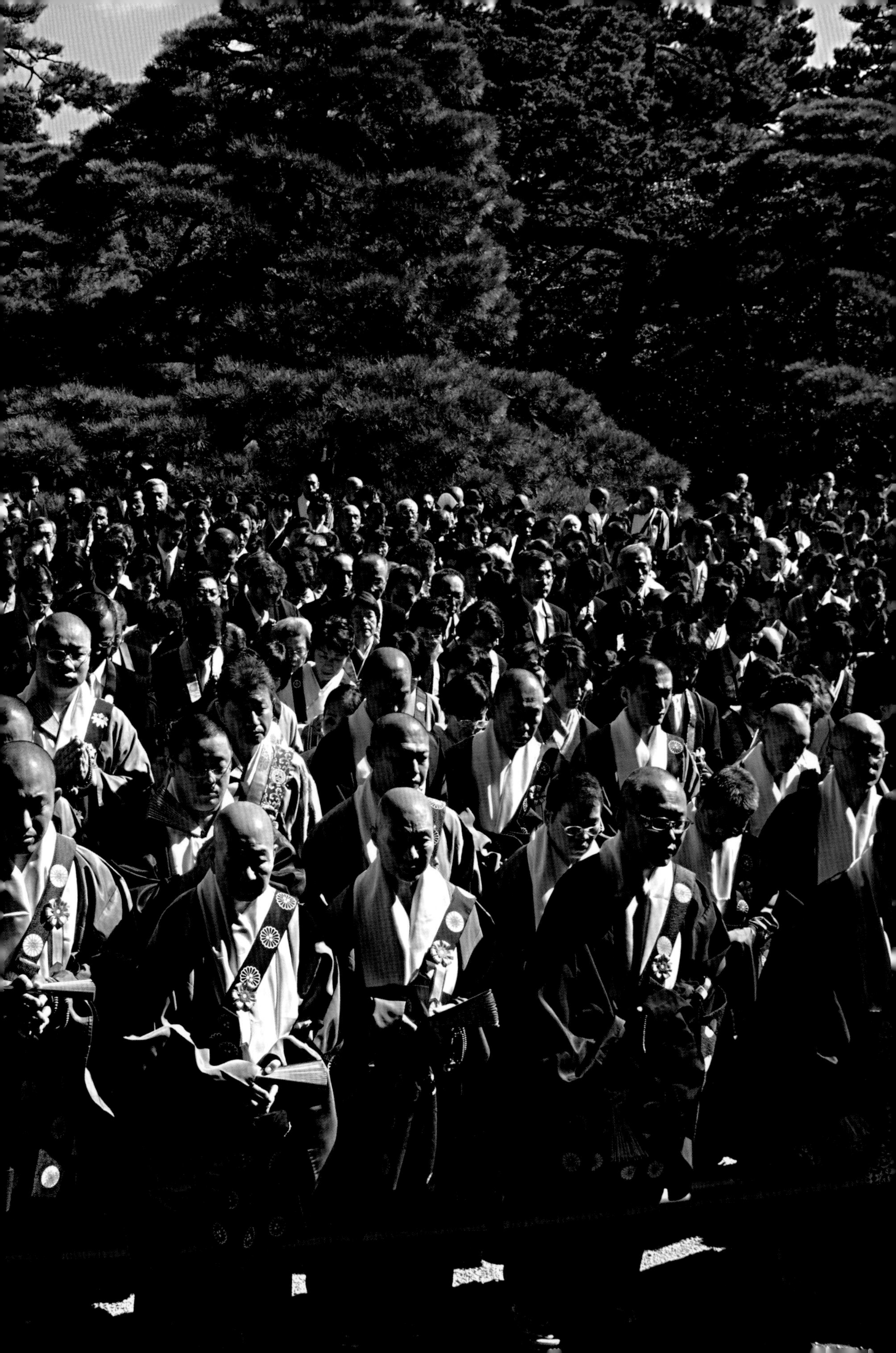

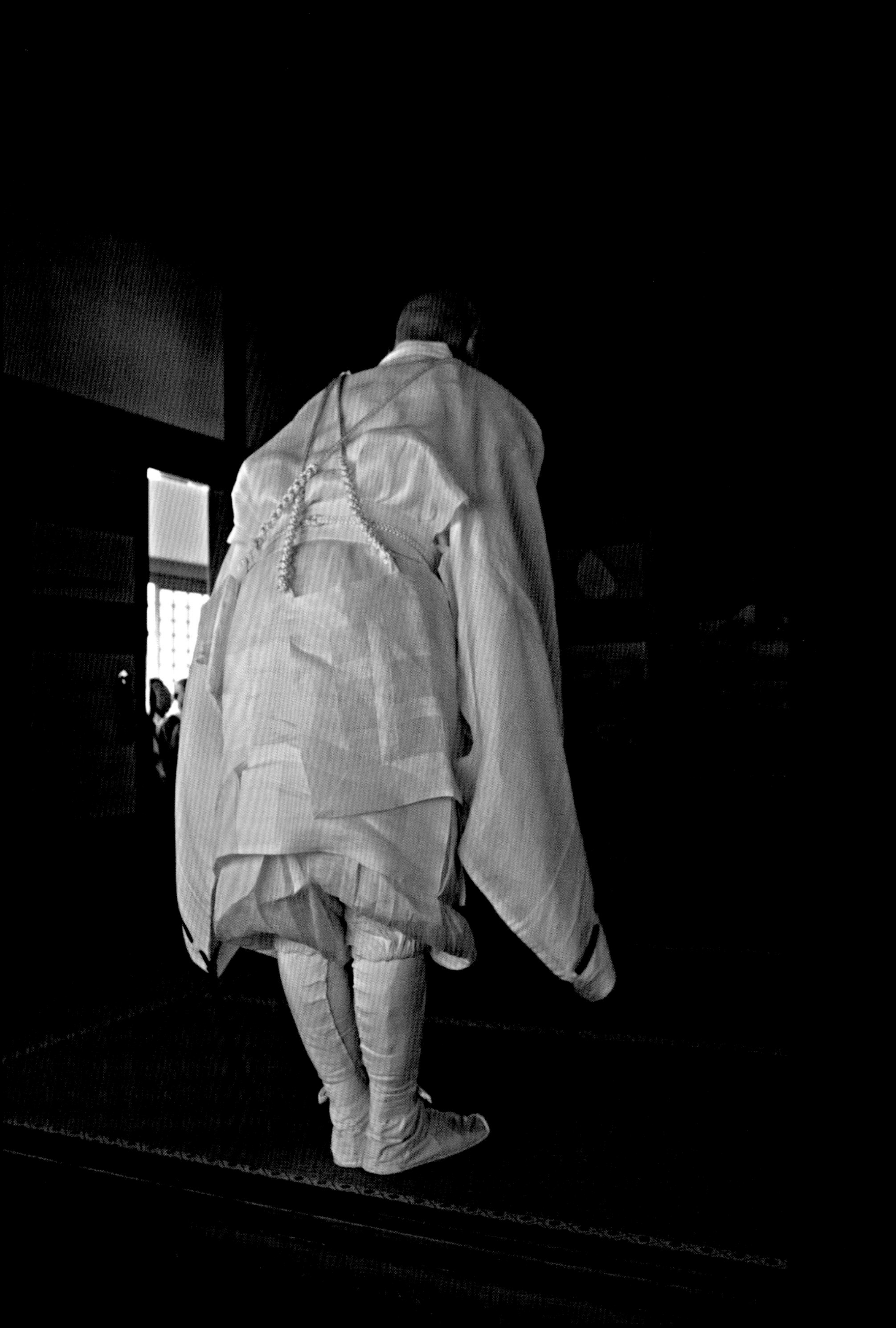

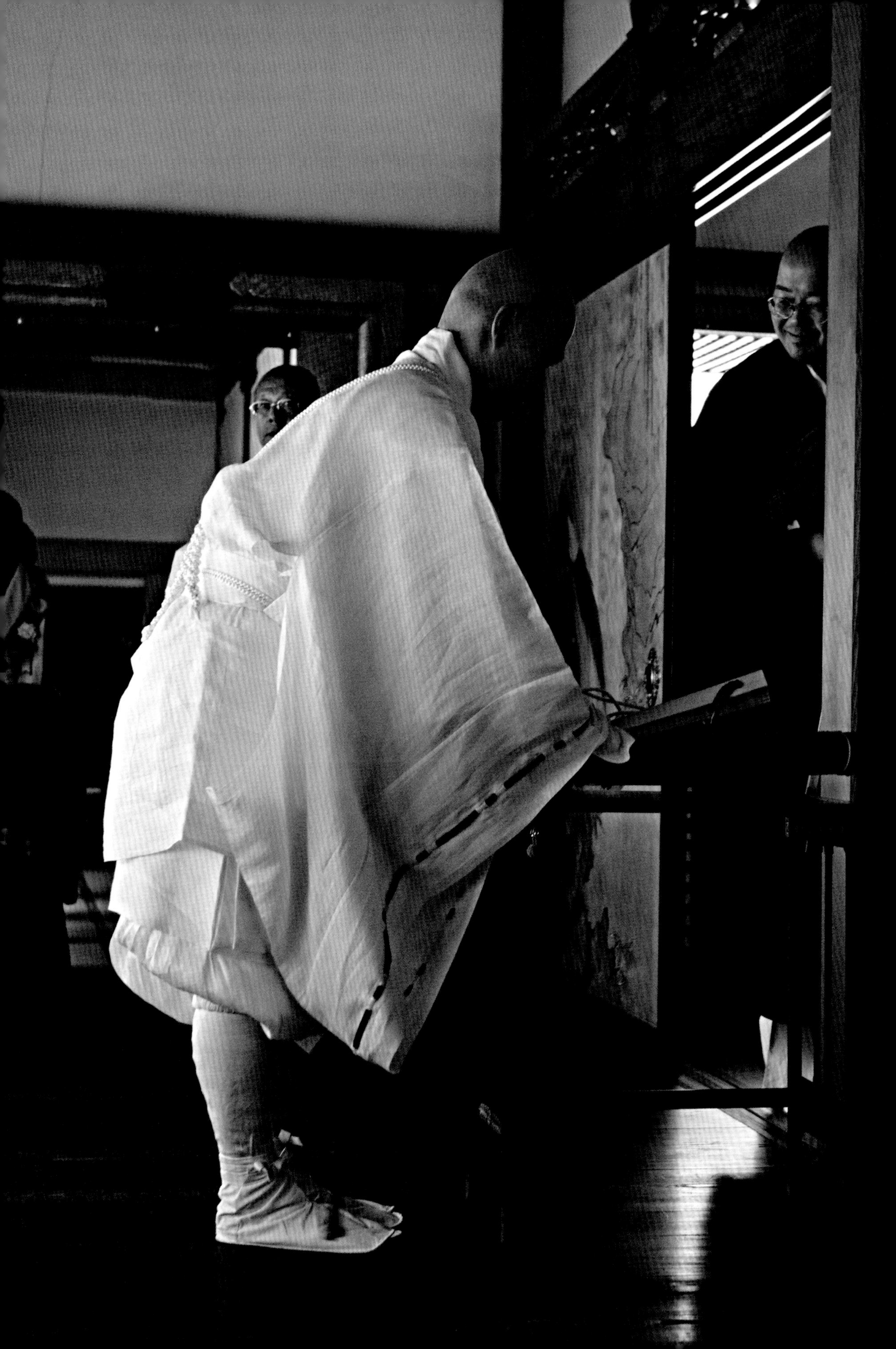

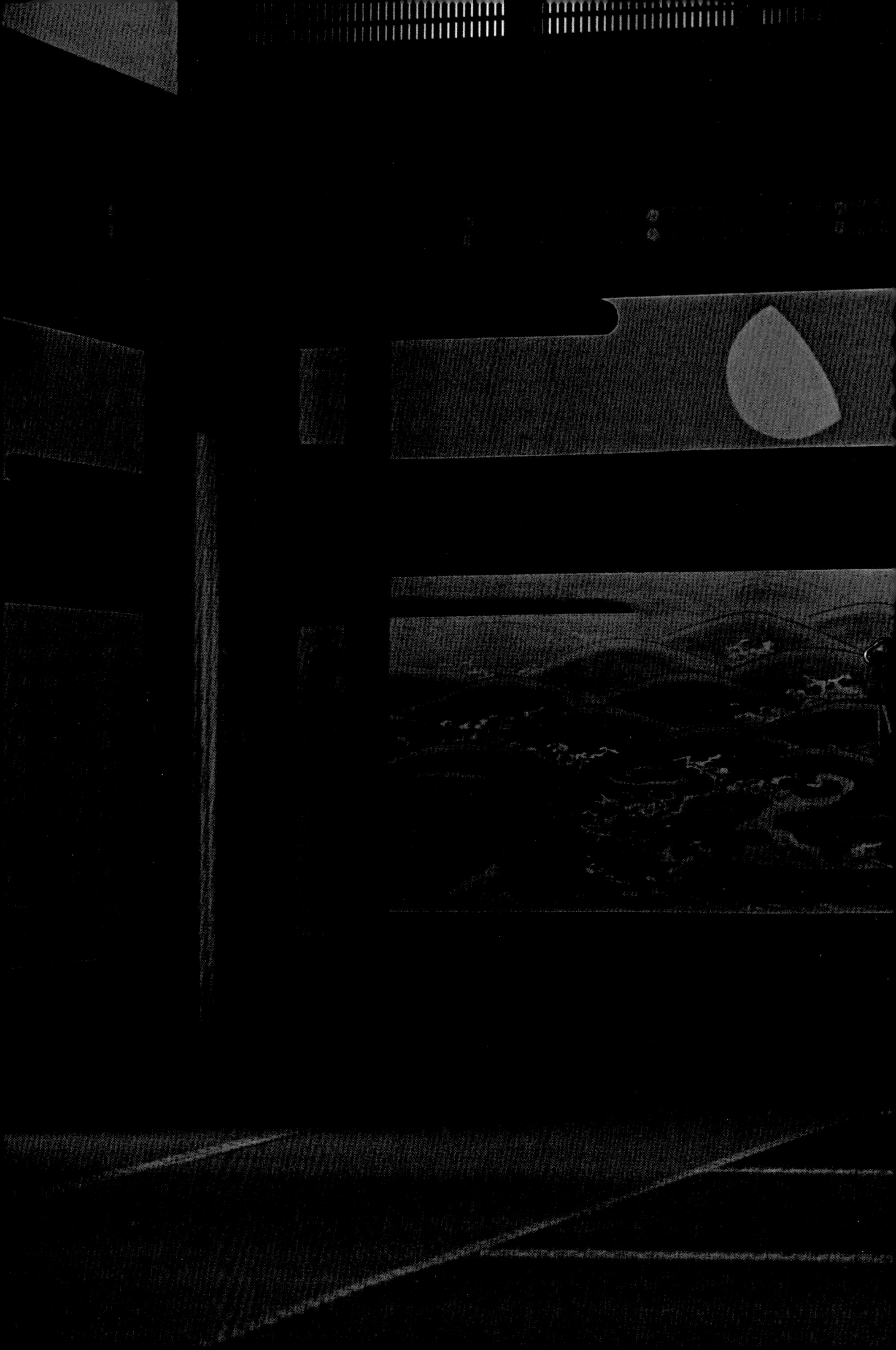

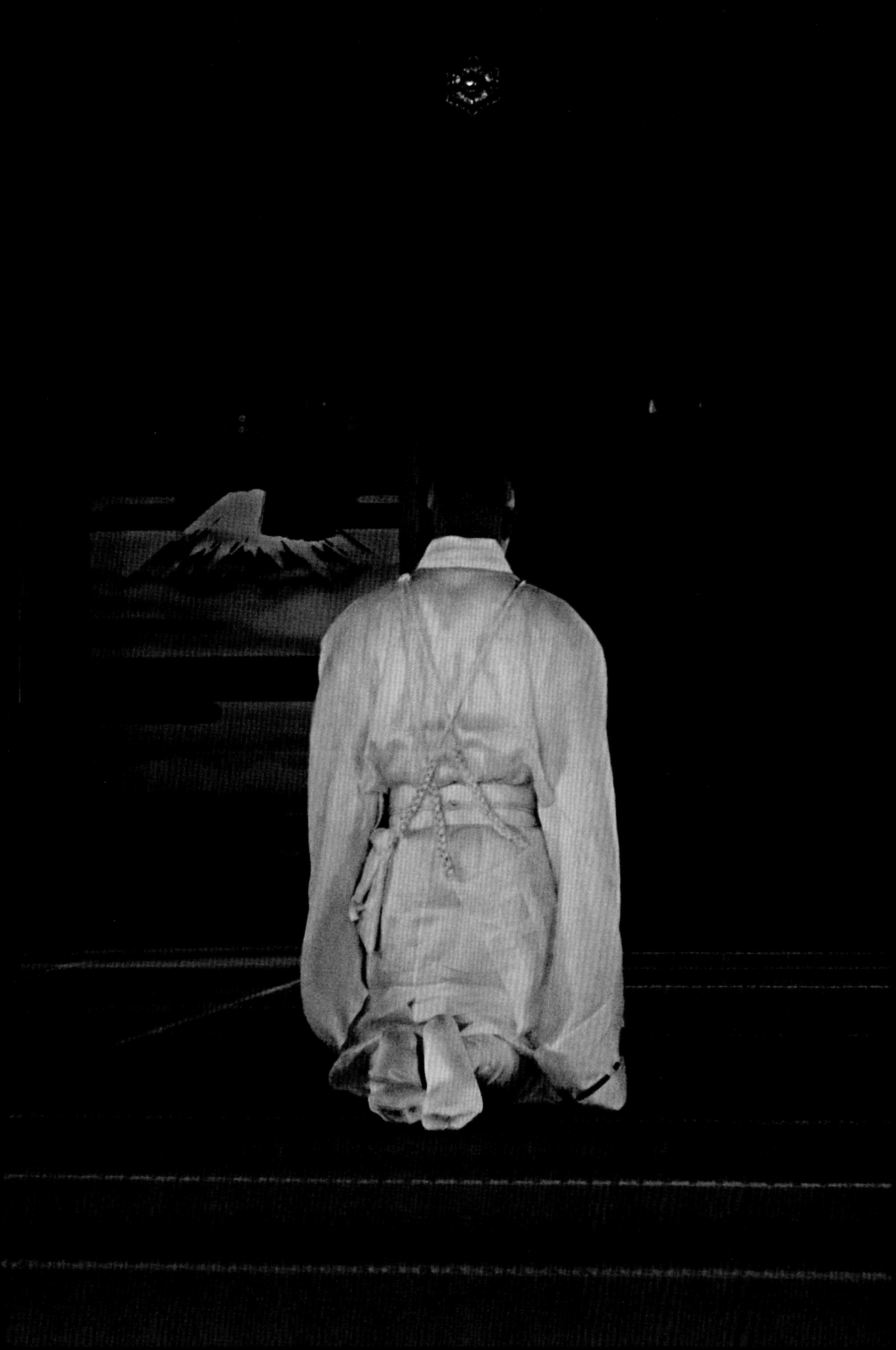

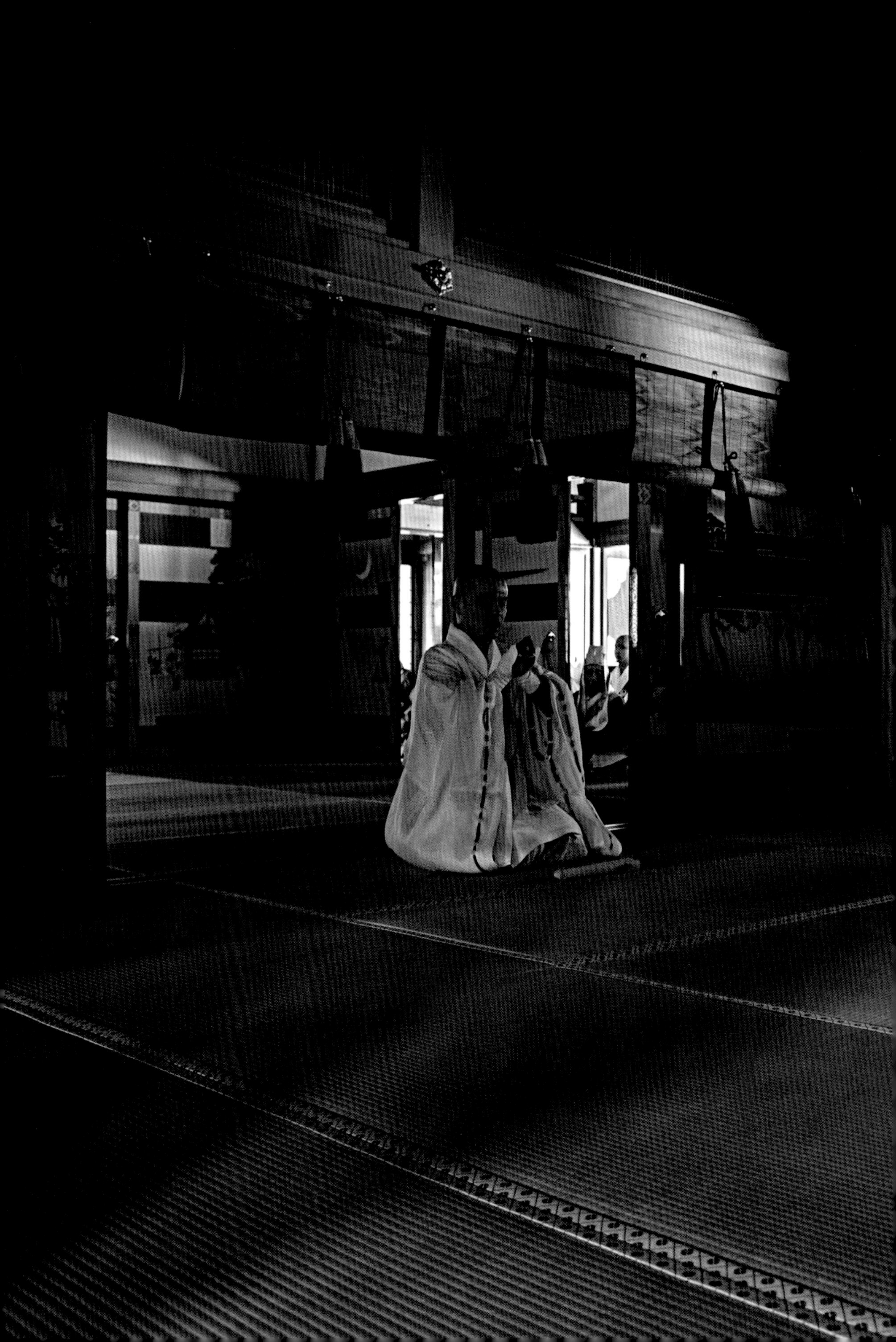

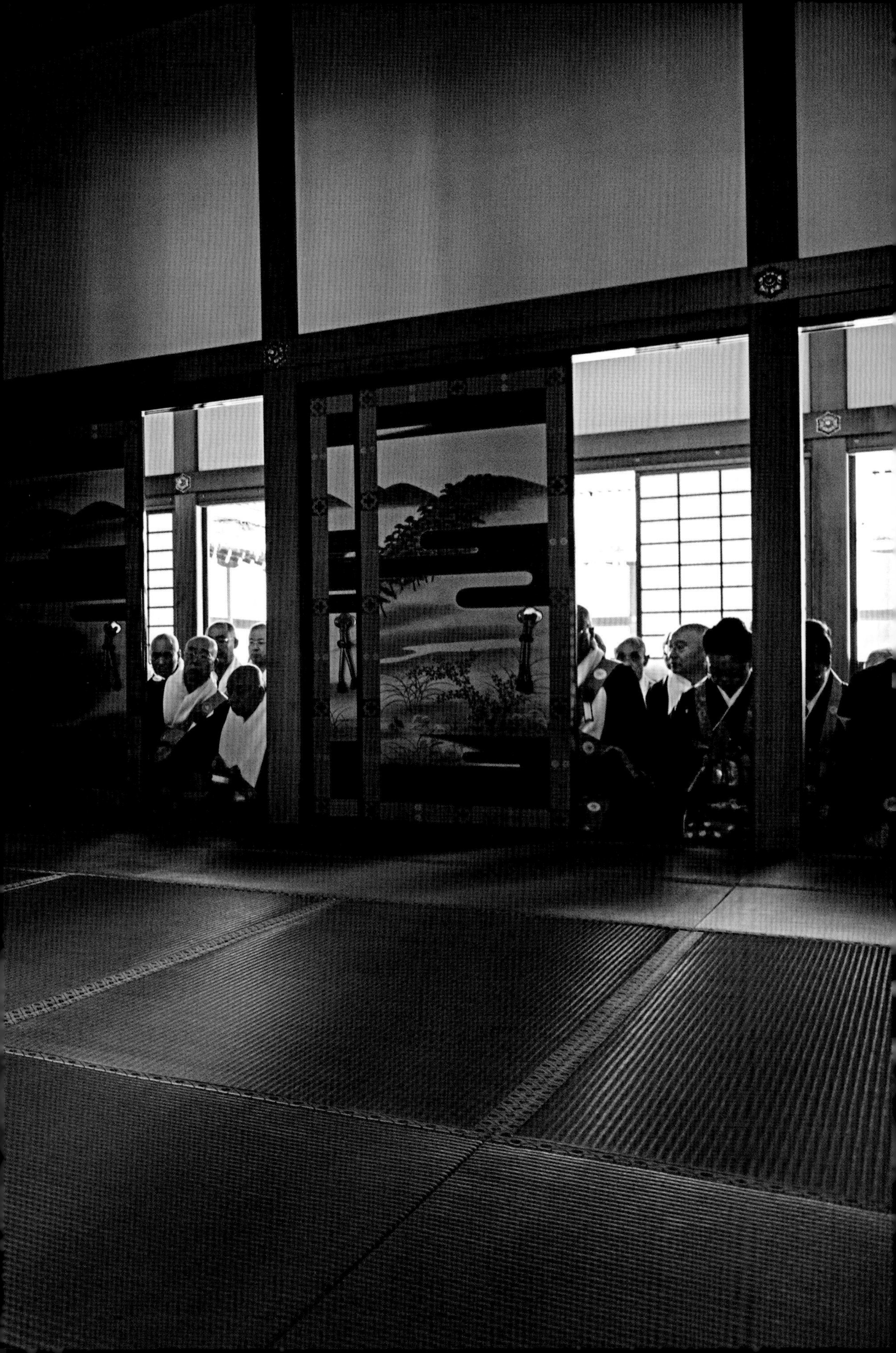

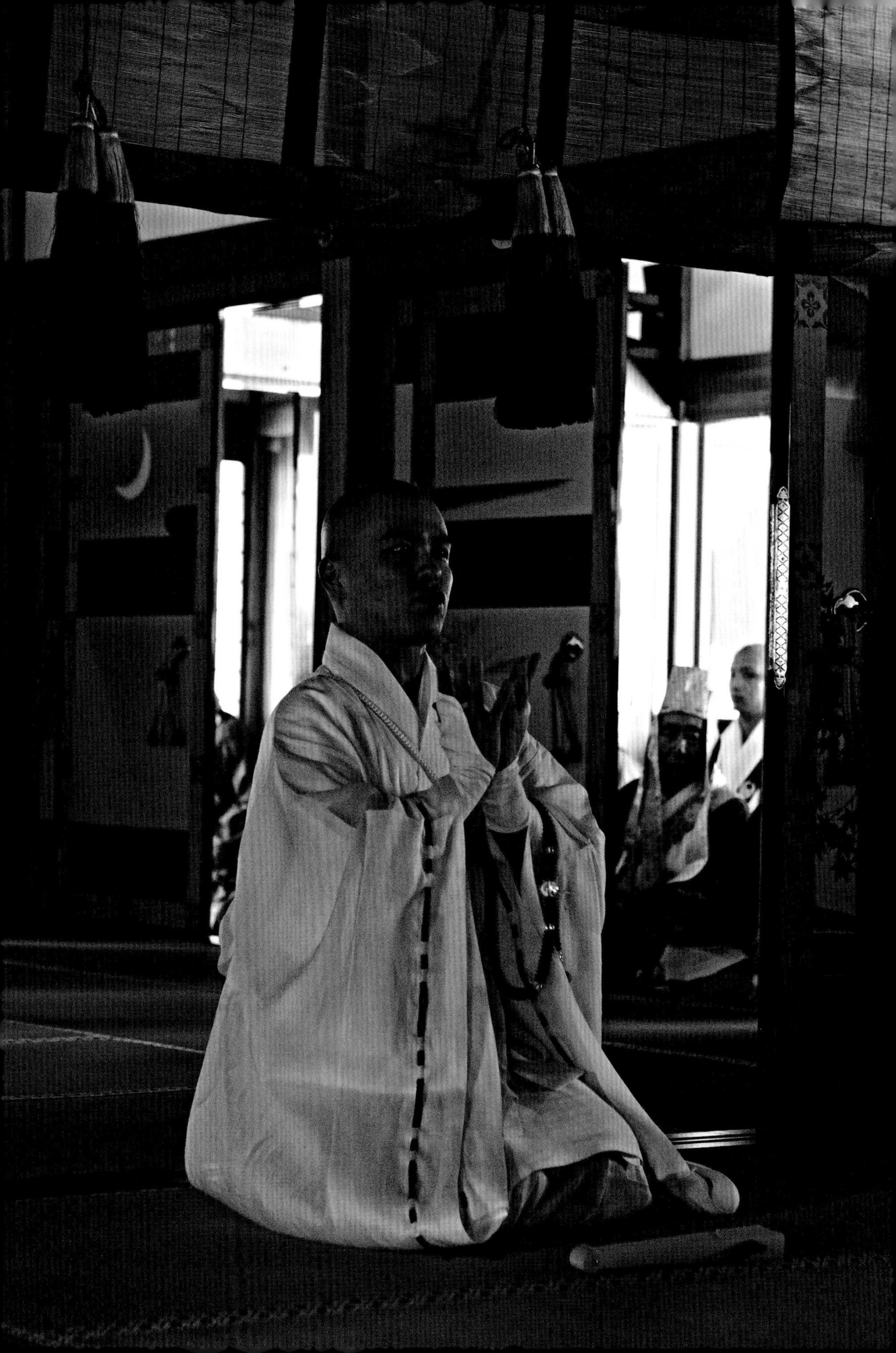

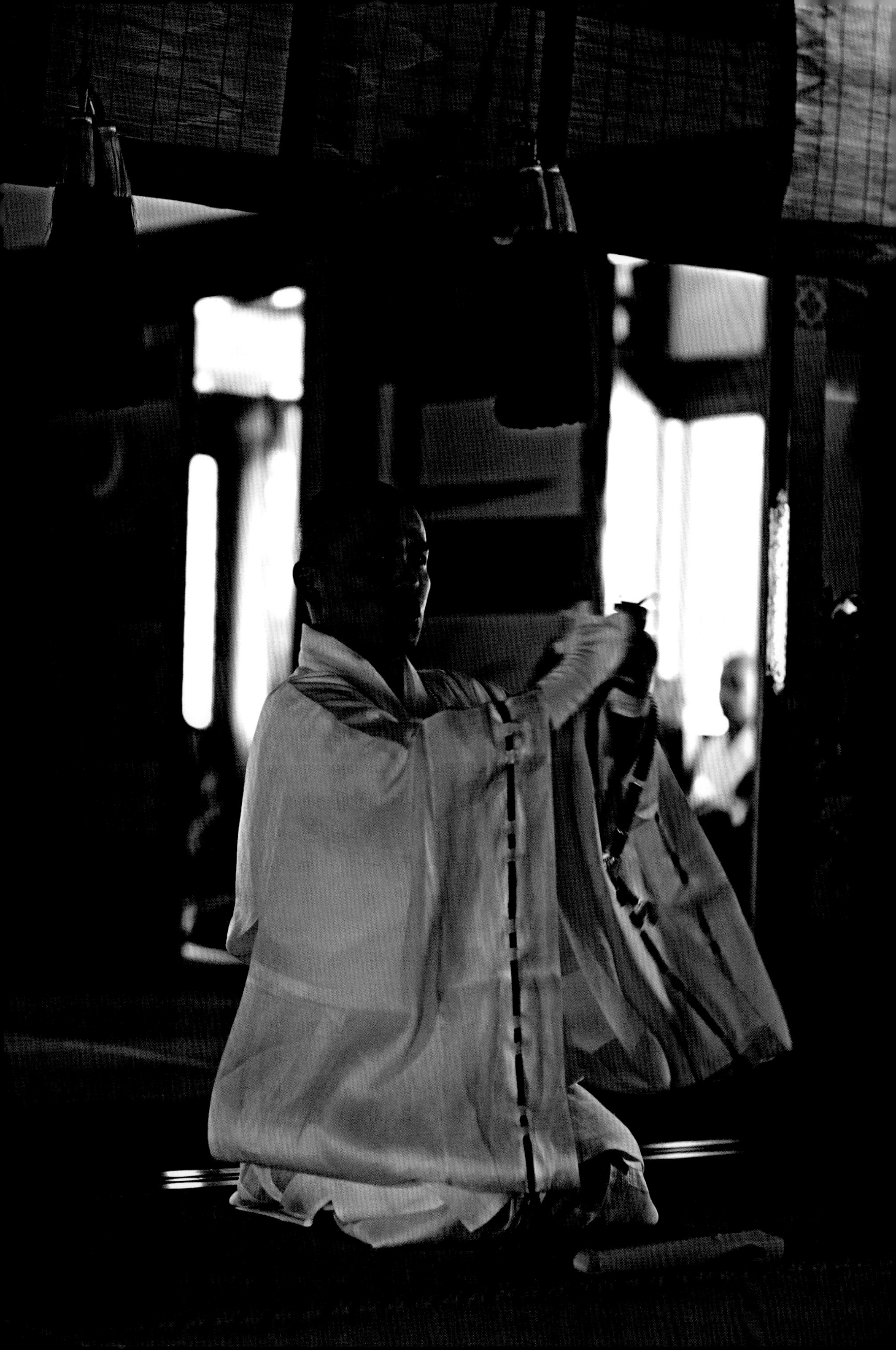

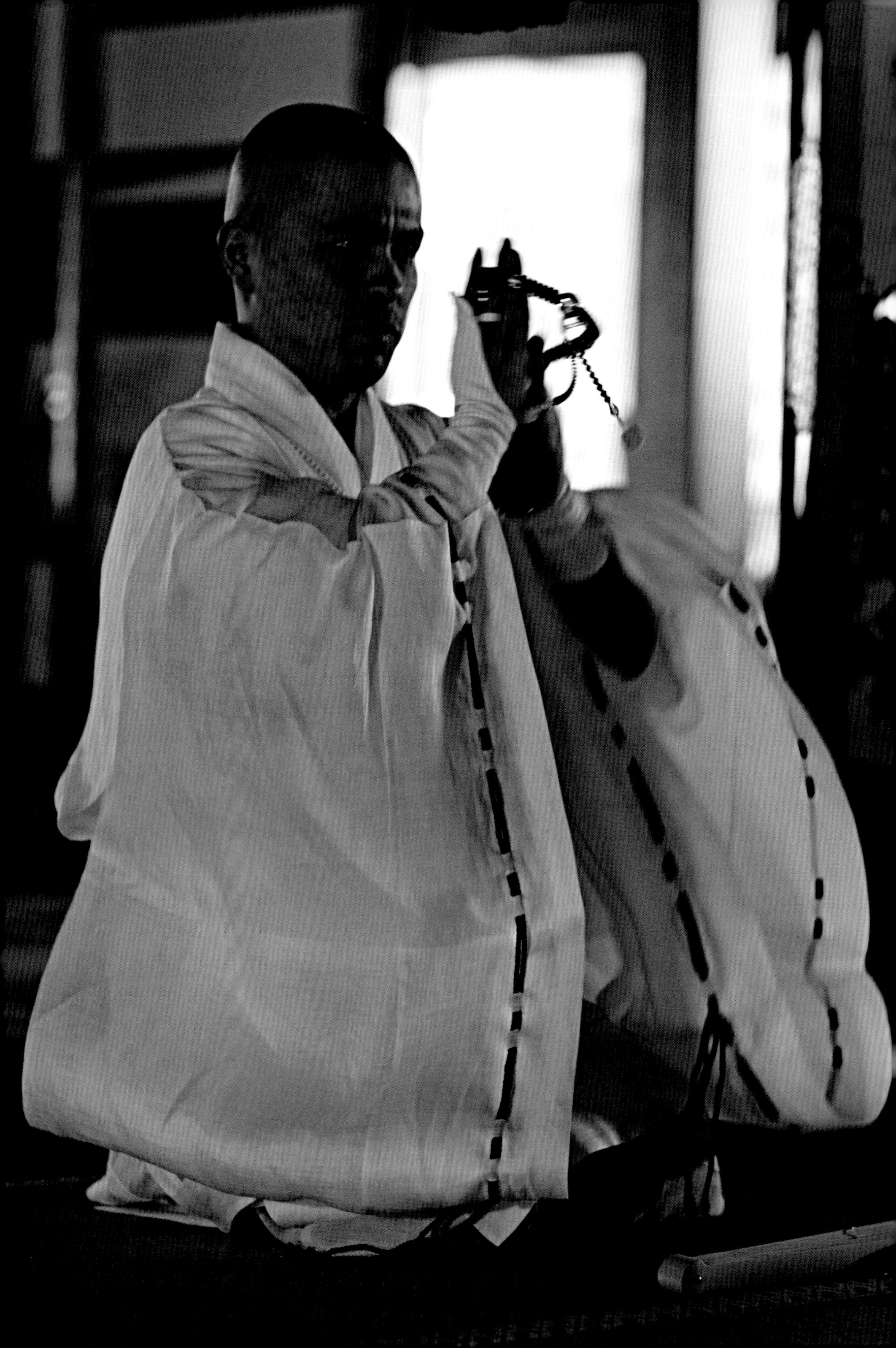

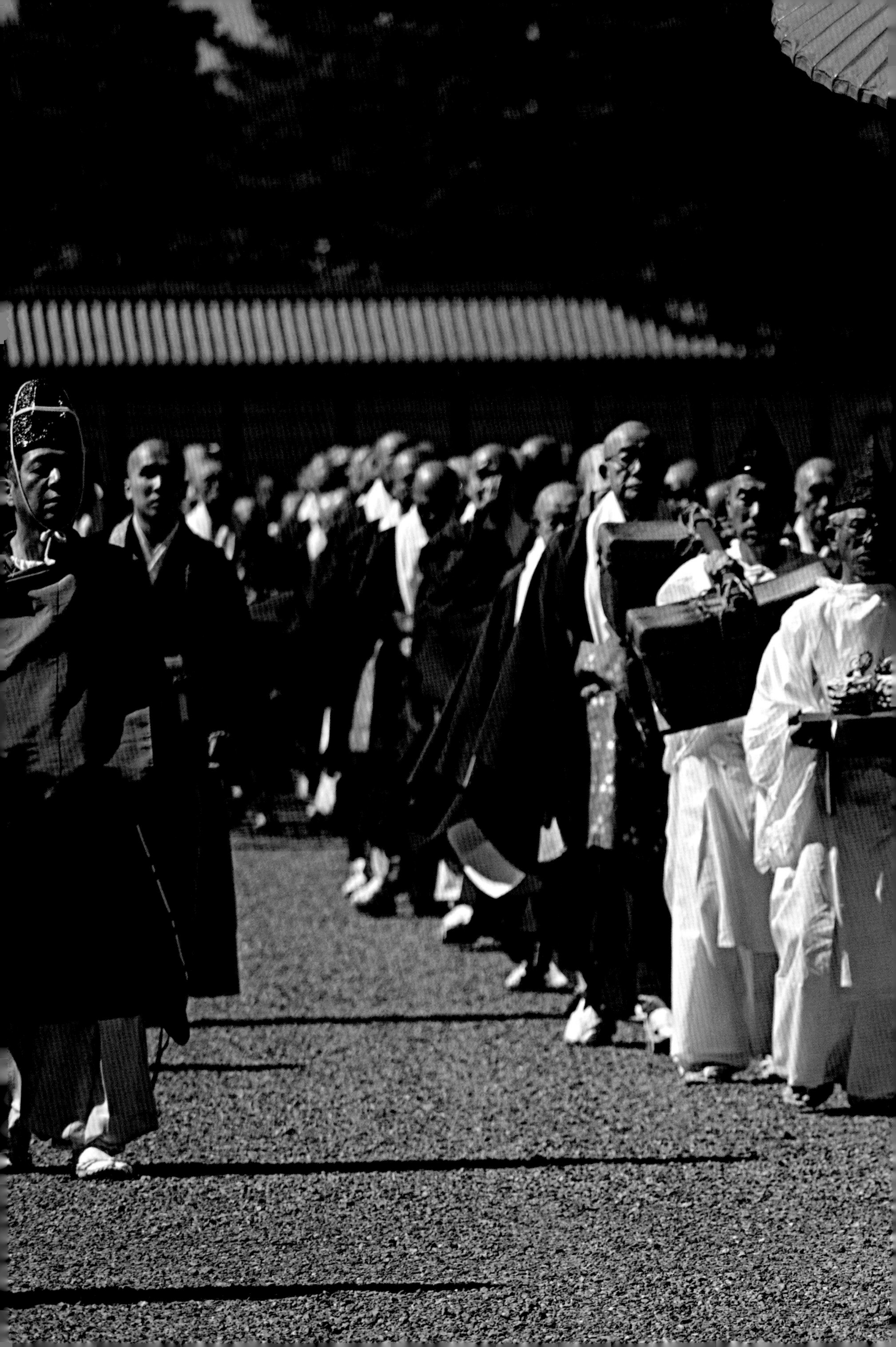

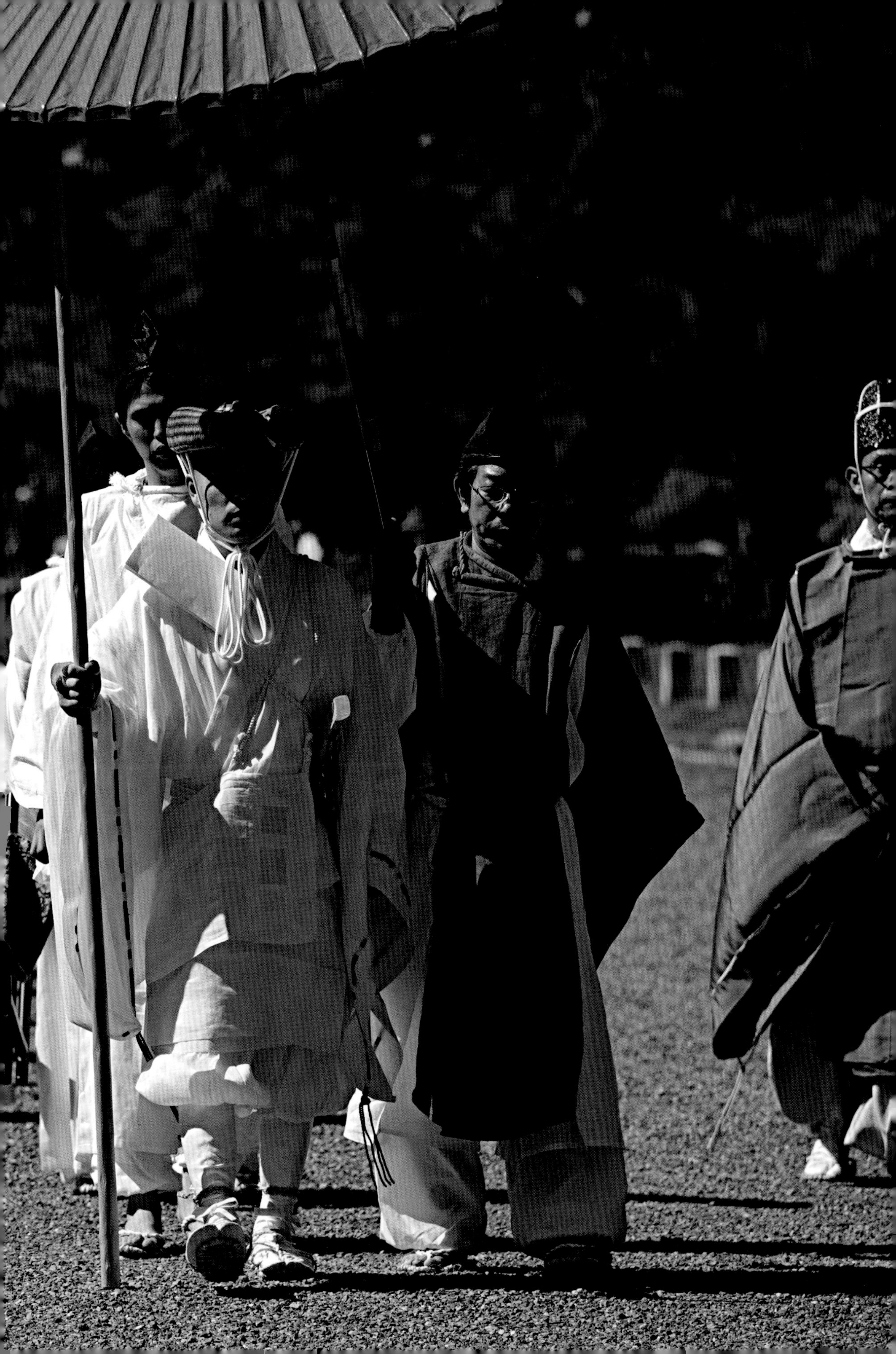

十萬枚大護摩供 | *Jyumanmai-ōgomaku*

圓道師にとっては堂入りに続いて、2度目の断食・断水・不眠の一週間におよぶ大苦行である。護摩供の火柱は護摩堂の天井近くまで立ち上り、火柱にうつる圓道師の姿は不動明王のようだ。援護してくれる僧侶たちの姿もまた不動明王に仕える童子のようだった。

谷中に響く不動明王の真言を唱和する声は、この行が成就するようにとの願いを込めた祈りの響きであった。

行は、僧俗を問わず、行を支える人々の存在があってこそ、成り立っているのだと思った。この祈りの声も大きな力となって圓道師を支えたのではないだろうか。

For Reverend Endō this was the second time that he had performed the great act of penance of depriving himself of food, water and sleep for one week. As he performed the *goma* ritual (a ritual where offerings are made using fire), the flame from the ritual bowl nearly reached the ceiling of the room. Through the column of fire, Reverend Endō's form looked like that of Fudō-Myōō's. The forms of the monks who were assisting him in the ritual also looked like that of Fudō-Myōō's disciples. The valley was filled with the sound of Fudō-Myōō's mantra, carrying the wish that Reverend Endō could complete his training safely.

I think that it didn't matter whether they were monks or normal people, they were there to support him. There isn't any doubt that hearing their prayers gave Reverend Endō great support.

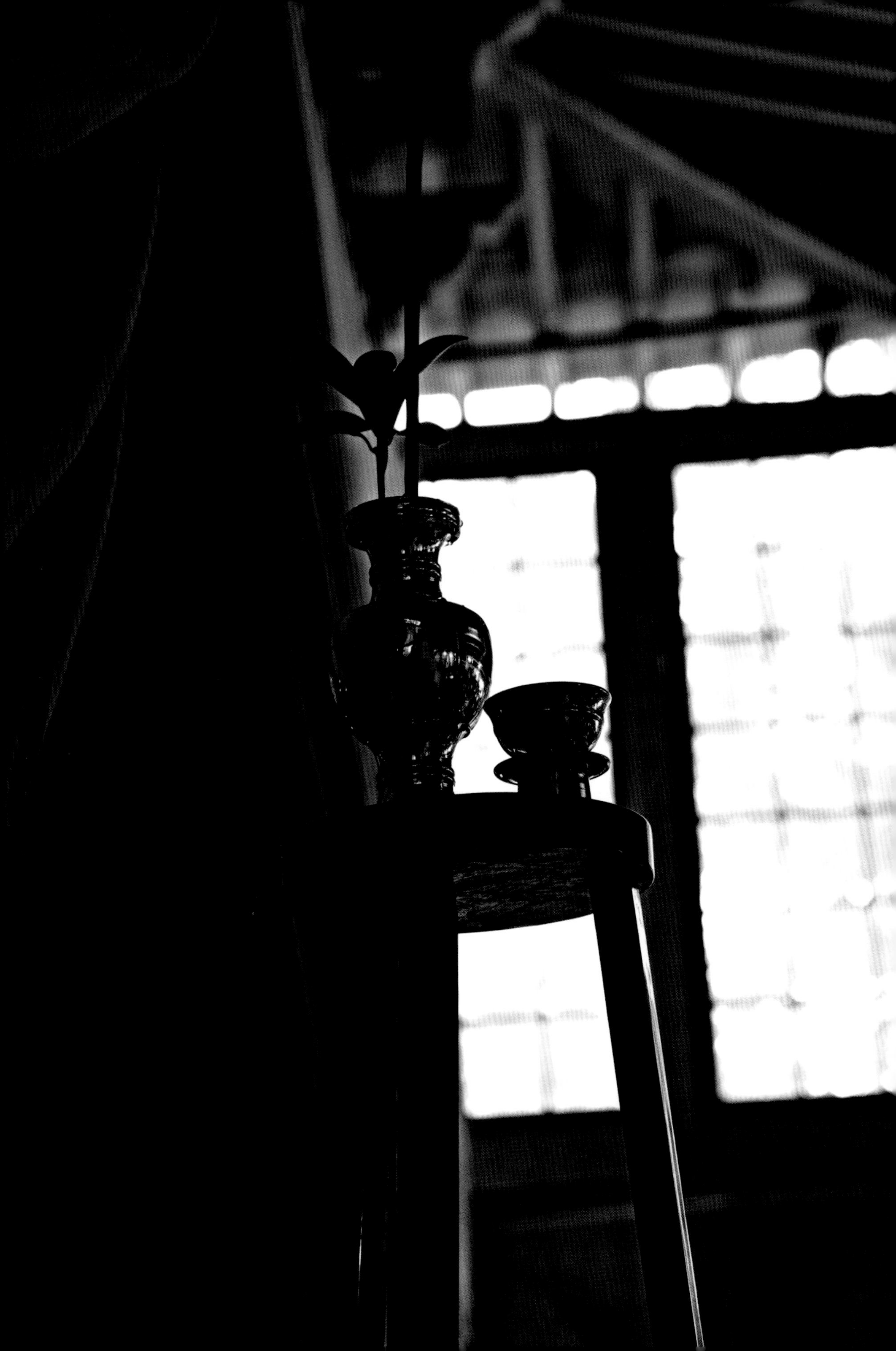

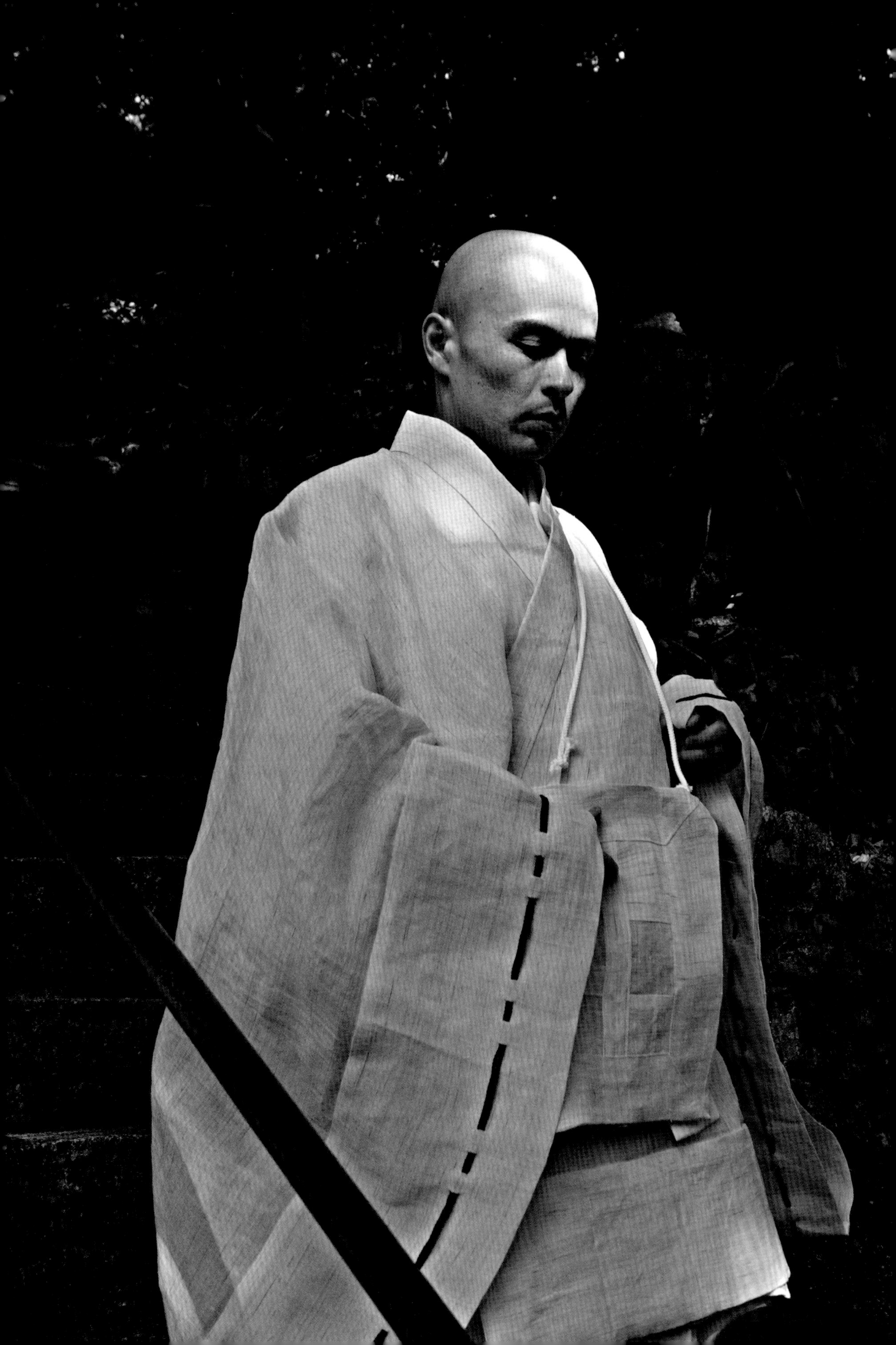

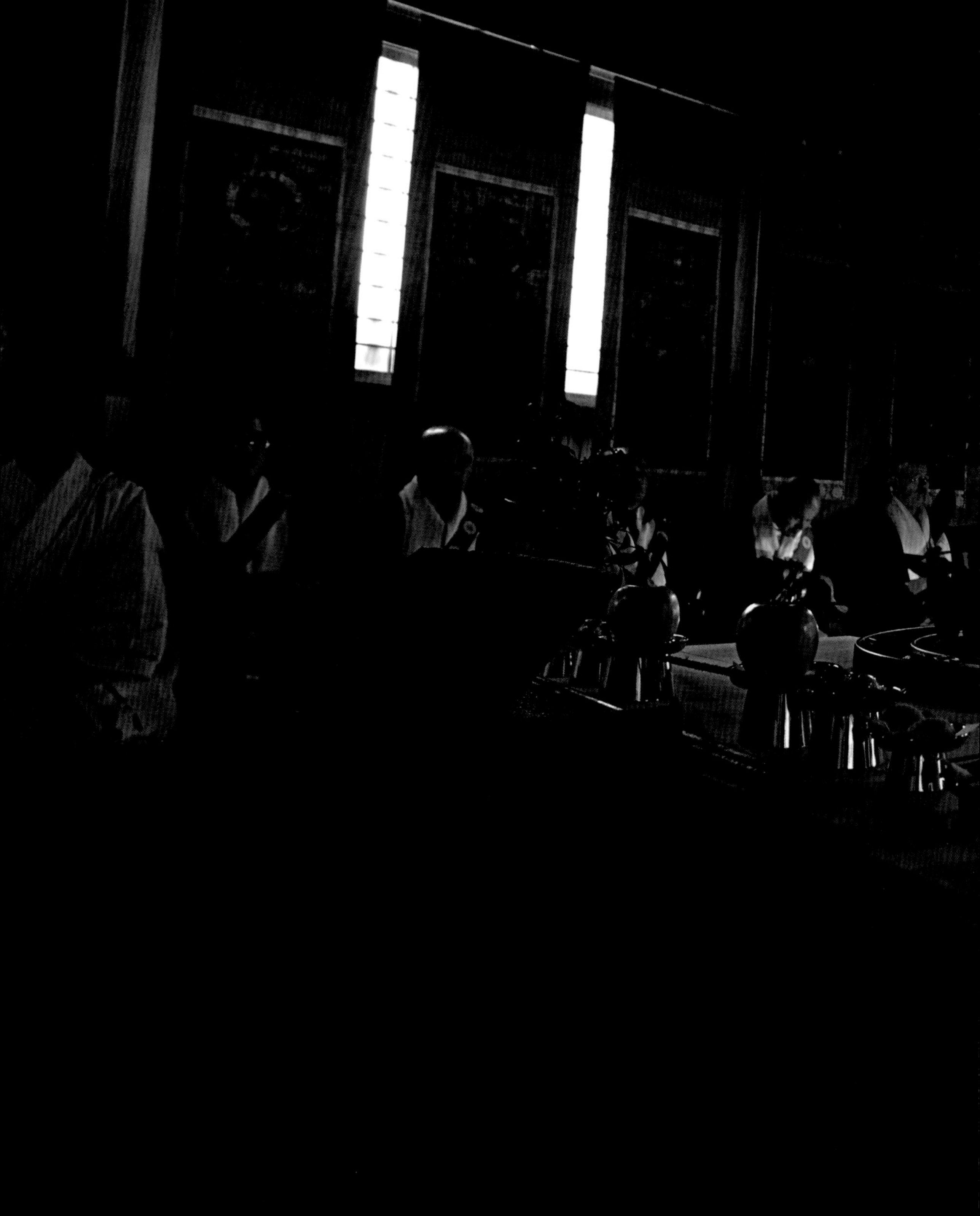

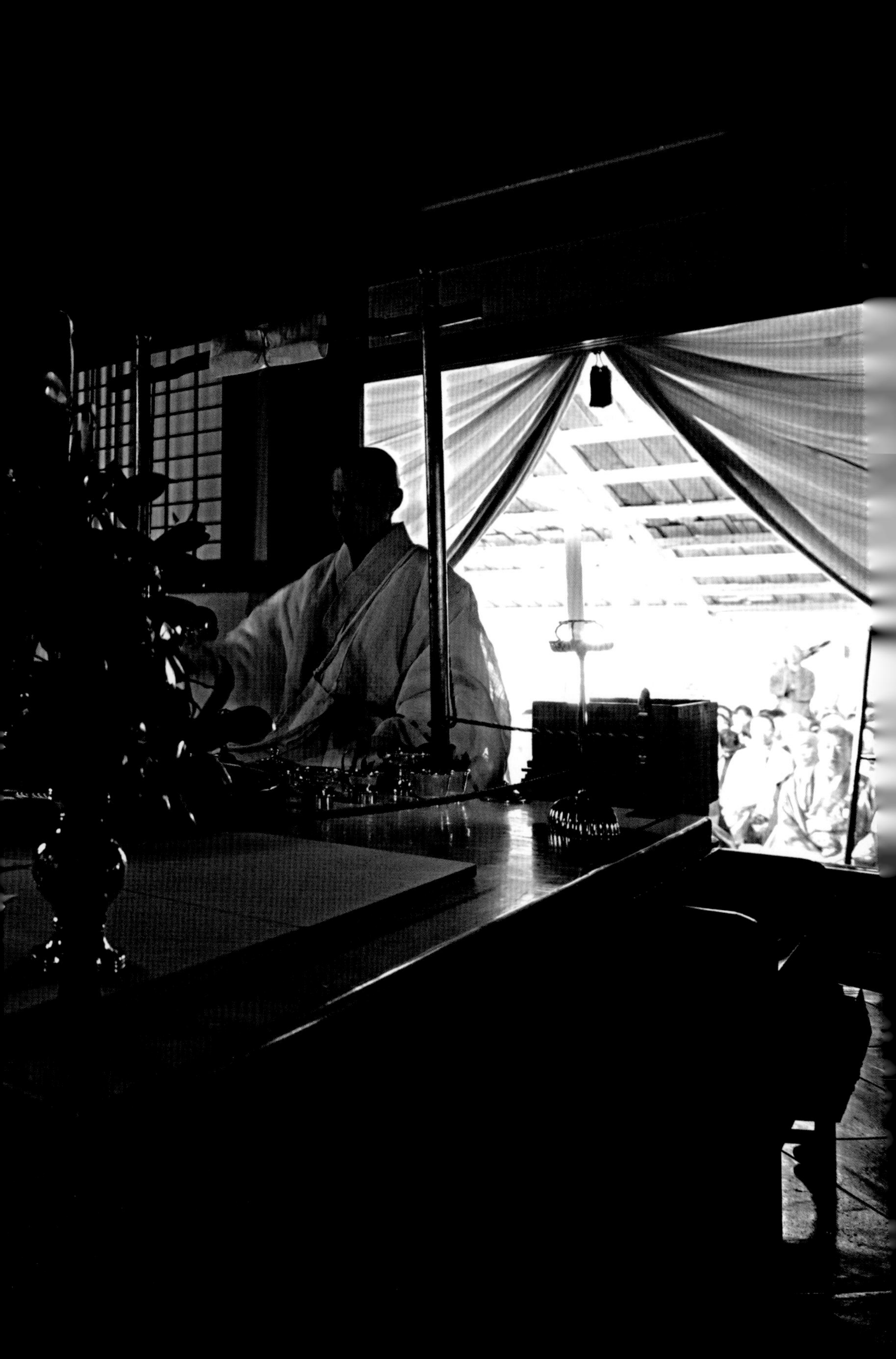

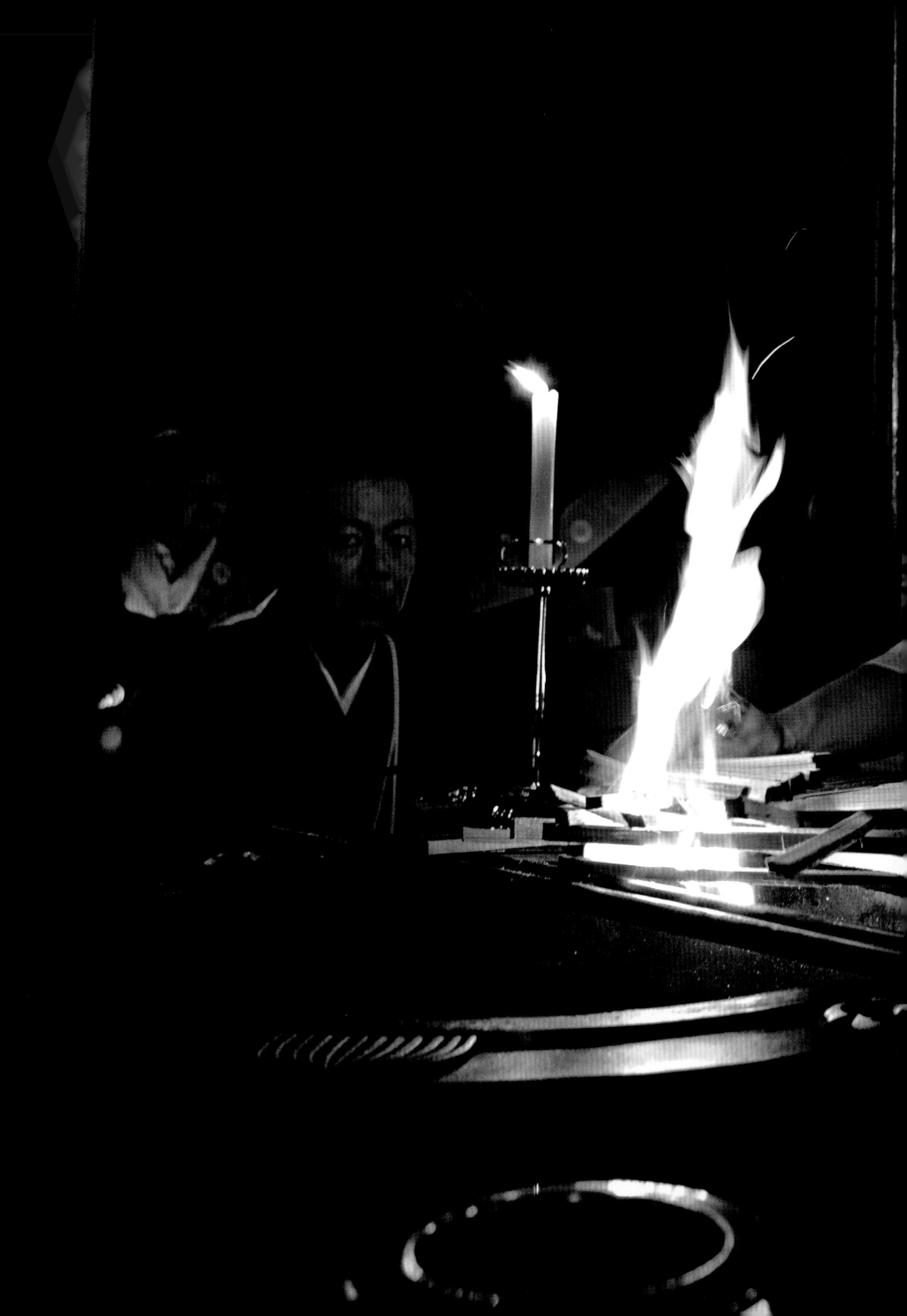

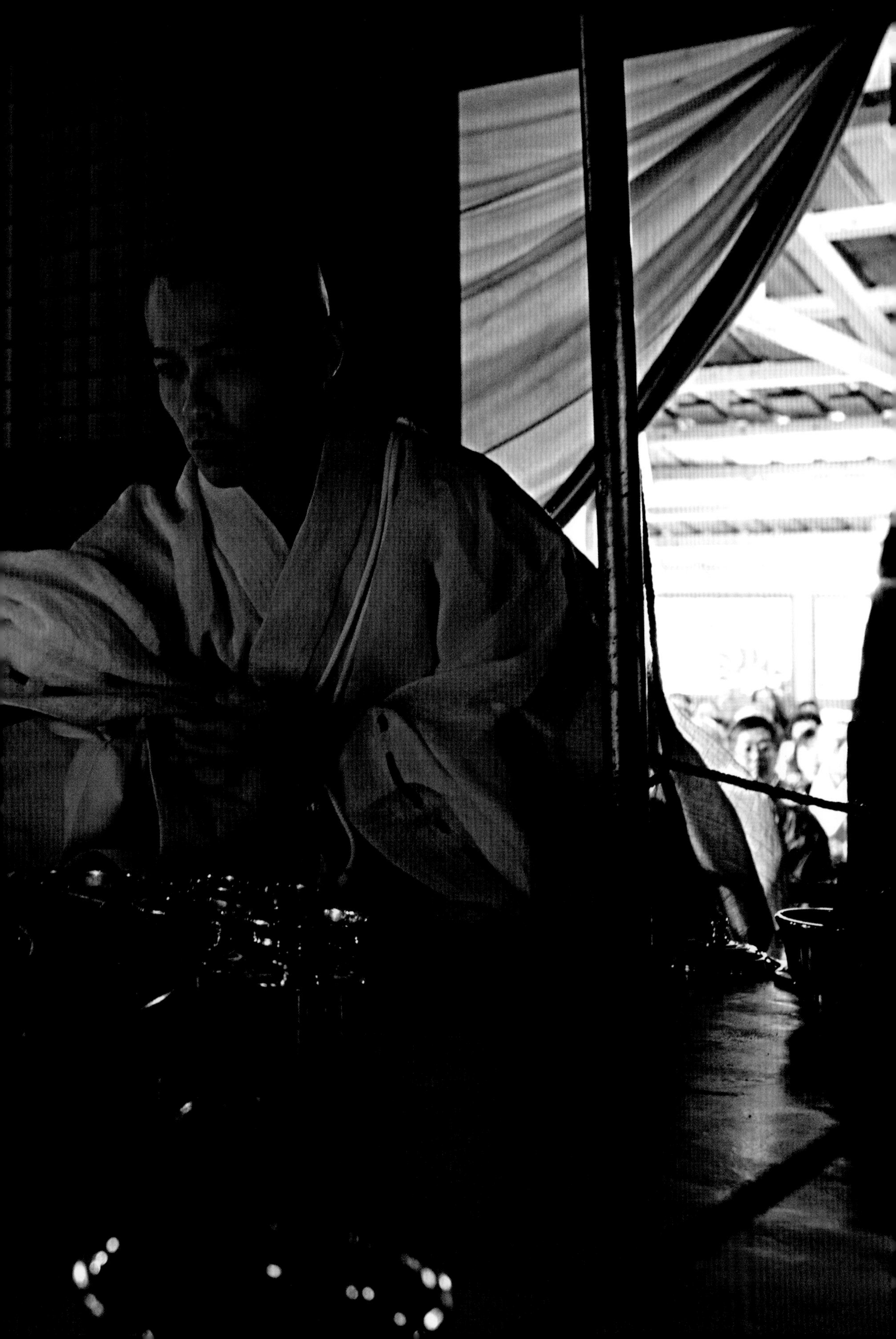

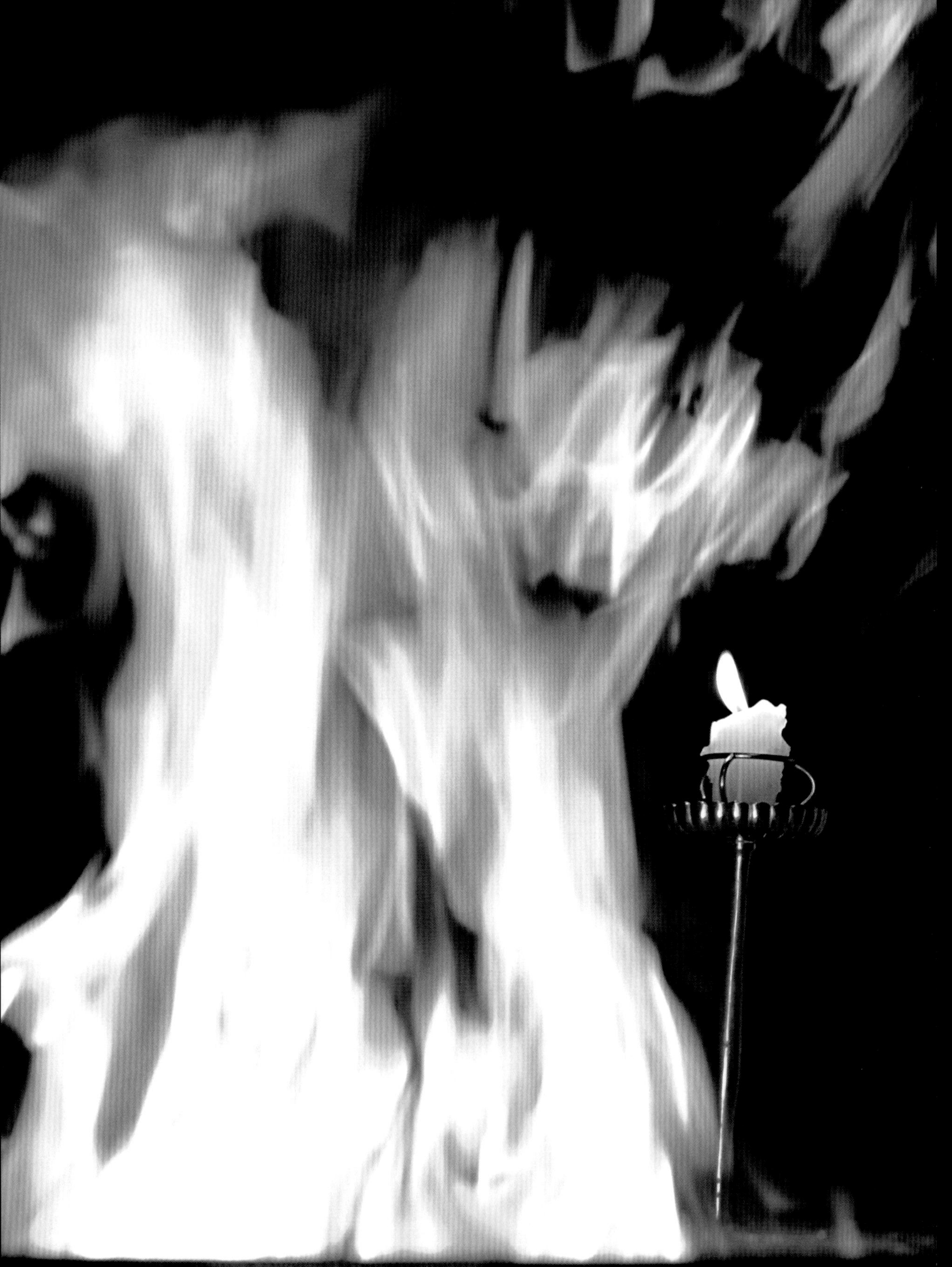

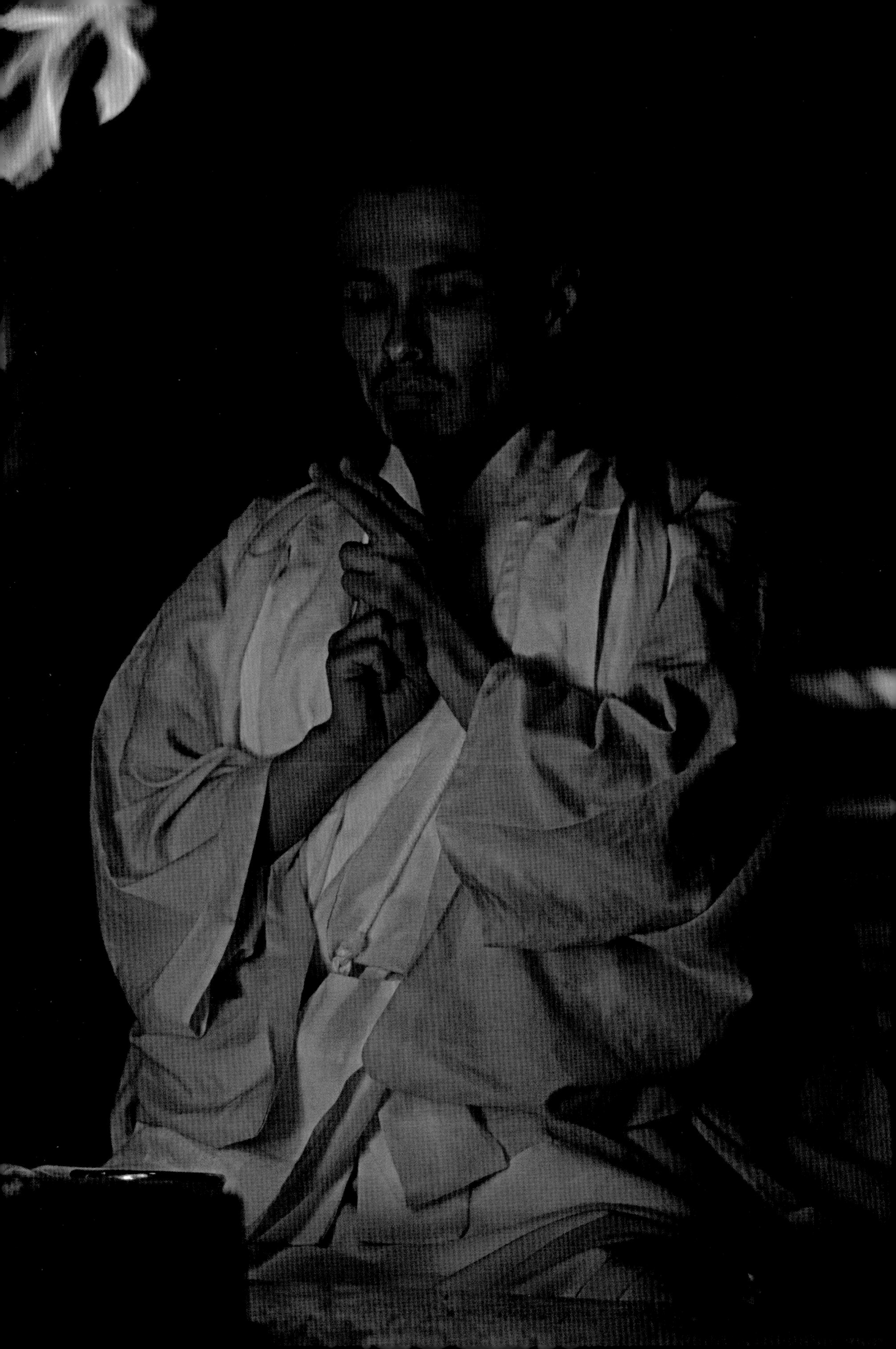

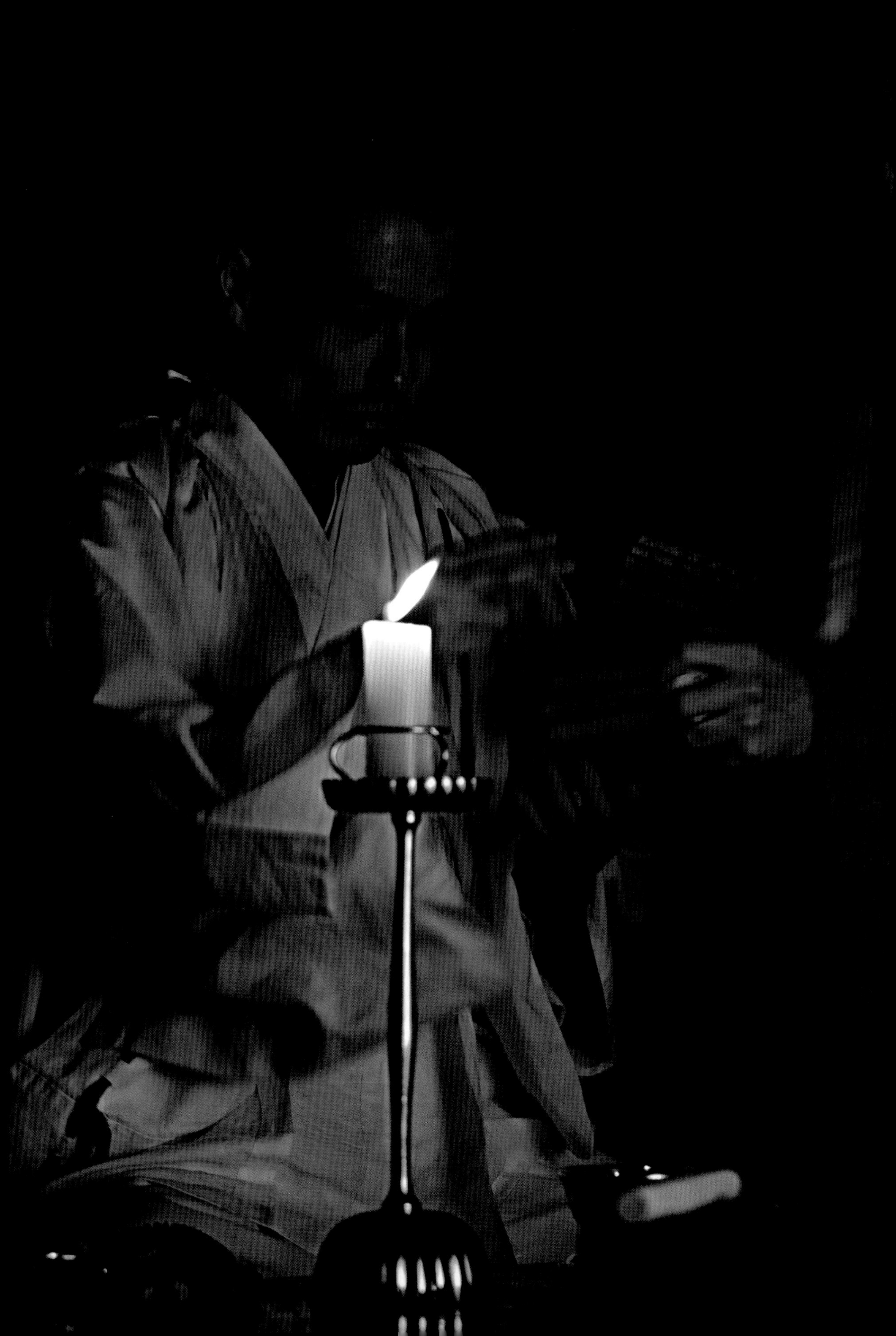

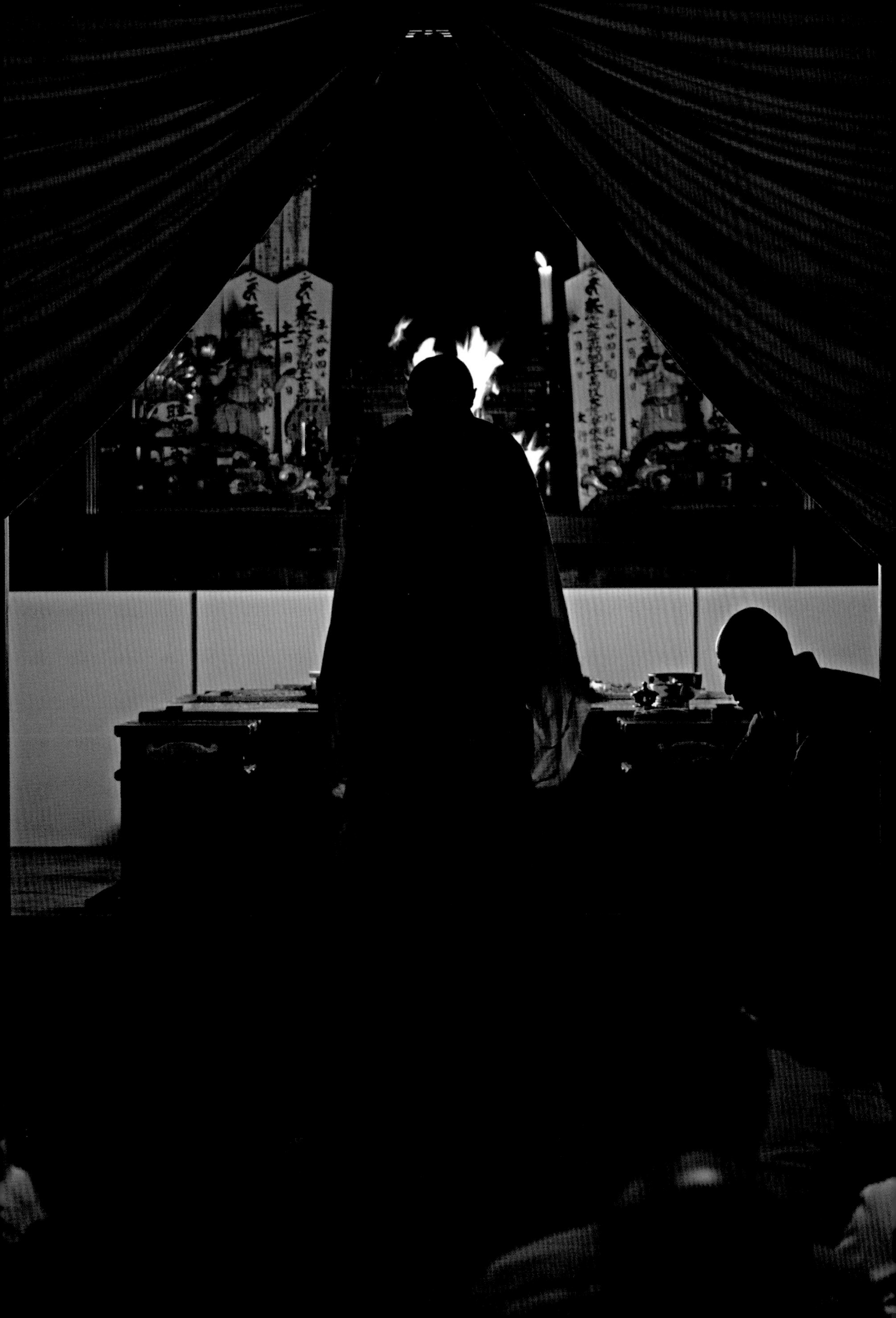

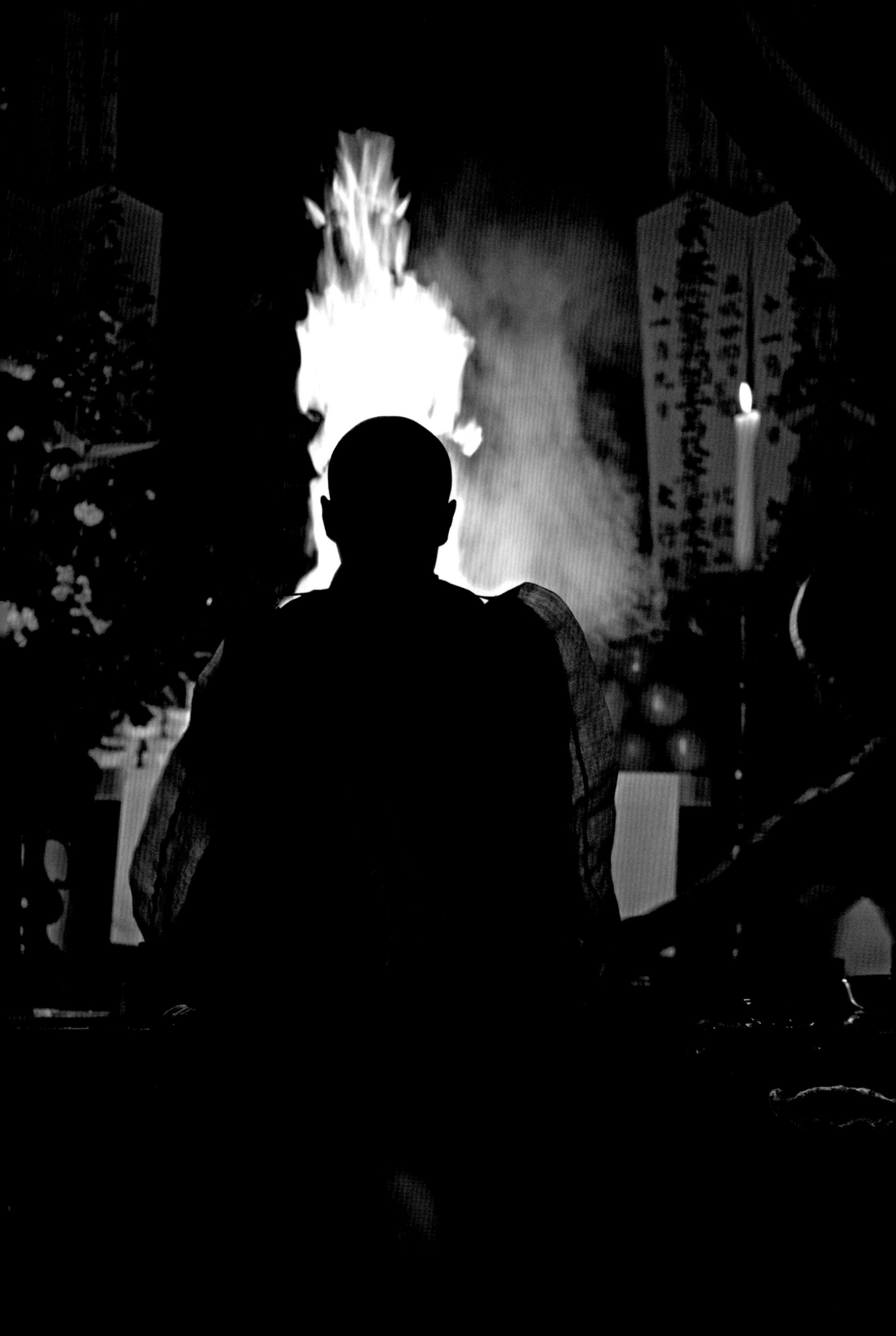

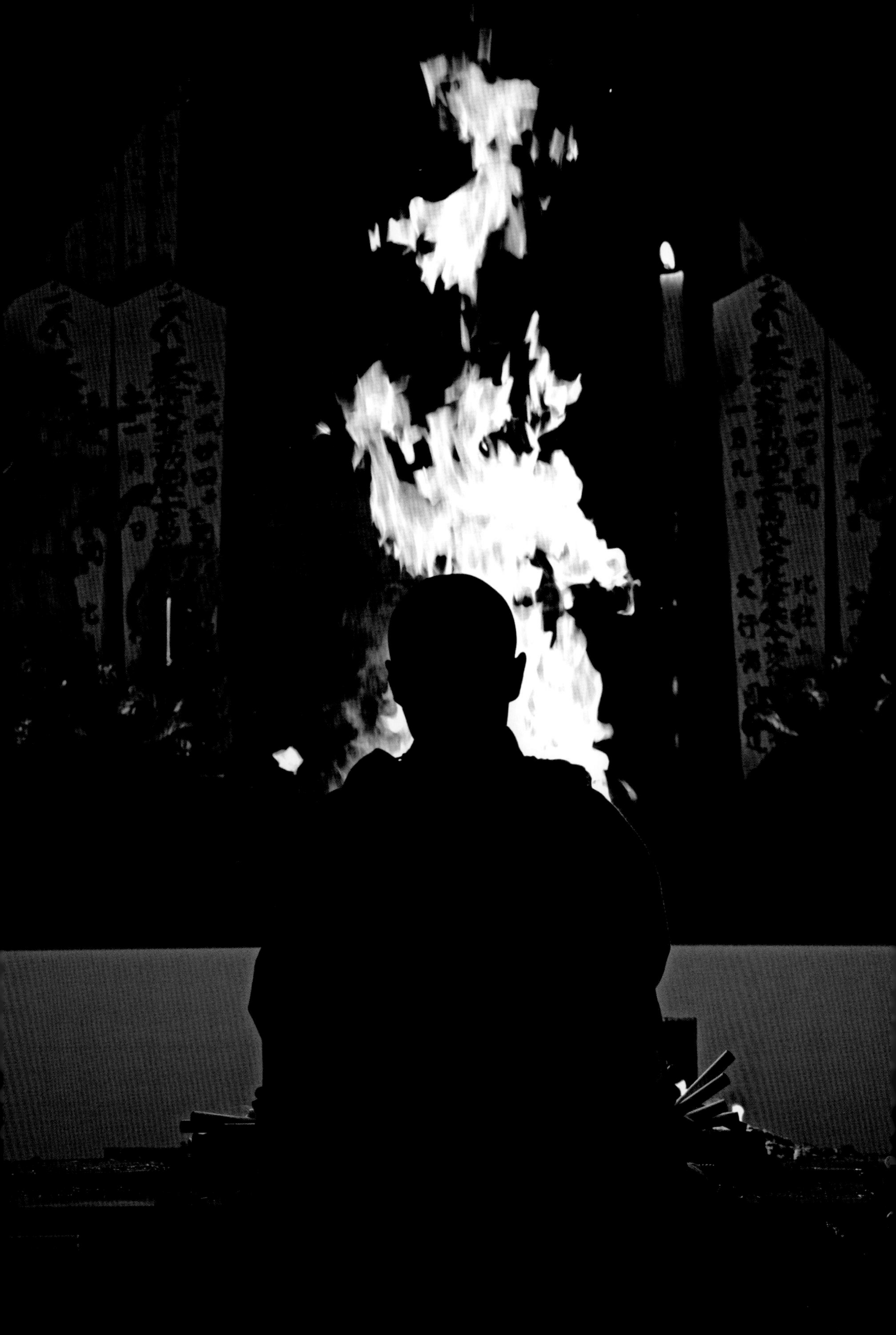

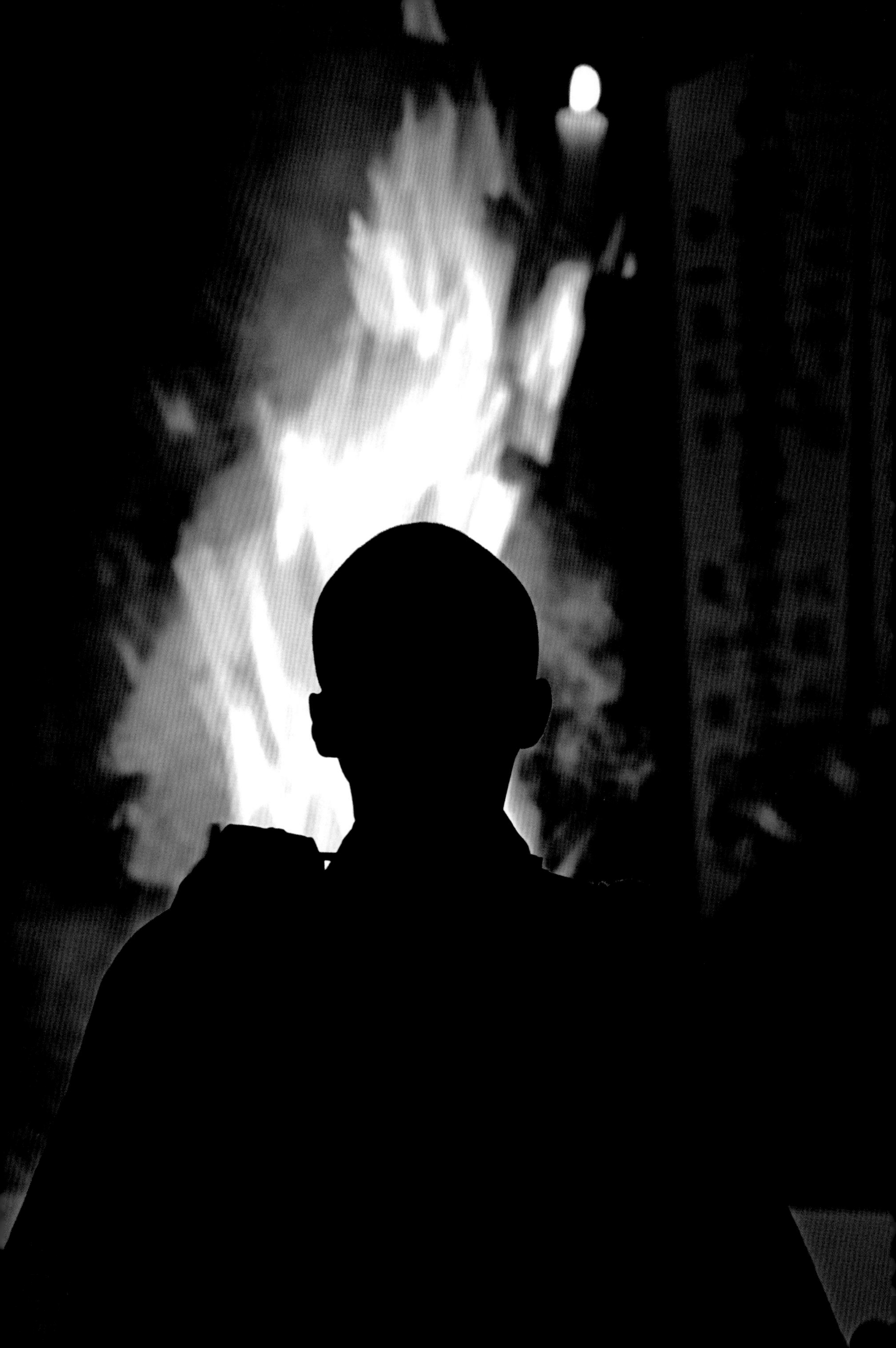

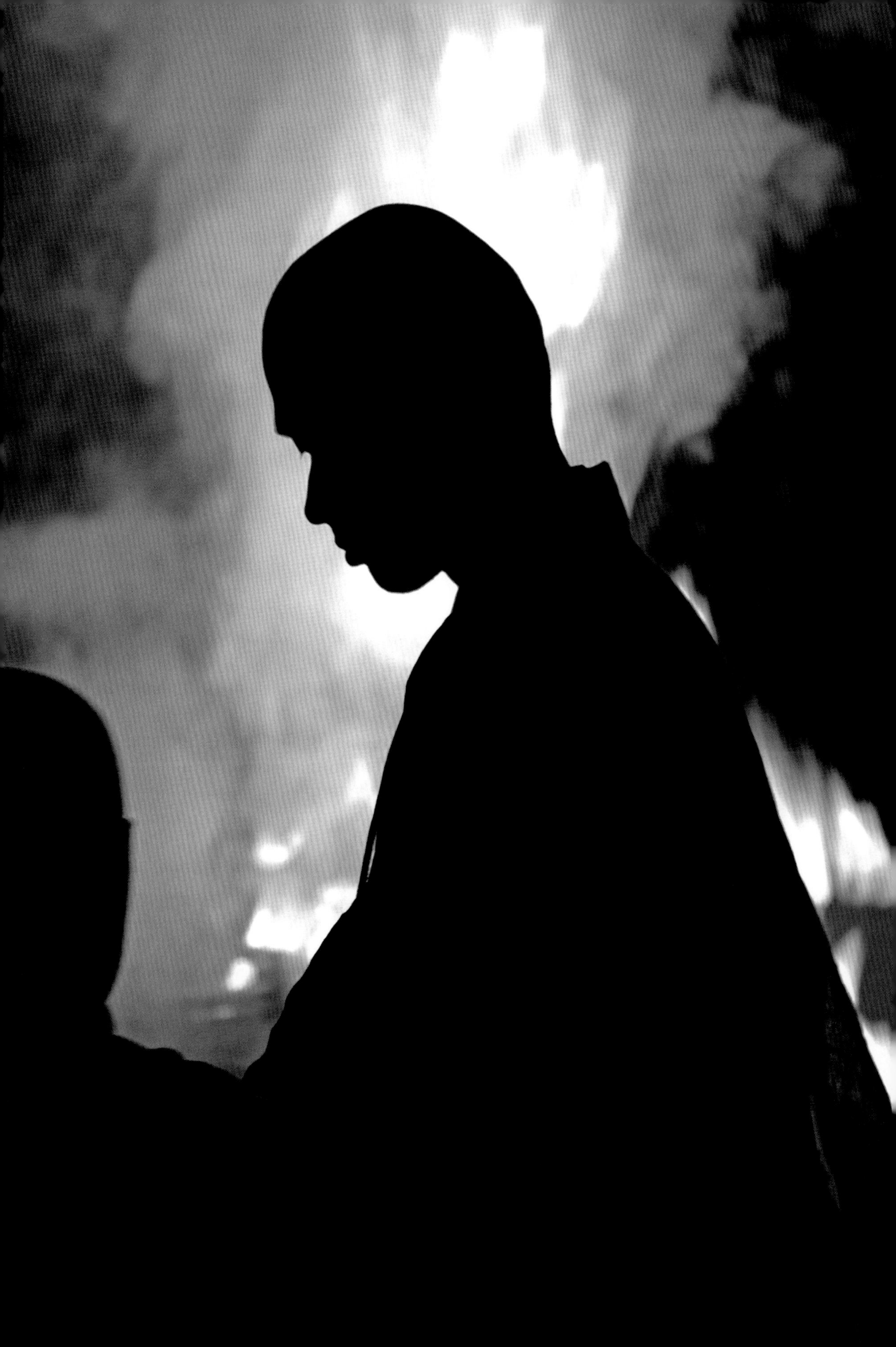

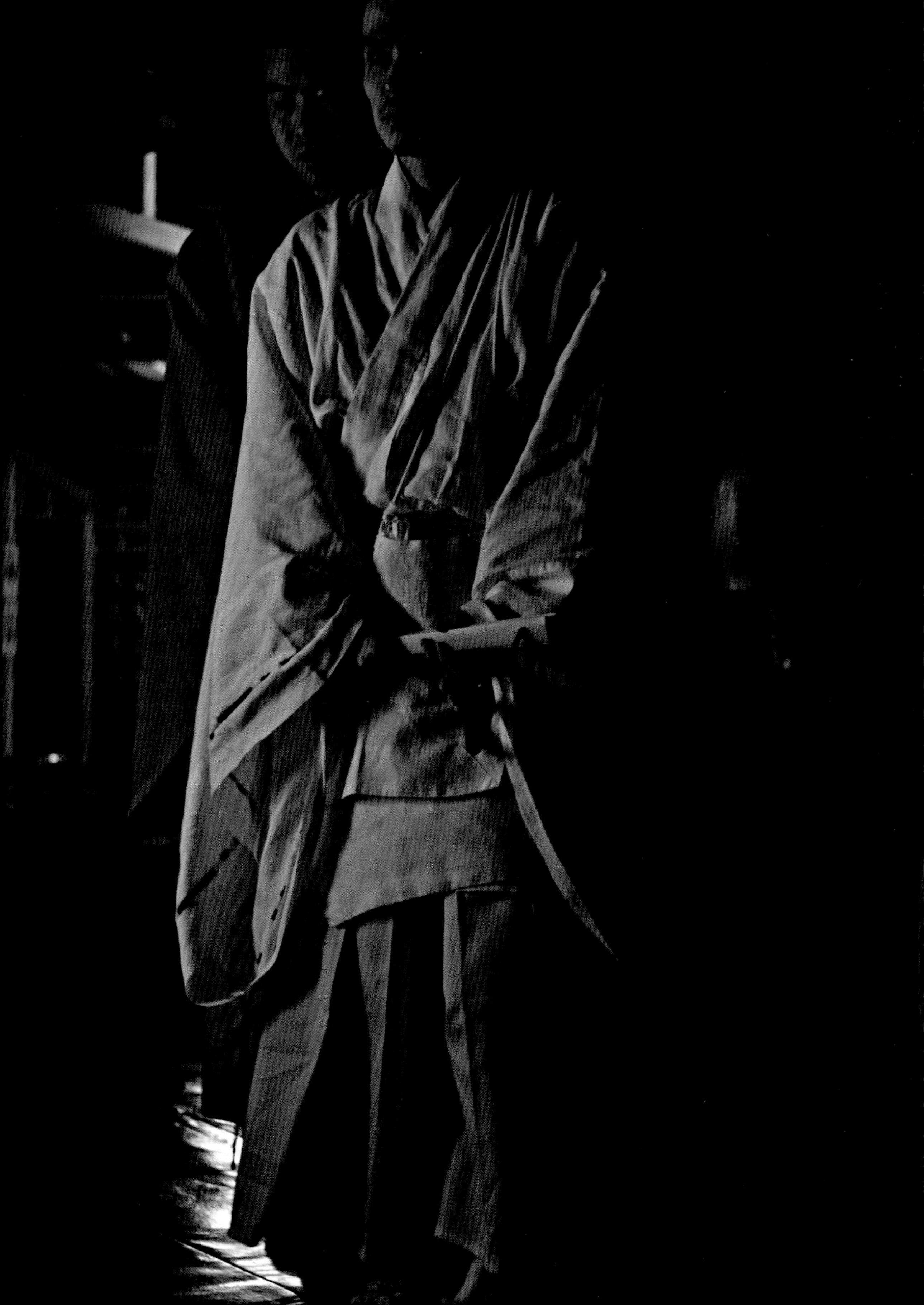

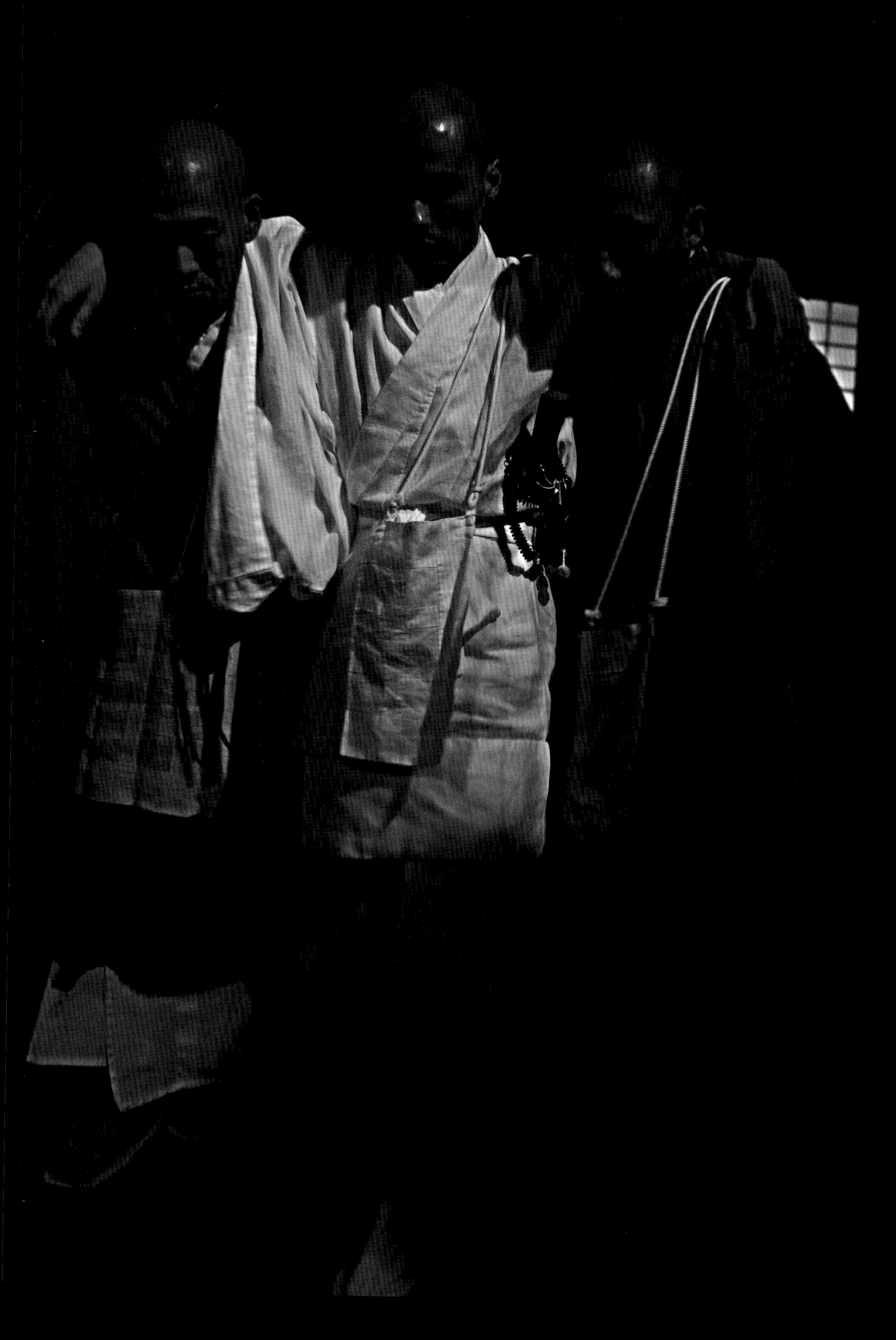

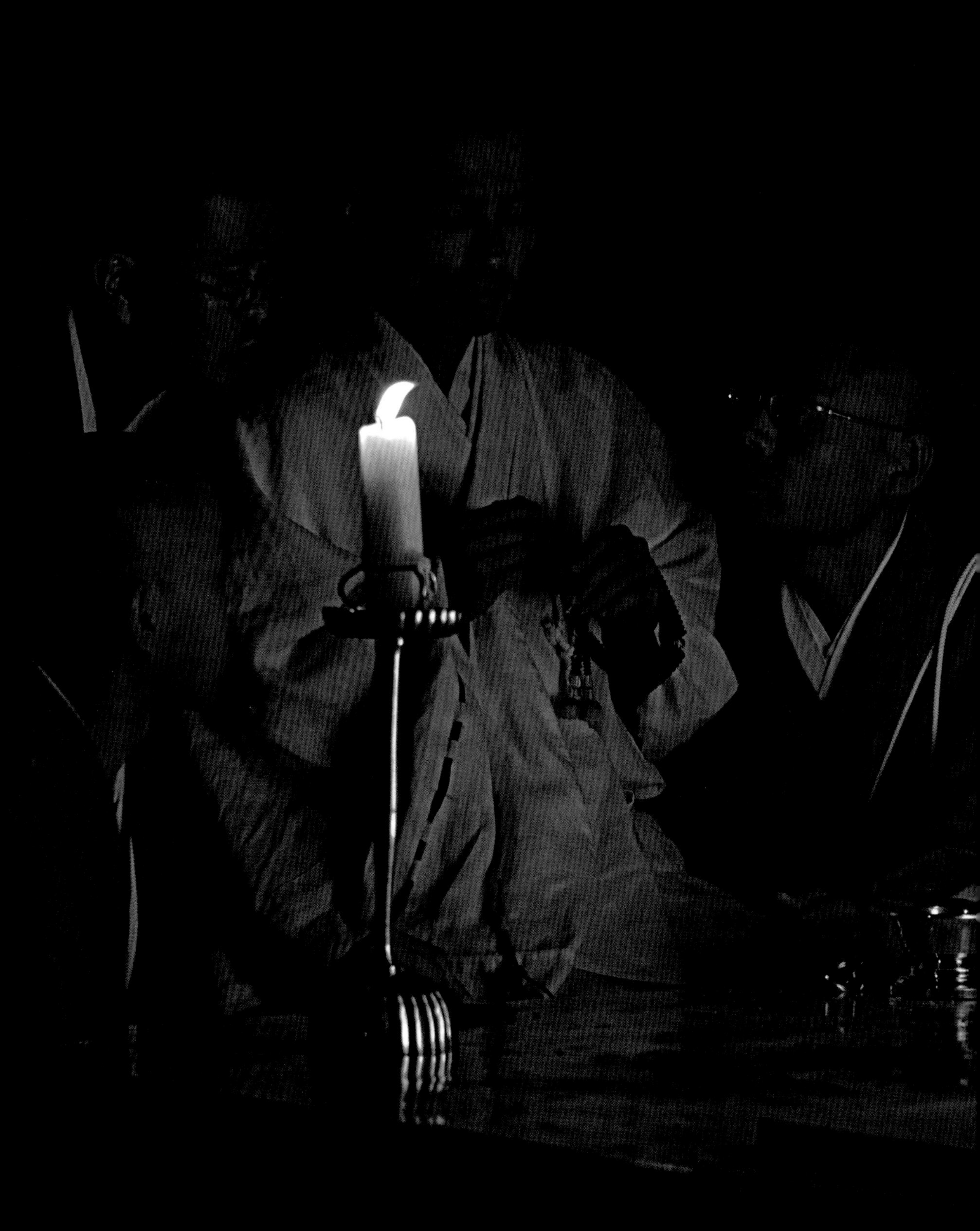

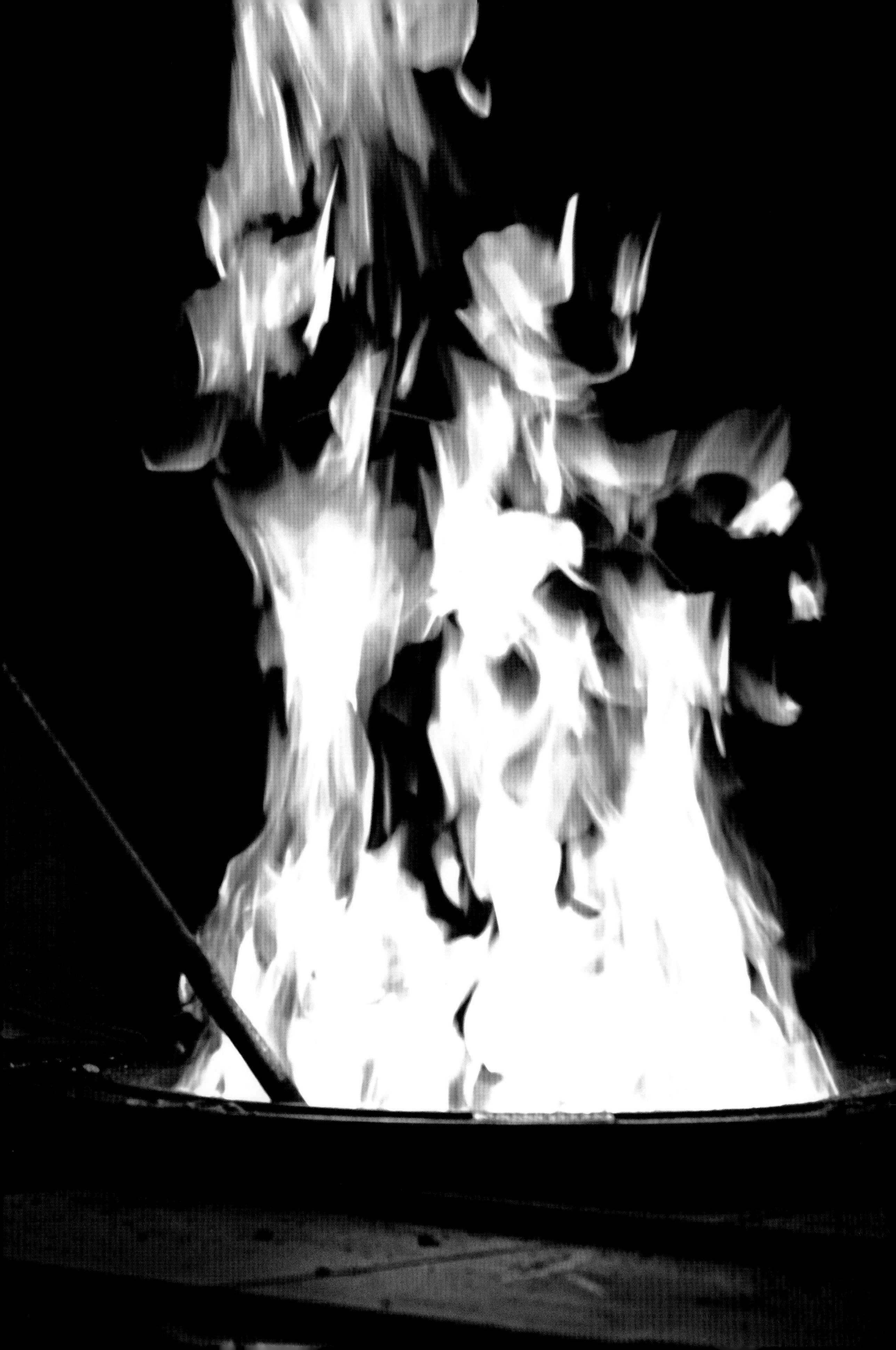

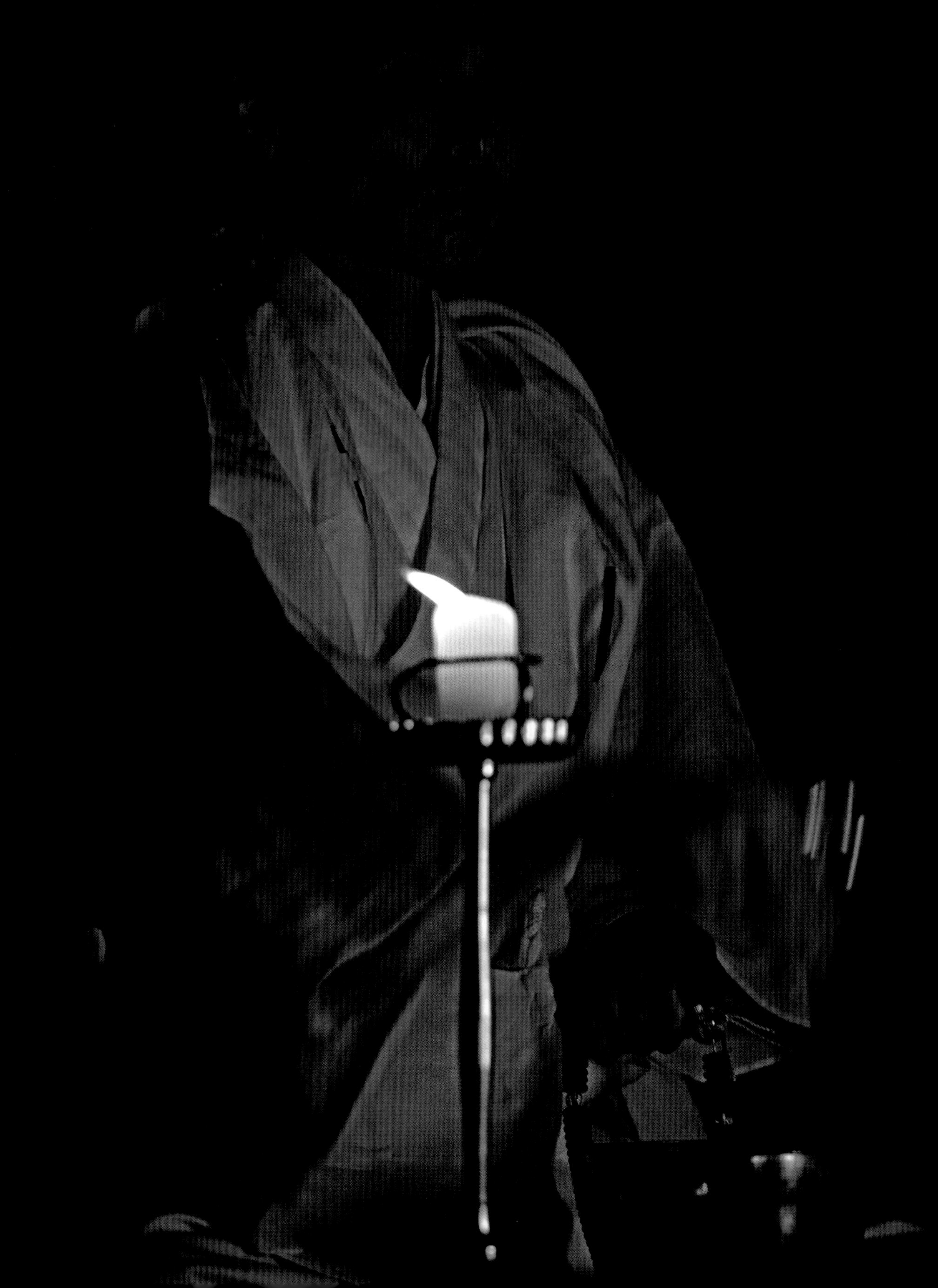

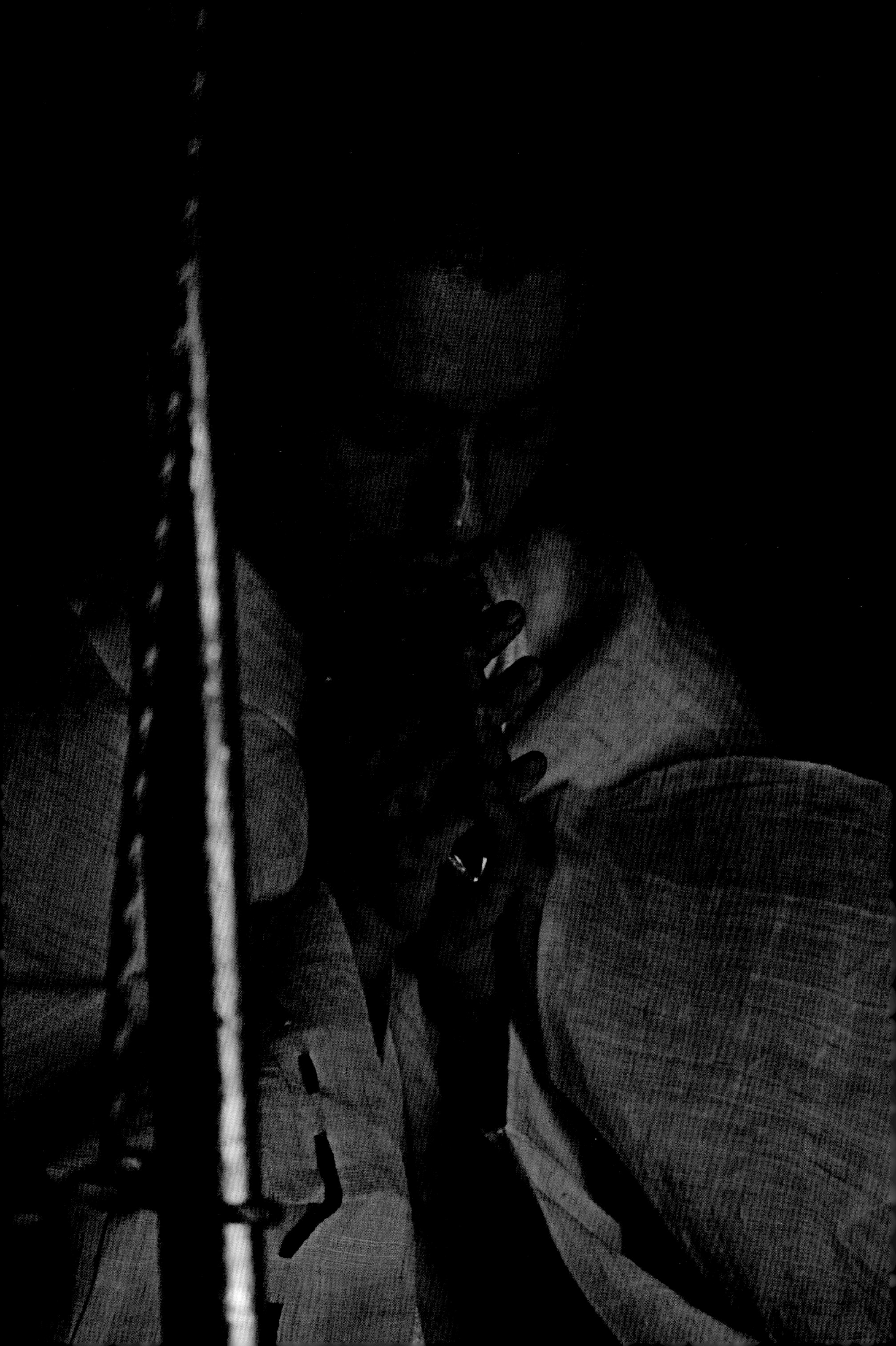

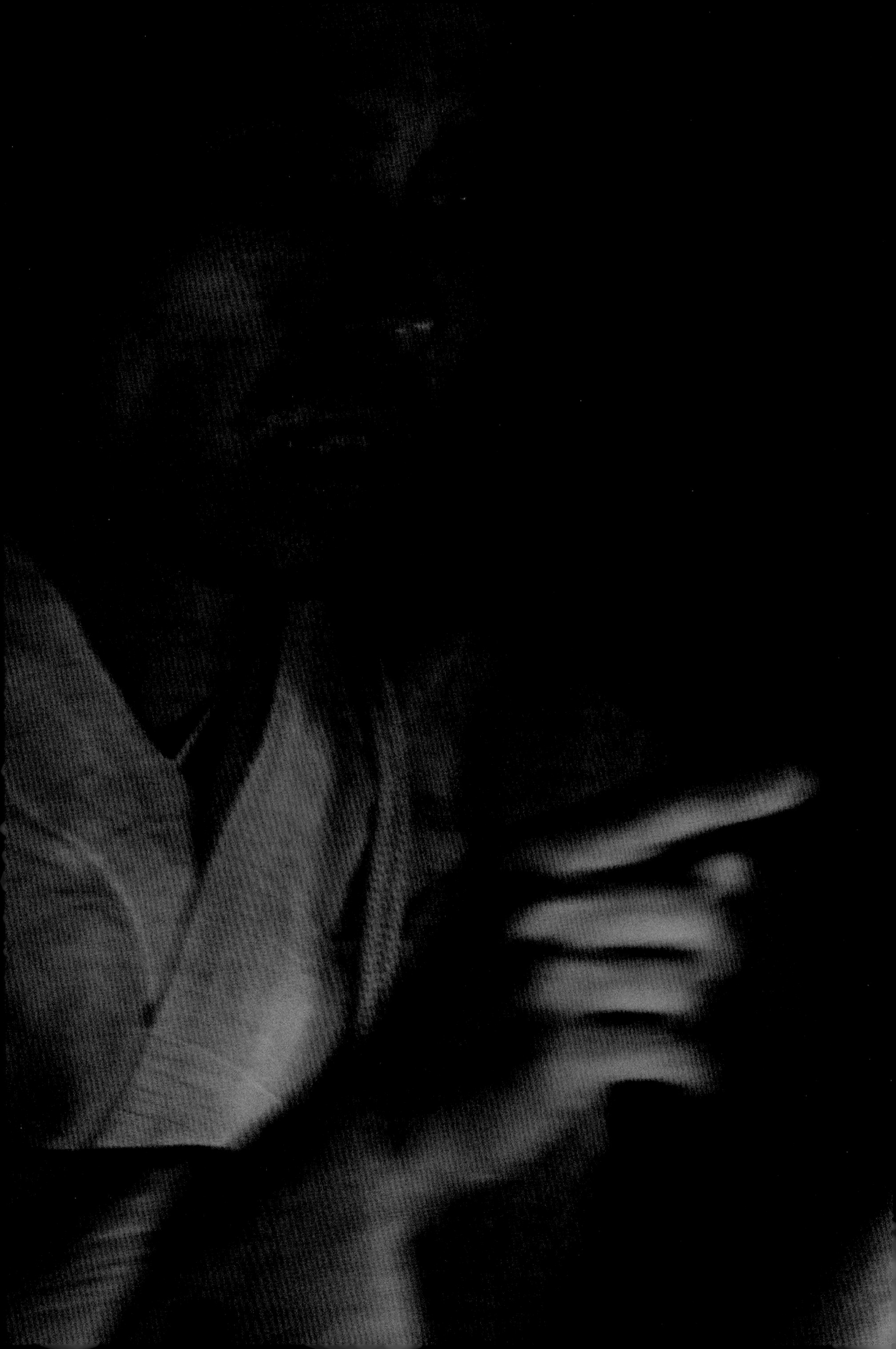

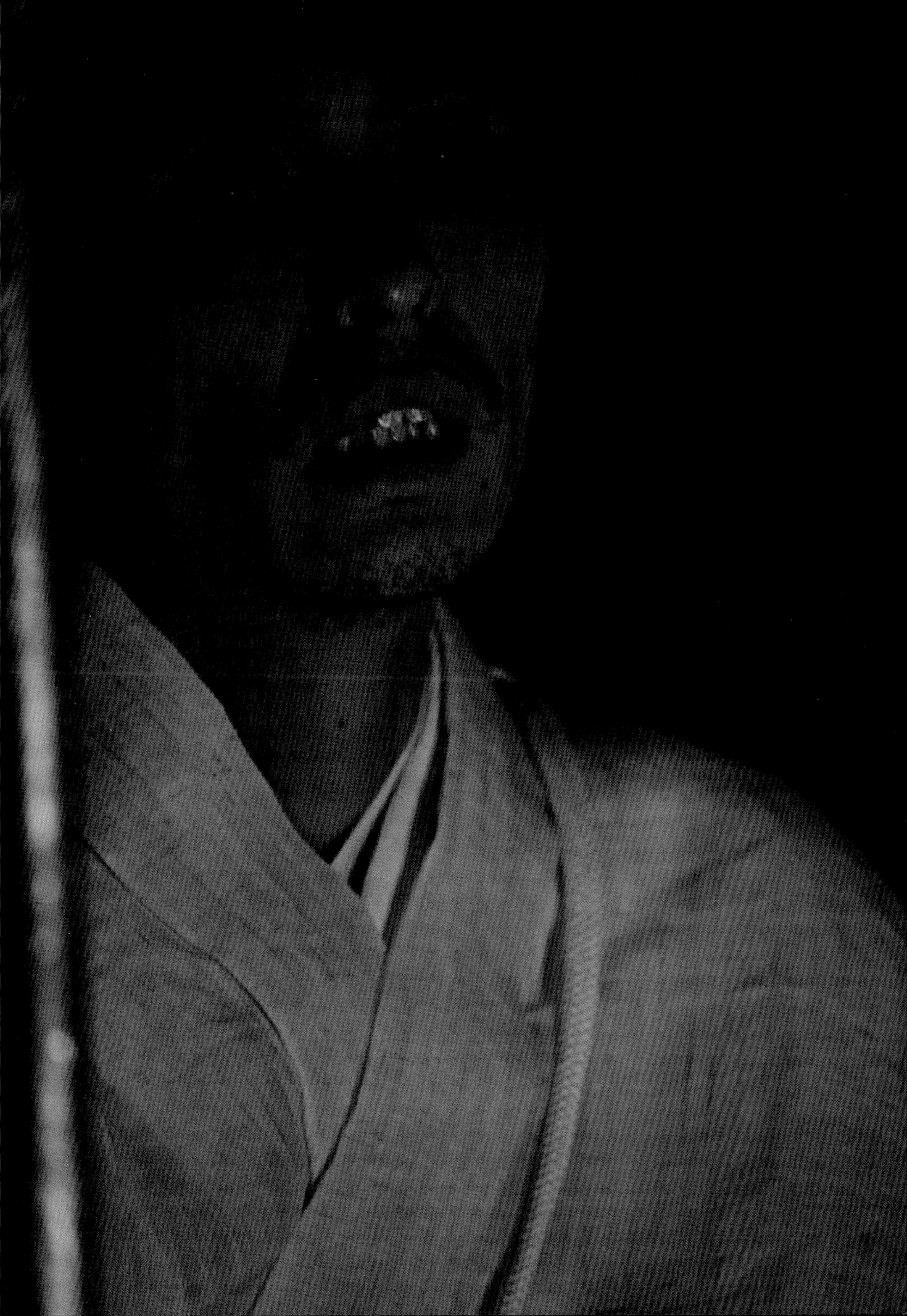

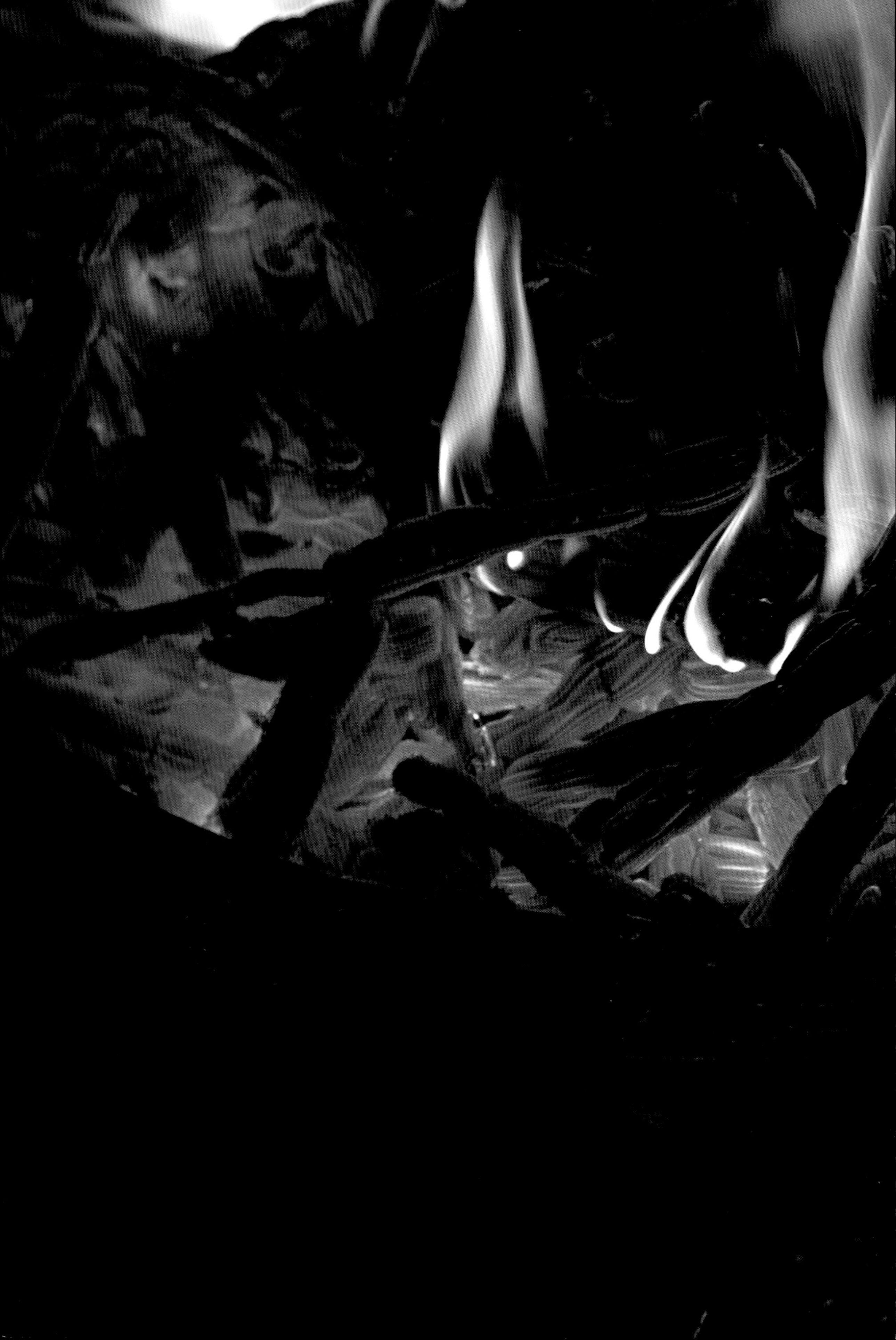

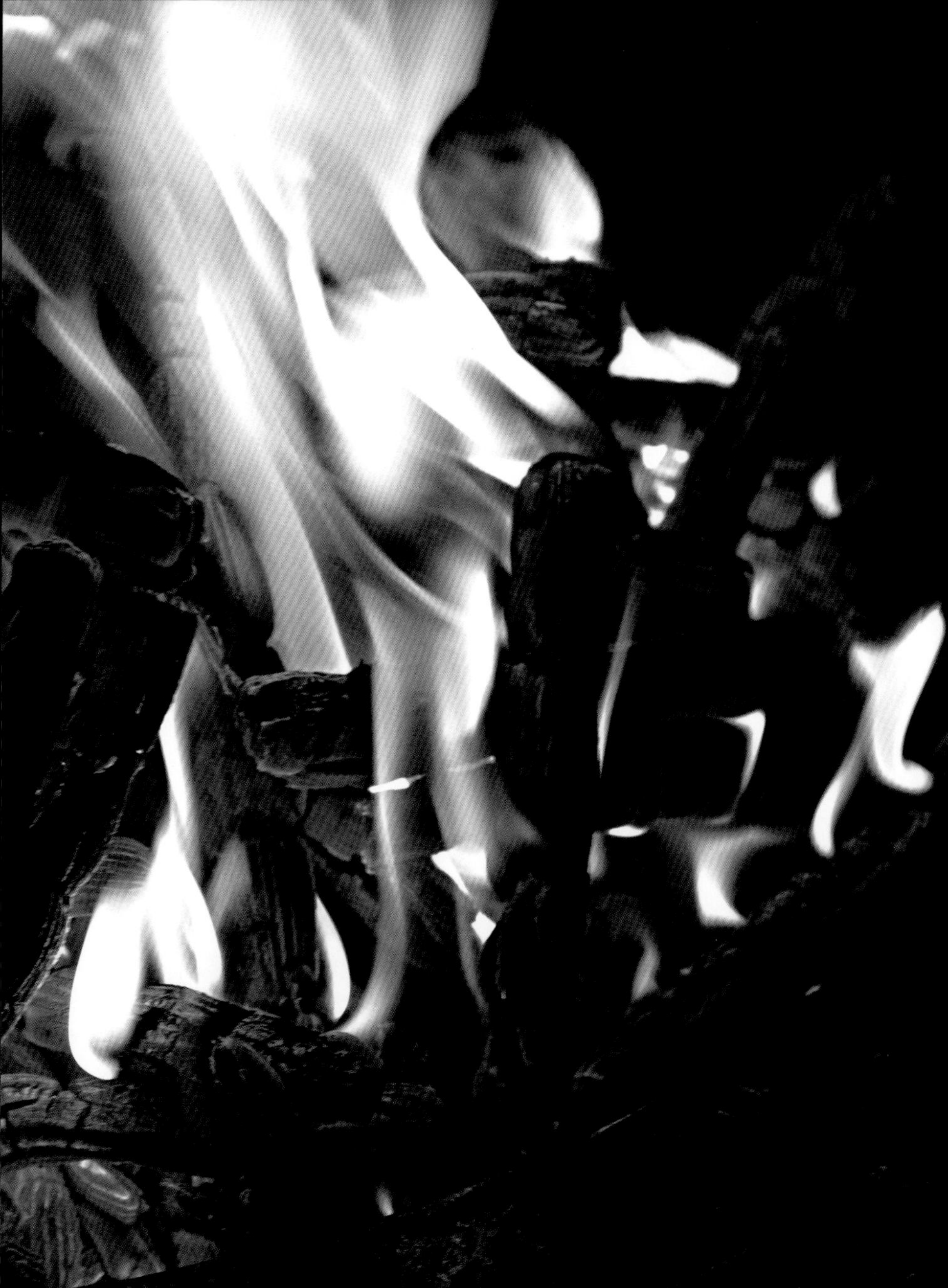

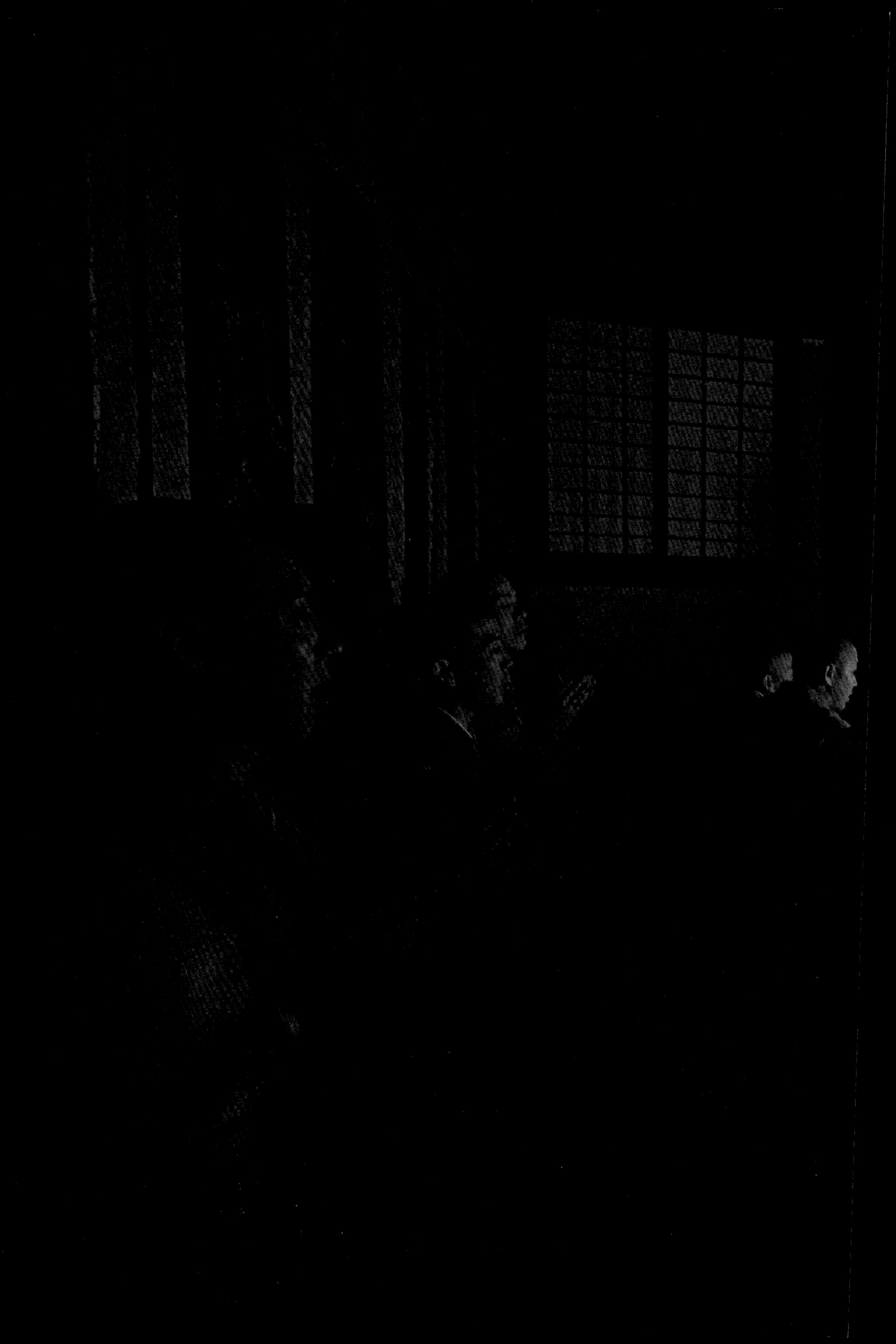

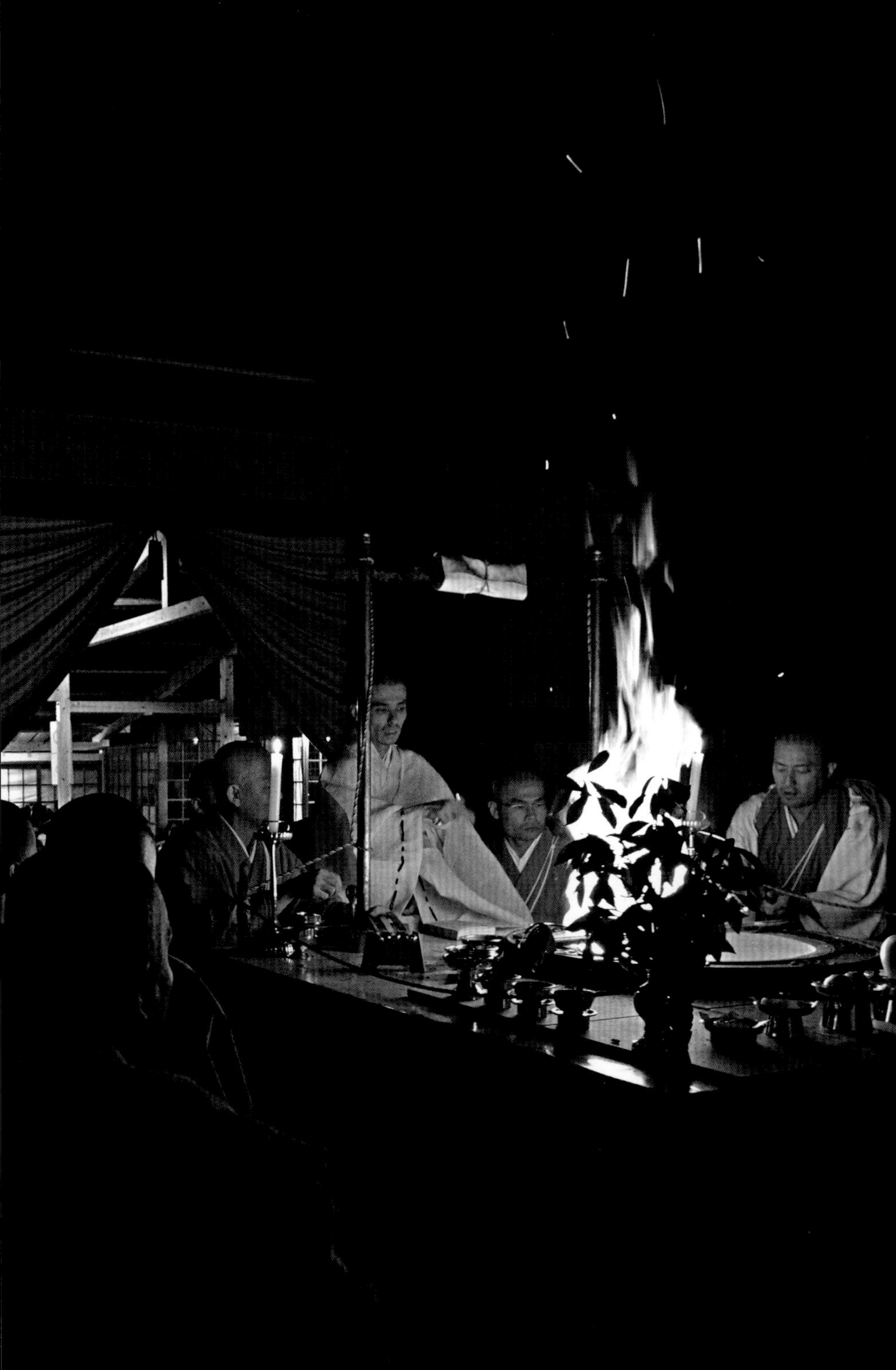

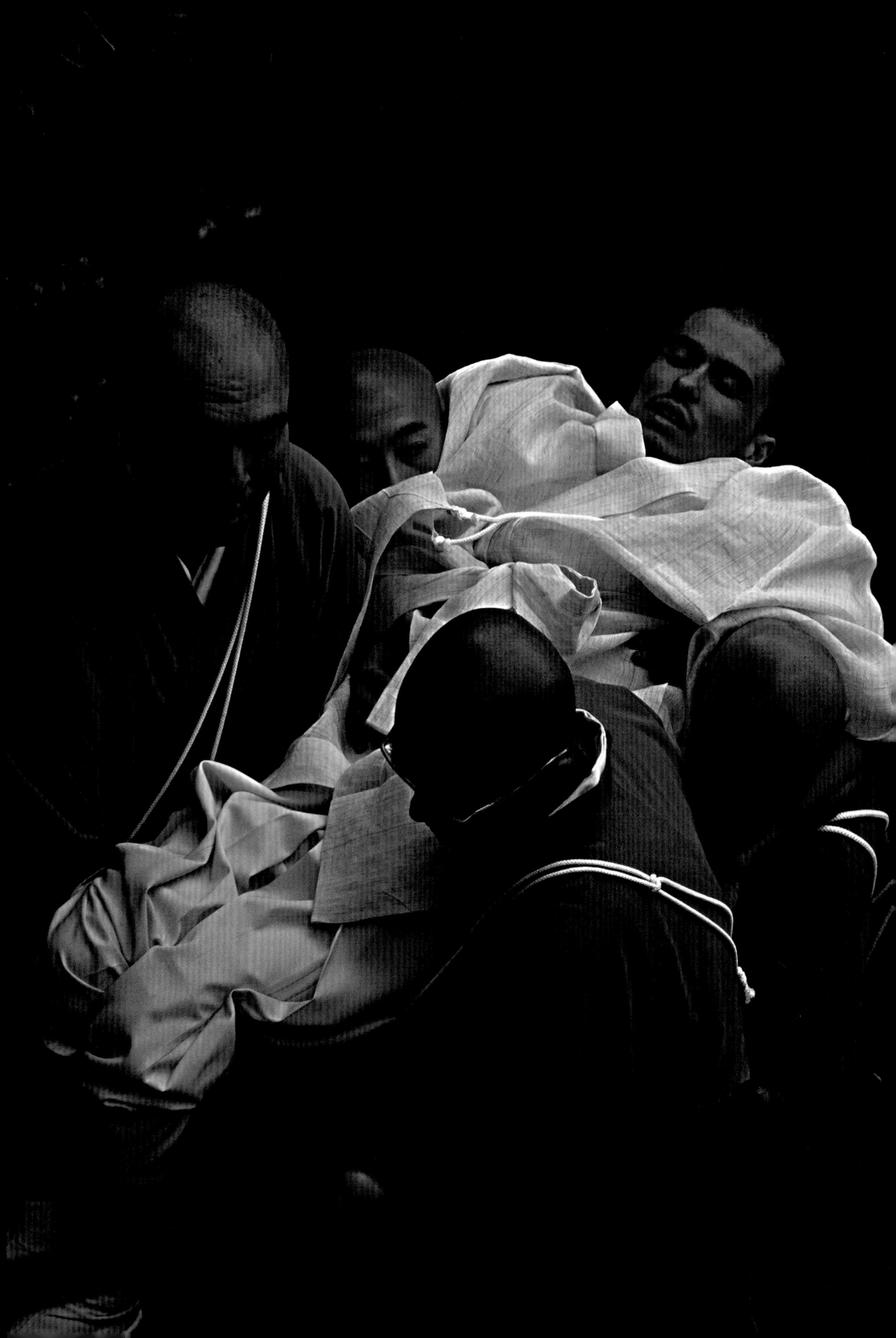

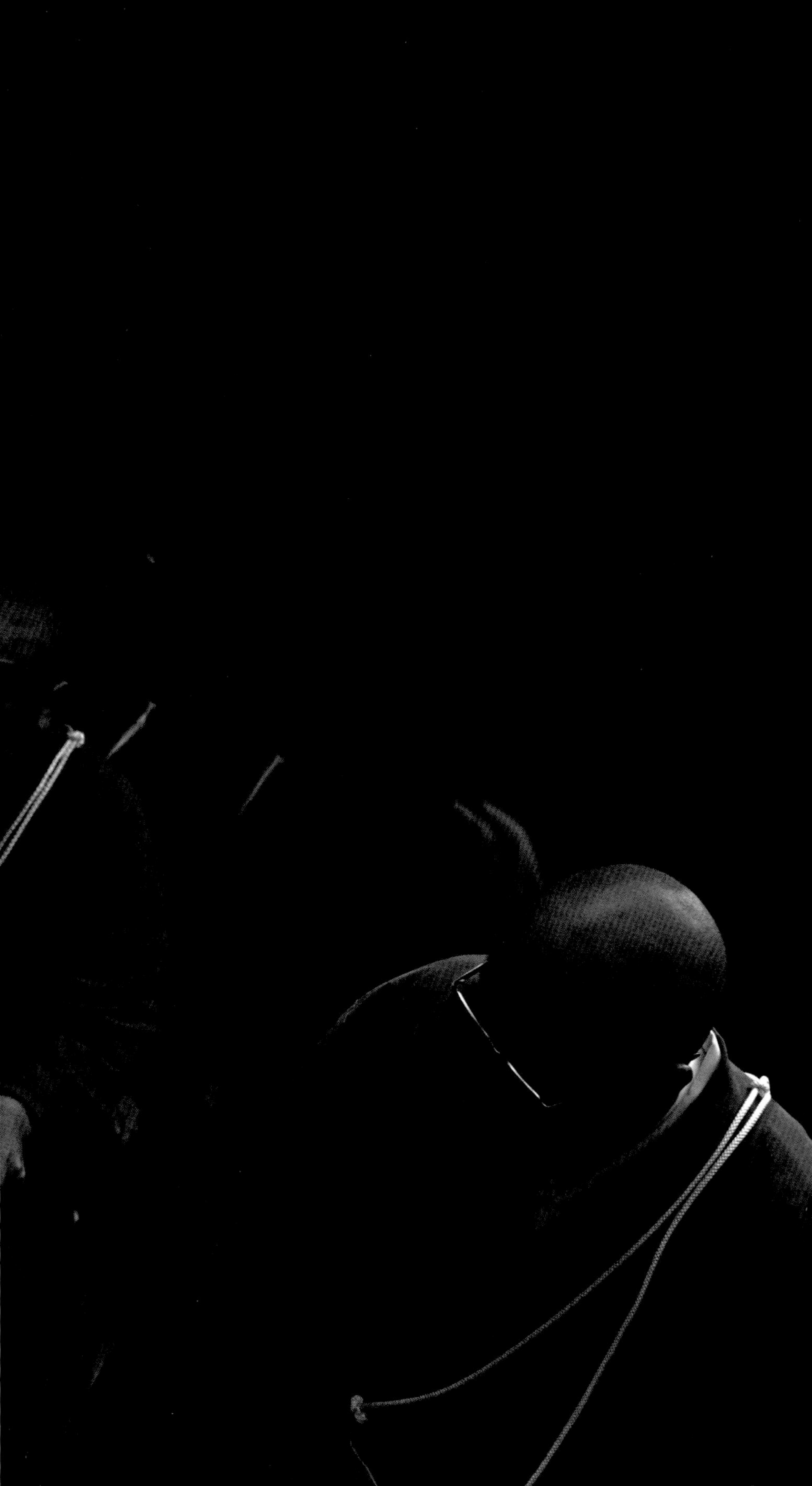

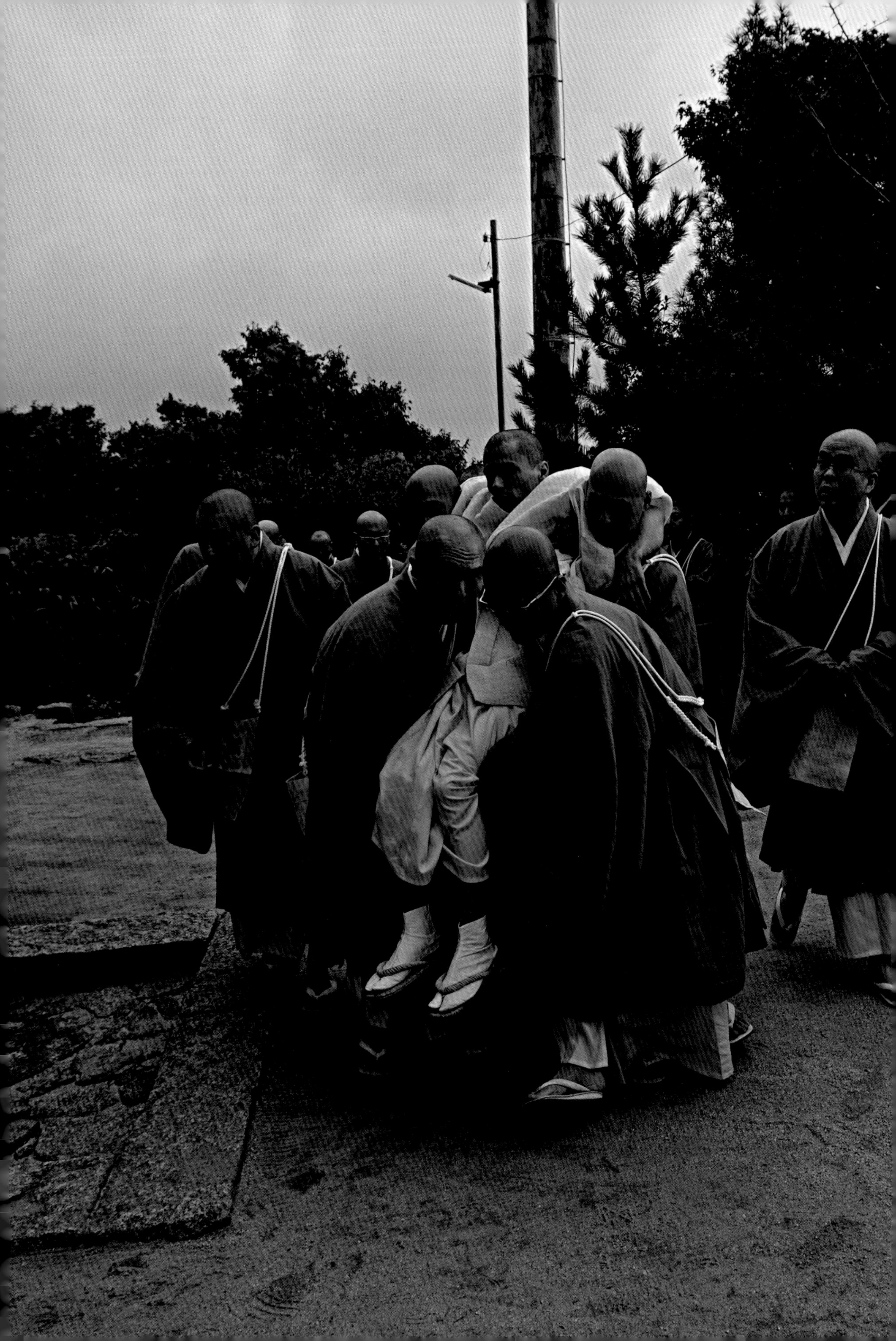

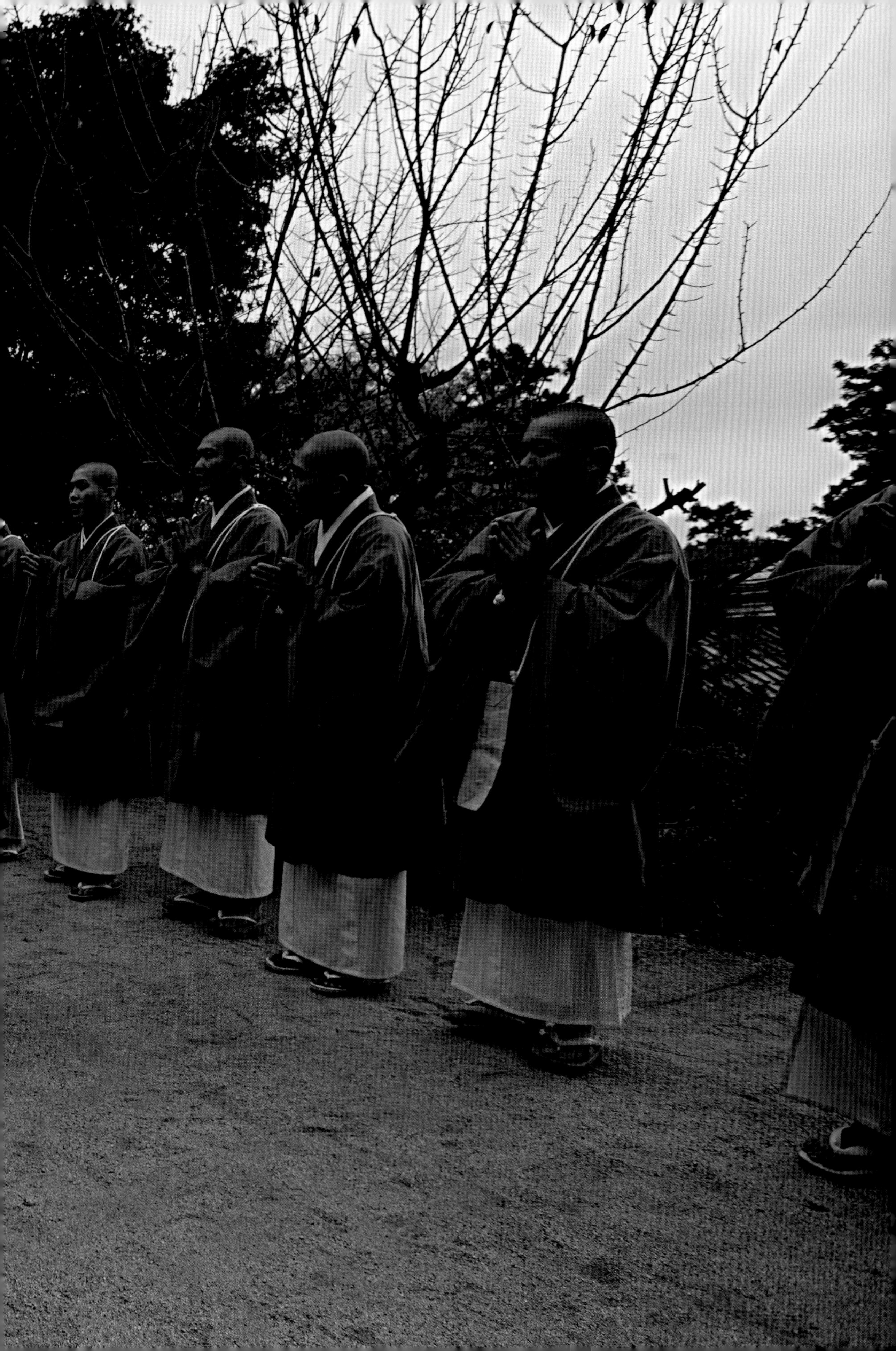

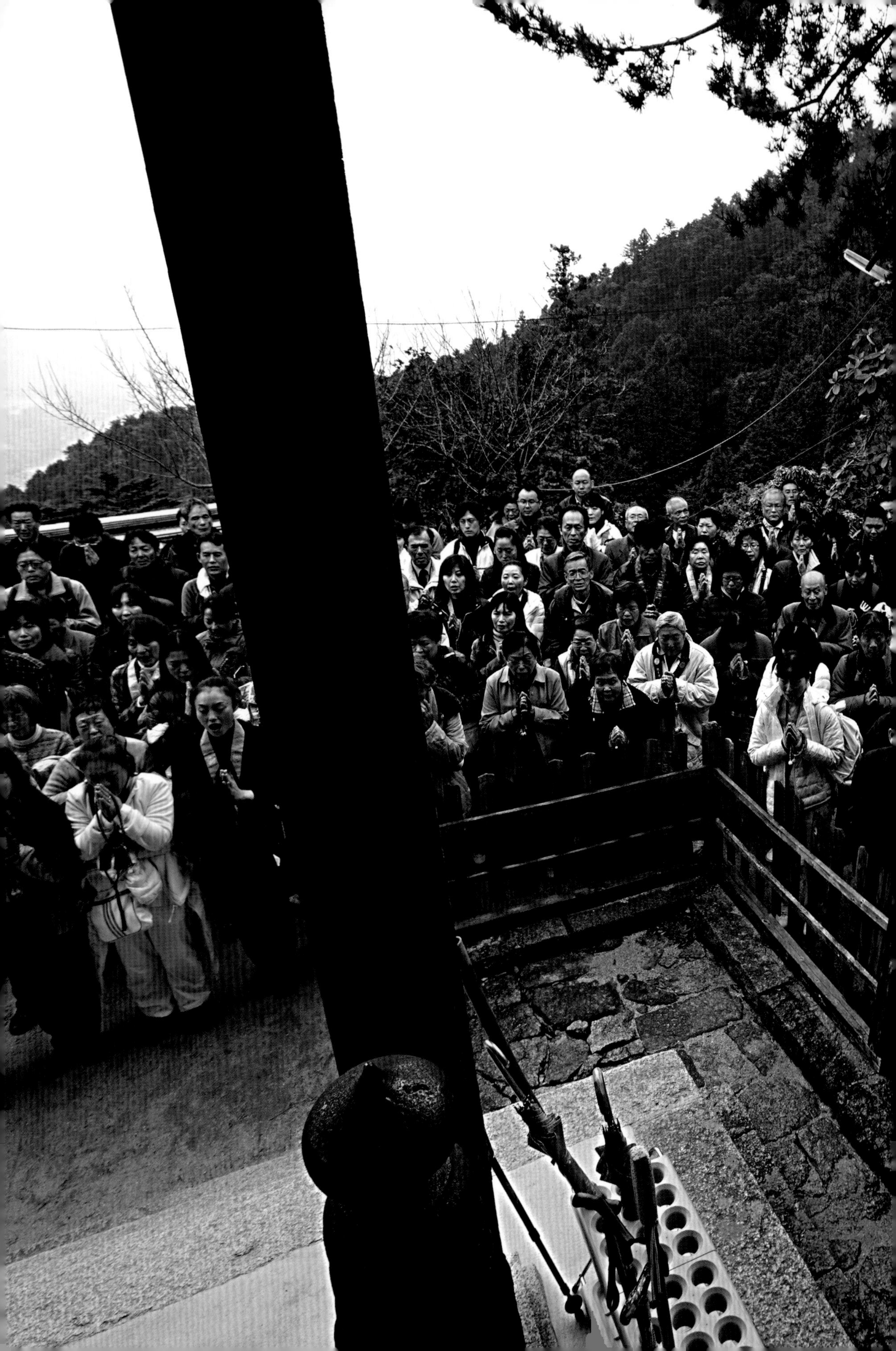

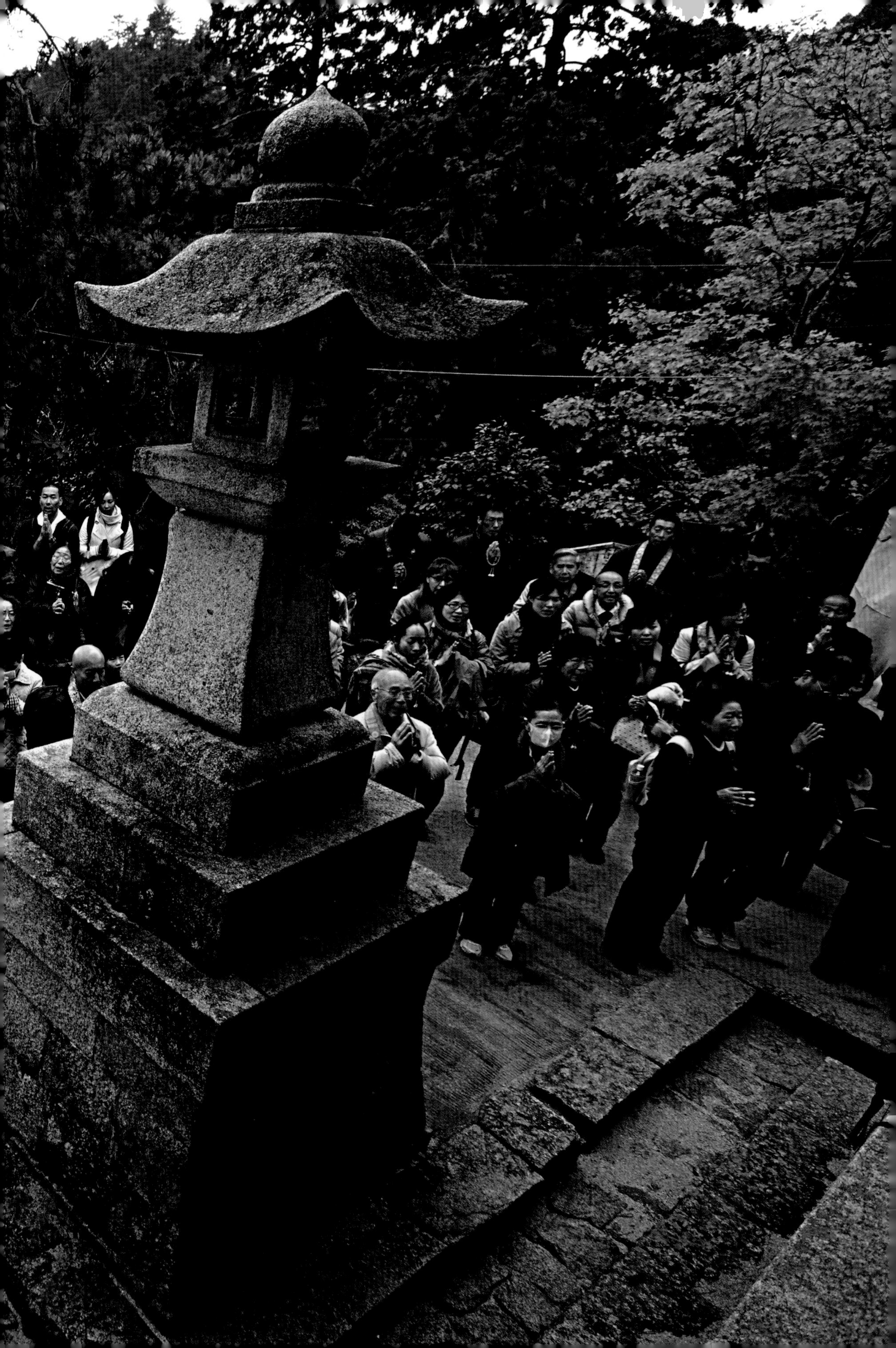

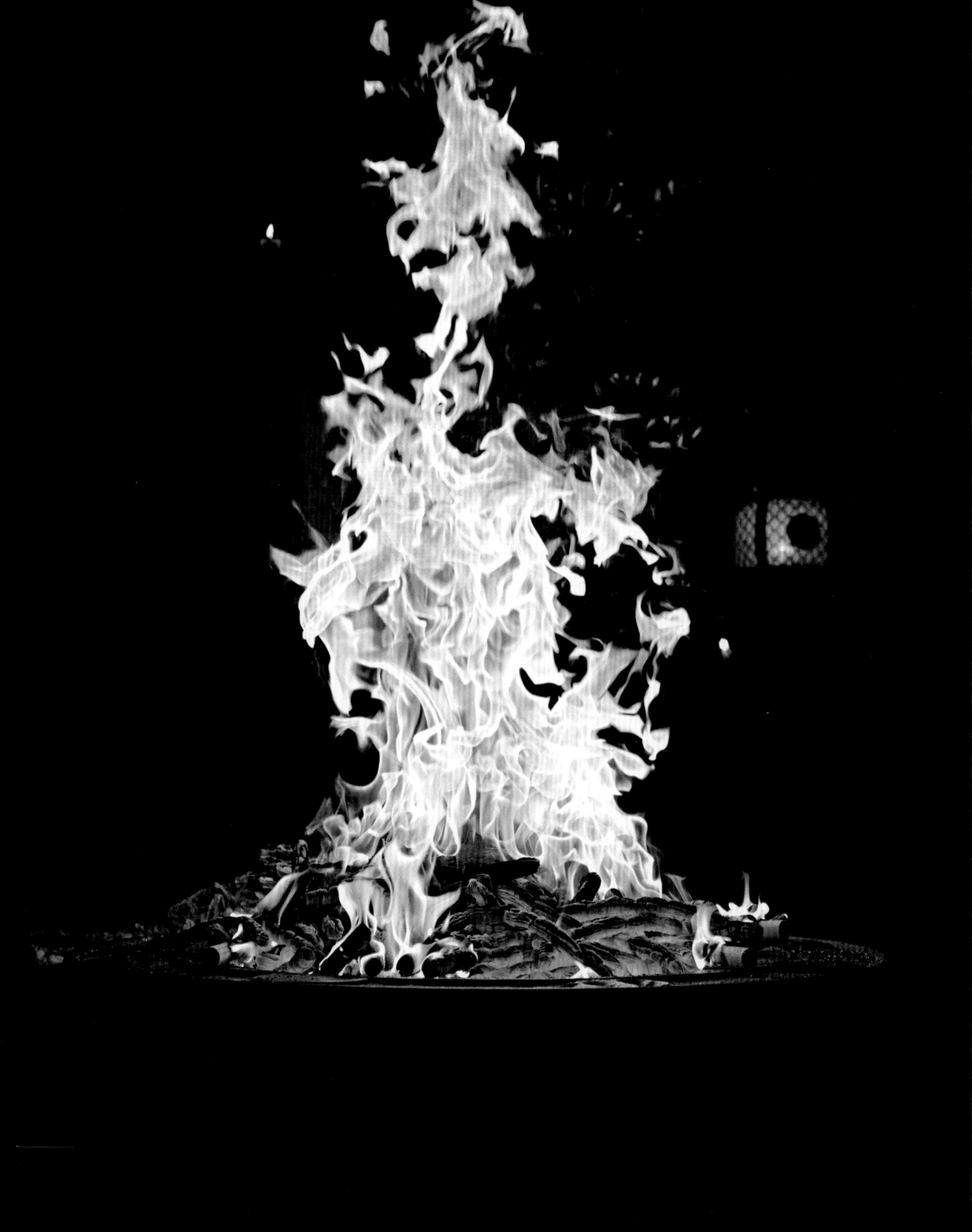

日本中がバブル景気で沸き立ったころ、NHKの特集番組「行〜比叡山 千日回峰〜」が放映され、回峰行が一躍有名になった。

そのころ、私の最大の関心事は黒人ブルースミュージシャンであった。彼らが奏でるギターそして魂の叫びといえるエネルギッシュな歌声の虜になり、アメリカまで撮影に出かけていた。バブル景気に陰りがみえはじめたころ、ふとしたことから圓道師の師匠・光永覚道阿闍梨と巡り合うことができた。あのドキュメンタリー番組の映像が蘇り、あの過酷な千日回峰行の行者さんが目の前に。それだけで感激であった。そして、この出会いが、2人の大行満の「千日回峰行」の足跡を撮影させていただくことになったのは、不思議な縁というほかはない。とくに、師匠の満行から13年の時を経て、圓道師を入行から遂業までの12年間、少年から青年、そして壮年へと至る心身の変化・成長、そして何よりも積み重ねられていく「行」の姿を追い続けられた幸運を今更ながらに噛みしめている。

最後に本書の出版にあたり、春秋社会長神田明氏、社長澤畑吉和氏、編集部佐藤清靖氏ならびにご協力いただいた聞真・ポール・ネエモン師、ハリエット・F・スタントン氏、伊藤賢映師西岡勉氏、千坂祐希氏、台麓息障講社、京都息障講社のみなさんに心から御礼申し上げます。

Around the peak of the Bubble period, an NHK special program was broadcasted about *kaihōgyō*. Overnight, *kaihōgyō* training became famous.

Around that time I had a strong interest in black blues musicians. I was captivated by them guitar and energetic singing voice which screamed life, so I went to America in order to capture them on film. Around the time when the end of the bubble period was in sight, by chance I was able to meet Reverend Endō's teacher, Kakudō Mitsunaga again. I was reminded of that documentary program, the determination of the thousand days *kaihōgyō* trainees was before my eyes. It was extremely moving. Furthermore, the fact that I became acquainted with those two incredible monks, and that I was able to capture their thousand days *kaihōgyō* training with my camera. I felt like our meeting was an incredible twist of fate. Particularly, I am thankful to have observed the 13 years since Kakudō completed his training, and the 12 years that Endō spent on his training. I was able to witness the prime of Endō's life, growing from a young man, changing in mind and body, flourishing into a splendid adult. I am truly thankful that I had the good fortune to follow his journey and capture it on film.

Finally, for the publication of this book I would like to give thanks to the chairman of Shunjusha, Mr. Akira Kanda, President Mr. Yoshikazu Sawahata, the editorial department, Mr. Kiyoyasu Sato. Also I would like to thank the cooperation of Reverend Monshin Paul Naamon, Ms. Harriet F. Stanton, Reverend Kenei Ito, Mr. Tsutomu Nishioka, Ms.Yuki Chisaka, Tairoku Sokushokosha, Kyoto Sokushokosha. To all of these people I would like to offer thanks from the bottom of my heart.

光永圓道阿闍梨・千日回峰行の歩み

平成9年(1997) 4月1日……………………三年籠山行入行
　　11年(1999) 3月29日～7月6日………回峰第初百日
　　12年(2000) 4月1日……………………三年籠山行遂業
　　15年(2003) 3月1日……………………十二年籠山行入行
　　　　　　　 3月27日～7月4日………回峰第二百日
　　16年(2004) 3月28日～7月5日………回峰第三百日
　　17年(2005) 3月28日～7月5日………回峰第四百日
　　18年(2006) 3月28日～7月5日………回峰第五百日　白帯行者となる
　　19年(2007) 3月28日～7月5日………回峰第六百日
　　　　　　　 7月6日～10月13日………回峰第七百日
　　　　　　　 10月13日～10月21日……明王堂参籠(堂入り)
　　　　　　　　　　　　　　　　　　　当行満阿闍梨となる
　　20年(2008) 3月28日～7月5日………回峰第八百日(赤山苦行)
　　　　　　　 12月1日…………………明王堂輪番拝命
　　21年(2009) 3月28日～7月5日………回峰第九百日(京都大廻り)
　　　　　　　 7月6日～9月18日………回峰第一千日満行
　　　　　　　　　　　　　　　　　　　北嶺大行満大阿闍梨となる
　　　　　　　 10月12日…………………土足参内(玉体加持)
　　24年(2012) 11月2日～11月9日………十萬枚大護摩供
　　27年(2015) 3月1日……………………十二年籠山行遂業

得度式、平成2年(1990)2月28日

出峰

　回峰行第一日目を出峰といい、広くは百日間、比叡山内の巡拝に出発することすべてをいう。日付の変わったことを確認して覚心（起床）し、後夜座の勤行を行い、衣体を整え、午前2時頃、出峰する。

　百日回峰行者の場合、出峰の日には「伝法」といって大行満が先達し、回峰のコース、巡拝する諸仏、諸菩薩の場所（堂塔伽藍を整えている場合は少なく、目印となるものが樹木や石などの場合もある）、陀羅尼などが伝授される。

　行者の姿は、回峰行者の本尊である不動明王そのものを表している。頭に戴く「お笠」は未敷蓮華（蓮は仏教において最も清浄な花とされている。お笠はその蕾のままの蓮の葉を象り、檜で網代に編まれている）を象り、千日回峰行者でも第四百日目に入ってからでないと頭に戴くことは許されず、大切に手に持って歩く。手に持つ念珠は不動明王の羂索、檜扇は明王の利剣を示し、八葉の草鞋は仏の蓮台をあらわす（第四百日目からは行者足袋という特殊な足袋を履くことが許されるが、それまでは素足に草鞋ばきである）。衣体は麻の浄衣に野袴、手甲、脚半、四手紐、手巾（行なかばで断念せねばならぬ時は、四手紐で首をくくり、手巾は死後の顔を覆うのに用いられる）を帯びる出で立ちで、すべて白一色で整えられる。行者の装束は死装束を意味し、お笠のなかには三途の川の通行手形の六文銭がつけられているのである。行者は毎夜、室内から草鞋を履いて出峰する。回峰行は「不退の行」とか「捨身の行」とかいわれるように、いかなるアクシデントにみまわれようとも一日たりとも休むことはできない。断念するときは、自ら命を絶つ定めとなっている。

　出峰からはじめの一週間は「順七日」といって、出発点の明王堂の前にある急勾配の80段あまりある石の階段を三匝（三往復）する。百日の最終日から一週間前も三匝は繰り返される。

[回峰コースのあらまし]
　明王堂→根本中堂→阿弥陀堂→大講堂→浄土院（伝教大師御廟）→西塔・釈迦堂→峰道→横川中堂→大師堂（四季講堂）→八王子山→坂本・日吉大社→無動寺坂→明王堂

堂入り（明王堂参籠）

　回峰第七百日目が満行した当日から九日のあいだ回峰行者の根本道場である明王堂に参籠することをいう。

　断食、断水、不眠、不臥により人間の三欲を断って本尊大聖不動明王と一体となることを願って、九日間、一日三座の勤行以外は、「逆屛風」のなかで、禅定（座禅）の姿勢を崩さず、不動明王の陀羅尼（真言）を一洛叉（十万遍）唱え続ける。ただし、毎夜午前2時、「取水の儀」といって不動

明王にお供えする水を明王堂から数100m離れた閼伽井まで汲みに行く儀式があり、この時だけは明王堂の外に出ることが許される。

斎食儀

入堂の儀式に先立ち、法曼院では行者を正座に据え、歴代の大行満や有縁の僧侶たちと今生の別れとなるかもしれないという意味を込めた会食の儀式をいう。堂入りは生き葬式といわれ、行者は一切、食べ物に箸をつけない。会食を前に座奉行と呼ばれる総責任者役の僧侶が「下根満となった圓道行者が不動明王と一体とならんがための浄行であり、不動明王の意に適ったならば、魔事なく満行できる。もしも、不動明王が否と判断されたならば、皆様と相まみえることもこれが最後となる。今生に別れを告げる会食である」というような挨拶をし、水を打ったような静けさのなかで、会食が摂られていった。以後の九日間は生くるも死ぬも不動明王の掌に委ねられるのである。

出堂

入堂の日より9日目の未明、最後の取水の儀があり、堂内に戻って結願の作法を行う。こののち、明王堂内で参籠遂業を証明する証明文が法曼院政所職・無動寺谷長老故井深観讓大僧正によって読上げられ、行者は内陣を自力で三匝（三周）する。九弁の花を咲かせるという「朴の湯」という薬湯に口をつけ、行者の発音（発声）により、「般若心経」を誦して内陣での儀は終える。こののち、参籠していた明王堂正面の扉が開けられ、両脇から助僧に支えられ出堂する。

赤山苦行（回峰八百日）

回峰第七百日までの比叡山内7里半の巡拝の行程に加えて、比叡山の西の守護神である京都・洛北赤山禅院まで足を延ばして諸仏諸菩薩を巡拝する百日間のことをいう。赤山禅院往復を加えると15里と言われる。比叡山内の巡拝は自利の行（自らを高めるための行）であるが、堂入りを終えた行者は化他の行（自らのためではなく他人のために生き、一切衆生の済度を願う行）となり、赤山苦行は化他行となる。

そもそも、赤山禅院は慈覚大師圓仁が新羅より請来した赤山明神を本尊とする。比叡山から赤山禅院に至る道は雲母坂と呼ばれる険しい坂道であるが、京の都から比叡山に登るときは雲母坂が最短で、白河上皇に強訴した叡山の僧兵の御輿振りも、親鸞聖人が百日間、六角堂に通ったのも、この坂を下ってきたのである。美しい清水の湧き出たという「水飲み」という場所辺りから「浄刹結界」といって、古くは女人はもちろん、牛馬も登叡することが適わなかった。

明治政府の廃仏棄釈にあっても、赤山禅院が神仏習合のまま寺院として存続したのは「赤山苦行」の拠点であったからといわれている。

京都大廻り

　千日回峰行中、801日から900日までをいう。比叡山内より結界（戒律護持僧が修行専心のため一定の地域を区画制限することをいう。籠山中の回峰行者は、東麓は日吉大社の一の鳥居まで、西麓は赤山禅院の鳥居までを結界とする）を出て、旧京都市内にある神社仏閣を巡拝する。

　その主旨は、堂入りを成満したことによって化他の門に入った行者が、広く衆生済度を願うものである。その行程は次の通りで、出峰の日は明王堂から清浄華院（宿舎）、翌日はその逆コース（宿舎から明王堂へ）を辿る。一日の行程はおよそ21里となり、京都の宿舎での睡眠は2〜3時間の仮眠である。

　明王堂→比叡山内巡拝→雲母坂を経て赤山禅院→真如堂→八坂神社→庚申堂→清水寺→六波羅密寺→因幡薬師→北野天満宮→西方尼寺→上御霊神社→下鴨神社→河合神社→清浄華院（宿舎）

土足参内（玉体加持）

　起源は貞観3年（861）までに遡る。相応和尚が類い希なる加持力を持っているとの噂が清和天皇の耳にまで及び、勅命によって修行中の和尚を宮内裏に呼び寄せ、染殿皇后の病気平癒を祈願させたところ、即座に「息障の験」が現れたという。

　その時、和尚は草鞋履きのまま参内したという故事にならい、千日回峰行を円成した大行満が土足のまま京都御所に参内し、天皇の玉体安穏を祈願する。

　古来、殿上人でも宜秋門で履物を履き替えて参内したが、大行満は宜秋門の内で結草履と呼ばれる特殊な履物に替える。

十萬枚大護摩供

　千日回峯行を満行した大行満が、一代に一度だけ奉修する大護摩供である。開闢より結願にいたる七日のあいだ断食、断水、不眠の状態で行われる。正行・七ヶ日に先立ち、百日のあいだ五穀（米、大麦、小麦、小豆、大豆）・塩断ちの前行を修し、精進専一して正行に入る。

　大行満が修法する七日間の正行もさることながら、十萬本という未曾有の護摩木勧進を信者にあおぐことが、この大護摩供を成満することの大前提となる。

（千坂祐希）

Ajari Endō Mitsunaga's 1000 days *kaihōgyō* journey

April 1st, 1997 .... Start of 3 years of training on Mt. Hiei
Mar 29th to July 6th, 1999 ... completed first 100 days *kaihōgyō*
Apr 1st, 2000 .... completed 3 years training on Mt. Hiei
Mar 1st, 2003 .... started 12 years training on Mt. Hiei
Mar 27th to July 4th, 2003 ... completed 200 days *kaihōgyō*
Mar 28th to July 5th, 2004 ... completed 300 days *kaihōgyō*
Mar 28th to July 5th, 2005 ... completed 400 days *kaihōgyō*
Mar 28th to July 5th, 2006 ... completed 500 days *kaihōgyō*
  (received the title of Byakutai-Gyōja)
Mar 28th to July 5th, 2007 ... completed 600 days *kaihōgyō*
July 6th to Oct 13th, 2007 ... completed 700 days *kaihōgyō*
Oct 13th to Oct 21st, 2007 ... completed *dōiri*
  (9 days fasting, no water, no sleep. Peak of the 1000 days *kaihōgyō*. Received the title of Togyōman-Ajari)
Mar 28th to July 5th, 2008 ... completed 800 days *kaihōgyō* (*Sekizankugyō*)
Mar 28th to July 5th, 2009 ... completed 900 days *kaihōgyō* (*Kyoto ōmawari*)
July 6th to Sep 18th, 2009 ... completed 1000 days *kaihōgyō*
  (received the title of Hokurei-Daigyōman-Daiajari)
Oct 12th, 2009 .... completed Dosoku-sandai
  (prayer for good fortune for Emperor and the nation)
Nov 2nd to Nov 9th, 2012 ... *Jumanmai-ōgoma* ceremony
Mar 1st, 2015 .... completed 12 years training on Mt. Hiei

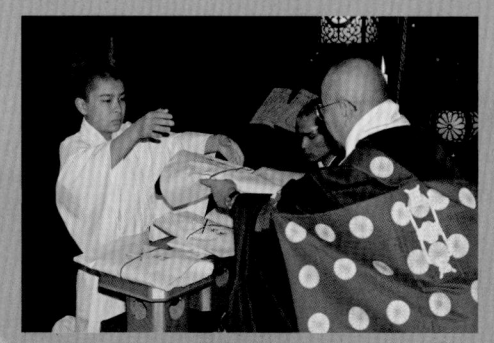

Tokudoshiki, February 28, 1990

Shuppō

The first day of every one hundred day period during *kaihōgyō* training is called *shuppō*, it essentially means 'departure' and signals the beginning of that 100 days segment. On the day of *shuppō*, the trainee wakes up, does the evening service, gets dressed and then at 2 a.m. departs and begins his training.

In the case of the one hundred days *kaihōgyō* the first day is called *denpō*, which roughly translates as 'teaching tradition'. On this day those that have completed their one thousand days training take the lead and show the new trainees the course, where to worship (there are structures included in the route, however at many of the worships spots the marker could be something as simple as a tree or a rock), and how to worship at the sacred sites along the route.

During the *kaihōgyō* training, trainees take upon the image of Fudō-Myōō, not only physically in dress but also mentally as well. On their heads they wear a hat called *okasa*, which is representative of a lotus, in Buddhism the lotus represents purity. The *okasa's* shape is that of an unfurled lotus leaf and is made of woven Japanese cypress wood. However until the 400th day of training the trainees are not permitted to wear the hat, instead they must carry it. They also carry in their hands a wooden rosary which is representative of Fudō-Myōō' s *kensaku* (a weapon used to destroy evil spirits) and a fan made of Japanese Cypress which is representative of his sword. On his feet he wears *rendai waraji*, straw sandals, which represents the lotus shaped base which Buddha statues are placed on. (After the 400th day of *kaihōgyō* trainees are permitted to wear special socks called *gyōja tabi*, however up until that point *waraji* are worn barefoot.)

The attire consists of a *jōe* (a robe made of hemp), *nobakama* (traditional style trousers), *tekkō* (wraps which cover the hands and loop through the thumb and middle finger), *kyahan* (wraps which cover the lower legs), *shidehimo* (a thick rope) and *shukin* (a handkerchief). All of these are white.

The *shidehimo* and *shukin*, which are tied around the waist, have a very special purpose. If a trainee wishes to quit his training, the only way out is death. He can use the *shidehimo* to hang himself, when his body is discovered the *shukin* would then be used to cover his face (it is a Japanese funerary practice to cover the face of the deceased). The clothing carries the same meaning as burial clothing (which in Japan are white), furthermore in the *okasa* are six old fashioned coins. This is so that should the trainee decide to end his training he would be able to pay the boatman to cross the river into the afterlife. Every night before he departs, the trainee will put on his *waraji* inside his room. Traditionally in Japanese culture only the deceased are permitted to wear shoes indoors.

Kaihōgyō is a practice which is *shashinnogyō* (an act in which you throw your body away for others) and *futainogyō* (an act which has no ending), because of this even if an accident occurs, the trainee cannot take even one day's rest. If a trainee has to quit for any reason, he must pay with his life.

During the first and last week of each one hundred day period *junnanuka* is observed. In front of Myōōdō Temple there is a set of steep stone steps, 80 steps in length. During *junnanuka* before the trainee sets out on his route he must go up and down those steps three times (6 times in total).

Course:
 Myōōdō Temple, Konponchudō Temple, Amidadō Temple, Daikōdō Temple, Jōdoin Temple (Dengyō great master priest), Shakadō Temple, Minemichi trail, Yokawachudō Temple, Daishidō Temple (Shikikodō Temple), Mt.Hachiōji, Hiyoshitaisha Shrine, Sakamoto Town, Mudōjizaka Pass, Myōōdō Temple.

Dōiri

Immediately after finishing the first 700 days of the thousand days *kaihōgyō* training, *dōiri* is performed for 9 days. The *kaihōgyō* trainee stays in the main hall of Myōōdō Temple. During the 9 days the trainee is not allowed to eat, drink or sleep; he requests to Fudō-Myōō to become one with him for his training. With the exception of rituals which must be performed three times a day, the trainee sits in a meditative position in front of a reversed folded screen, reciting mantras.

In Japanese culture a reversed folded screen is used when preparing the dead for their funeral rites, it is used in this context to represent a transition in the *kaihōgyō* training. In a way the trainee has 'died', he cannot return to that old aspect of himself, but at the same time when he has finished *dōiri* he will have been reborn.

For the 9 day duration the trainee is not permitted to leave the temple except to perform a single rite. Every night at 2a.m. he must make a 200m journey to a well to draw water to offer to Fudō-Myōō, this is known as '*shusui no gi*'. As the training progresses, this journey will become harder and harder for him to complete.

Saijikigi

Before entering the temple to carry out *dōiri*, there is a final meal which is called *saijikigi*. *Saijikigi* is like the trainee's 'last supper'. There is the possibility that this could be 'farewell', so he dines with monks who are close to him. (It is worth noting that the human body normally can only survive without water for around 7 days, therefore performing *dōiri* will literally push the trainee to the brink of death.)

Because *dōiri* is representative of the death of the trainee, this meal is like a 'living funeral'. He is not allowed to eat, nor is he permitted to pick up his chopsticks.

At Reverend Endo's *saijikigi*, the *zabugyō* (the person responsible for the supervision of the *dōiri*) announced that the trainee had just completed the first aspect of his training. He then went on to say that *dōiri* is the purest way to become one with Fudō-Myōō, therefore if Fudō-Myōō accepts the trainee he will be able to complete his *dōiri* safely. However if Fudō-Myōō decides that the trainee is unworthy, this would be the last chance for those who are present to see Reverend Endo. This meal is a farewell to his life thus far. Following this speech, the lunch was held in a tense silence. The consequences of the next 9 days were in Fudō-Myōō's hands.

Shutsudō

Early in the morning of the 9th day, after the last journey to the well and the last *shusui no gi* has been performed, the trainee returns to the temple in order to perform one last ritual (known as *kechigan*). After this is completed, the most senior priest in Mudōji Valley goes into the temple with the *shōmeibun* (a document of confirmation) and announces that the trainee has completed his *dōiri*. (At Reverend Endo's *shutsudō* the priest who confirmed his *dōiri* was the late Kanjo Ibuka, who was also the Master priest of Hōmanin Temple.)

The trainee then circuits the interior of the temple three times unassisted. Next medicinal water made from Japanese magnolia is brought to him and he cleanses his mouth. Following this, he chants the Heart Sutra together with the others who are present at the temple. Once this has been completed the gates at the front of Myōōdō Temple open, supported on both sides by monks, the trainee exits the temple.

Sekizankugyō

Sekizankugyō is the period from the 701st day to the 800th day of *kaihōgyō*, in which the pilgrimage route changes. In addition to the route which was walked during the first 700 days, Sekizanzenin temple in Kyoto, which is the guardian of West Mount Hiei, is added to the list of pilgrimage sites. This is done in order to worship the deities who reside there. The route in total becomes 15*ri* (approx. 60km). The first 700 days of the *kaihōgyō* training are for self-practice (*jirigyō*). After *dōiri*, the remainder of the training is a practice done for others (*ketagyō*), including the salvation of other sentient beings.

Originally, Jikaku Master Priest Ennin brought back Sekizan Myōjin (a mountain god) from China, which became the principal deity at Sekizanzenin Temple. There is a steep mountain trail from Mount Hiei to Sekizanzenin Temple which is called 'Kirarazaka', which is the shortest route from Kyoto to Mount Hiei by foot.

Kirarazaka is historically significant to the monks of Mount Hiei. Long ago an Emperor called Shirakawa made a law that the monks of Mount Hiei would not abide by. In direct protest the monks carried down relics from the mountain and left them in the city of Kyoto. This was very troubling for the Emperor as no one except the monks could touch or move the relics. Furthermore, a priest named Shinran visited Rokkakudō Temple in Kyoto for 100 days. The route that the monks used in both of these incidences was the Kirarazaka path.

Surrounding Mount Hiei there are several points which form the '*jyōsetsukekkai*'. This is a kind of spiritual barrier which surrounds the temple complex on the mountain. Long ago women and animals such as horses and cattle were not permitted to enter the barrier.

Along the Kirarazaka Path there is a beautiful spring known as 'Mizunomi'. Mizunomi is one of the points along the barrier.

Lastly, Sekizanzenin Temple is significant as it was able to escape reformation during the Meiji Government's *haibutsukishaku*. The *haibutsukishaku* was an attempt to destroy Buddhism in Japan, as Shintoism was declared the official state religion at the time. However, as Sekizanzenin Temple was the base for *sekizankugyō*, the Shinto shrine and the Buddhist temple were not separated during the *haibutsukishaku*. The *sekizankugyō* involves visiting both Buddhist and Shinto establishments on the grounds, therefore if the two were separated it would have become impossible to perform *sekizankugyō*.

Kyoto Ōmawari

The Kyoto ōmawari is the practice which lasts from the 801st day to the 900th day of the *kaihōgyō* training. Up until that point the *kaihōgyō* training route stays within the perimeter of the mountain, however during *Kyoto ōmawari* the route extends beyond that into Kyoto city, where shrines and temples are visited. Monks who are in the process of doing a dedication training are restricted to the space inside the boundary, this includes those doing *kaihōgyō* training. The boundary in the East is marked by the torii gate at Hiyoshi Taisha Shrine, and in the West by another torii gate at Sekizanzenin Temple.

The intent of *Kyoto ōmawari* is to practice for others, this is called *ketagyō*. The practitioner's aim for prayer is the salvation of all sentient beings. The route runs from Myōōdō Temple to the lodging house at Shōjyōkein Temple. The route is run only one way per day, the following day it is then done in reverse. (The route up until that point is like a circuit, so it was not necessary to run a reverse route.)

One day's route is 21*ri* (approx 84km), the trainee only has 2-3 hours in Kyoto at the temple dormitory, before the return journey is made.

Myōōdō Temple, the Mount Hiei circuit, pass through Kirarazaka to Sekizanzenin Temple, Shinnyodō Temple, Yasaka Shrine, Kōshindō Temple, KiyomizuderaTemple, Rokuharamitsuji Temple, Inabayakushi Temple, Kitanotenmangu Shrine, Saihōniji Temple, Kamigoryō Shrine, Shimogamo Shrine, Kawai Shrine, Shōjyōkein Temple (Temple dormitory)

Dosokusandai

This practice originates from one of Sōō's acts. In the 3rd year of the Jōgan Era (861), stories of Priest Sōō's incredible ability to heal reached the ears of the Emperor Seiwa. The Empress Dowager Somedono was sick, so the Emperor called Priest Sōō to the Royal Residence. It is said that when he prayed for her recovery, she was immediately cured. According to the story Priest Sōō entered the palace wearing straw sandals (outdoor shoes). In accordance with the story, those who have completed their thousand days *kaihōgyō* enter the palace wearing straw sandals, and pray for the wellbeing of the Emperor. It is a time-honored tradition that court officials when entering the Gishumon (an area in the palace), that they would change their shoes. However, those that have completed their *kaihōgyō* change their shoes to a particular type of straw sandal called *yuizori*.

Jyumanmai-ōgomaku

Those who have finished the thousand day's *kaihōgyō*, just once have to perform a ceremony called *ōgomaku*. From the opening of the ceremony to its closing, which is seven days, the monk must go through a process of no eating, drinking or sleeping (same as *dōiri*). During the one hundred days leading up to the *ōgomaku* (called *zengyō*), the monk is not allowed to eat rice, wheat, barley, red beans, soy beans or salt. As soon as *zengyō* has been completed, *ōgomaku* begins.

During *ōgomaku* the monk will offer 100,000 sticks of cypress wood. All of the sticks of wood must be made by donation by patrons, therefore without the support from patrons the monk would not be able to complete his training.

Yuki Chisaka / Translated by Monshin Paul Naamon, Harriet F. Stanton, Kenei Ito

比叡山千日回峰行――光永圓道阿闍梨写真集
kaihōgyō
photographed by Kōichi Uchida

2016年11月30日　第1刷発行

著者…………打田浩一
発行者…………澤畑吉和
発行所…………株式会社 春秋社
　　　　　　　〒101-0021 東京都千代田区外神田 2-18-6
　　　　　　　電話：03-3255-9611（営業）03-3255-9614（編集）
　　　　　　　振替：00180-6-24861
　　　　　　　http://www.shunjusha.co.jp/

印刷所…………萩原印刷株式会社
ブック・デザイン…西岡 勉

Ⓒ Kōichi Uchida 2016. Printed in Japan
ISBN 978-4-393-95320-4
定価はカバー等に表示してあります。